Web Standards Solutions

The Markup and Style Handbook
Special Edition

Dan Cederholm

friendsof

DESIGNER TO DESIGNER™

an Apress® company

Web Standards Solutions: The Markup and Style Handbook, Special Edition

ISBN-13 (pbk): 978-1-4302-1920-0

ISBN-13 (electronic): 978-1-4302-1921-7

Printed and bound in the United States of America (POD)

Distributed to the book trade worldwide by Springer-Verlag New York, Inc., 233 Spring Street, 6th Floor, New York, NY 10013. Phone 1-800-SPRINGER, fax 201-348-4505, e-mail orders-ny@springer-sbm.com, or visit www.springeronline.com.

For information on translations, please visit www.apress.com.

Apress and friends of ED books may be purchased in bulk for academic, corporate, or promotional use. eBook versions and licenses are also available for most titles. For more information, reference our Special Bulk Sales–eBook Licensing web page at http://www.apress.com/info/bulksales.

The source code for this book is freely available to readers at www.friendsofed.com in the Downloads section.

Credits

Lead Editor	**Associate Production Director**
Ben Renow-Clarke	Kari Brooks-Copony
Technical Reviewer	**Production Editor**
Matt Heerema	Laura Cheu
Editorial Board	**Compositor**
Clay Andres, Steve Anglin, Mark Beckner, Ewan Buckingham, Tony Campbell, Gary Cornell, Jonathan Gennick, Jonathan Hassell, Michelle Lowman, Matthew Moodie, Duncan Parkes, Jeffrey Pepper, Frank Pohlmann, Douglas Pundick, Ben Renow-Clarke, Dominic Shakeshaft, Matt Wade, Tom Welsh	Lynn L'Heureux
	Proofreader
	Lisa Hamilton
	Indexer
	Broccoli Information Management
Project Manager	**Interior and Cover Designer**
Richard Dal Porto	Kurt Krames
Copy Editor	**Manufacturing Director**
Liz Welch	Tom Debolski

CONTENTS AT A GLANCE

Foreword xvii

About the Author.. xviii

About the Technical Reviewer xix

Acknowledgments... xx

Introduction.. xxi

PART ONE **GET DOWN WITH MARKUP** 1

Chapter 1 **Lists** 3

Chapter 2 **Headings**...................................... 17

Chapter 3 **Tables are Evil?** 29

Chapter 4 **Quotations** 49

Chapter 5 **Forms** 61

Chapter 6 **<Strong>, <Em>, and Other Phrase Elements**..... 83

Chapter 7 **Anchors**...................................... 103

Chapter 8 **More Lists** 119

Chapter 9 **Minimizing Markup**............................ 133

PART TWO **SIMPLEBITS OF STYLE** **147**

Chapter 10 **Applying CSS**. **149**

Chapter 11 **Print Styles**. **167**

Chapter 12 **CSS Layouts** **179**

Chapter 13 **Styling Text** **207**

Chapter 14 **Image Replacement**. **223**

Chapter 15 **Styling <body>** **243**

Chapter 16 **Next Steps** **255**

Index. **263**

CONTENTS

Foreword . . . .**xvii**

About the Author . . . .**xviii**

About the Technical Reviewer . . . . **xix**

Acknowledgments . . . . **xx**

Introduction . . . . **xxi**

PART ONE **GET DOWN WITH MARKUP** **1**

Chapter 1 **Lists** **3**

    Let's go shopping 4
    Quiz time 4
        Method A: The <br /> breakdown 4
        It's a wrap 5
        Method B: The bullet that bites 6
            Validation, please 6
        Method C: Getting closer 6
        Method D: Wrapper's delight 8
    Summary 8
    Extra credit 9
        Bite the bullet 9
        Getting fancier with custom bullets 10
        Lists that navigate 11
        Mini-tab shapes 14

Chapter 2 **Headings** **17**

    What is the best way to mark up the title of a document? 18
        Method A: Meaningful? 18
        Method B: The p and b combo 19
            Difficult to style 19

Method C: Style and substance 19
    Easily styled 19
    Default distaste 20
    Search engine friendly 20
    An aside on heading order 21
Summary 21
Extra credit 22
Simple styling 22
    Adding backgrounds 23
        Backgrounds and borders 24
        Tiled backgrounds 24
    Swappable icons 25
    Easy updates 25
    The chameleon effect 26
        Aligning the <img> element 26
Wrapping up 27

Chapter 3 **Tables are Evil?** **29**

Totally tabular 30
A table that everyone can sit at 30
Adding a summary 33
The head(s) of the table 33
Header and data relationships 35
Using the abbr attribute 36
<thead>, <tfoot>, and <tbody> 37
Are tables evil? 39
Extra credit 39
    Creating a grid 39
    Collapsing the gaps 40
        An IE/Mac note 41
        Spaced out 41
    Customizing the headers 42
    Headers with background images 43
        Tiny tile 43
        The CSS 43
    Assigning icons to IDs 44
        The icons 45
        The CSS 45
        Combining rules for simpler bits 46
More table style examples 47
Wrapping up 47

Chapter 4 **Quotations** **49**

Method A: Lacks meaning 50
Method B: A class act? 50
Method C: <blockquote> is best 51
Using a screwdriver to hammer a nail 51
Summary 52

Extra credit 52
  A cite for curious eyes 52
  Inline quotations 53
    No need for marks 53
    Nesting inline quotations 54
  Styling <blockquote> 54
    Background quote marks 54
    Three images 55
    Tagging the elements 55
    Three elements, three backgrounds 55
    The results 57
    Calling out special words 58
    How does it degrade? 59
Wrapping up 59

Chapter 5 **Forms** **61**

What are our options when marking up a form? 62
  Method A: Using a table 62
  Method B: Tableless, but cramped 63
  Method C: Simple and more accessible 64
    The <label> element 65
    Why <label>? 65
  Method D: Defining a form 66
    Defining style 67
Summary 68
Extra credit 69
  The fabulous tabindex 69
    Why tabindex? 70
  accesskey for frequented forms 70
    Easily accessed search 71
  Styling forms 71
    Setting the width of text inputs 71
    Using <label> to customize fonts 72
    No need to be redundant 74
    Use <fieldset> to group form sections 74
    Adding style to <fieldset> and <legend> 75
    Three-dimensional <legend> 76
    Borders and backgrounds on form elements 78
Wrapping up 80

Chapter 6 **<strong>, <em>, and Other Phrase Elements** **83**

Presentational vs. structural 84
  Why are <strong> and <em> better than <b> and <i>? 84
    Check in with the experts 84
    Method A 85
    Method B 85
    Bold and beautiful 85

What about <em>? 85
    Method A. 85
    Method B. 86
    Emphasis mine. 86
Just bold or italic, please. 86
    Worth its (font-)weight in bold. 87
    That's italic! 87
Both bold and italic. 87
    Generic <span>. 88
    Emphasis with class 88
Summary. 89
Extra credit. 89
  The phrase elements 89
  <cite> design 90
    The specification 90
    A change in <cite> style 91
    Leveraging the structure. 91
  <abbr> and <acronym> 92
    Define once 93
    The presentation. 93
    Compatibility issues. 94
  <code>. 94
  <samp> 95
  <var> 95
  <kbd>. 95
Microformats 96
  New growth 96
  A simple explanation. 96
  An hCard example. 97
    Code Creator. 97
    The markup 98
    The power of microformats 99
Final phrase 101

Chapter 7 **Anchors**. **103**

When pointing to a specific portion of a page, what is the best way to mark up an anchor? 104
  Method A: An empty name. 104
  Method B: It's all in a name 105
    Beware of global <a> styling 105
    Richer name attribute. 106
  Method C: Lose the name. 106
    Two birds with one stone 107
    Older browsers and the id attribute. 107
  Method D: The all-in-one 108
    Sharing names 108
Summary. 108

Extra credit 109
   The title attribute 110
      Title in action 110
      Tooltip titles 110
      Titles are spoken 111
   Styling links 111
      Backgrounds 112
      Dotted borders 112
      Where you been? 113
      Hovering 113
      Active state 114
      LoVe/HAte your links 114
      Fitts' Law 115
      A hack for IE6 116
   Anchors aweigh 117

Chapter 8 **More Lists** **119**
   What is the best way to mark up a numbered list of items? 120
      Method A: Unordered order 120
      The numbers game 121
      Rendered bullets 121
      Method B: An ordered list 121
      Automatic numbering 121
      Wrapper's delight II 122
      List types 122
   What is the best way to mark up a set of terms and descriptions? 123
      Method A 124
      Method B 124
      Structure leads to style 125
      Adding icons 125
      Other applications 126
   Summary 127
   Extra credit 127
      Identify the parts 127
      Custom numbers 128
      Adding the numbers to the CSS 128
      The results 130
   Wrapping up 130

Chapter 9 **Minimizing Markup** **133**
   How can we minimize markup when building sites with web standards? 134
      Descendant selectors 134
      Method A: Class happy 134
      Classified CSS 135

Method B: Natural selection 135
    Contextual CSS 136
    Not just for sidebars 136
    Fewer classes mean easier maintenance 137
The unnecessary <div> 138
Method A: <div> happy 138
Method B: Lose the <div> 139
Other examples 139
Summary 140
Extra credit 140
The raw markup 140
Adding style 141
Custom bullets 142
Adding a border 143
Conclusion 145

PART TWO **SIMPLEBITS OF STYLE** **147**

Chapter 10 **Applying CSS** **149**

How do I apply CSS to a document? 150
Method A: The <style> element 150
    Partial understanding 150
    Uncached 151
    Multiple changes 151
    Good for development 151
Method B: External style sheets 151
    Separate file = easy maintenance 151
    Download once 152
    Still not completely hidden 152
Method C: @import 152
    Hide and seek 152
    Styles on, styles off 153
Combining B and C for multiple style sheets 154
    The chameleon effect 154
    How it's done 155
Lo-fi and hi-fi styles 155
    Order is important 156
Embrace the cascade 156
Method D: Inline styles 157
    Style tied to markup 158
    Use with caution 158
Summary 158

Extra credit 159
    Alternate styles 159
        Three font sizes 160
        Still cascading 161
        Getting alternate styles to work 161
        More than just font sizing 162
        Courtesy of DOM 163
    Reset styles 163
        An example reset.css 164
    Conclusion 165

Chapter 11 **Print Styles** **167**
    How can we specify styles for print? 168
        Media types 168
        Two ways to target 169
        Method A: The media attribute 169
            Partial support 169
        Method B: @media or @import 169
            In the head or externally 170
        Multiple values allowed 170
        Separating screen and print styles 171
        Building a print style sheet 171
            Make a point 172
            Save ink by hiding unnecessary elements 172
            Expose links 173
            Link text 174
            Save ink with print preview 174
            How it looks 175
    Summary 177

Chapter 12 **CSS Layouts** **179**
    How can I use CSS to build a two-column layout? 180
        Method A: Floating the sidebar 181
            Styling the header and footer 182
            Floating the sidebar 183
            True columns 183
        Method B: The double float 186
            Clear both 187
        Method C: Floating the content 187
            The CSS 187
            Background woes 188
            Plain and simple 189

Method D: Positioning. 190
    Predictable height. 191
    Space for the column 191
    Drop in the sidebar. 192
    The footer issue. 193
    Three's company 196
Summary. 197
Extra credit. 198
    The box model problem 199
        Seeing is believing. 199
        Wavering widths 200
        The Box Model Hack. 200
        Code by example. 200
        Be nice to Opera 201
        Not just for widths 201
    Faux columns. 202
        Vertical stretch 202
        The cheat. 203
        The CSS 203
        Positioned columns. 203
        Whatever floats your boat 204
Wrapping up. 204

Chapter 13 **Styling Text** **207**
How can I make hypertext look cool?. 208
    Times they are a-changin' 208
    Adjusting leading (a.k.a. line-height). 209
    All in the family 210
        Font names with spaces 211
    Kerning (a.k.a. letter-spacing) 211
    Drop caps. 213
    Text alignment 214
    Transforming text. 216
    Small caps. 217
    Paragraph indentation. 218
    Contrast 219
Summary. 220

Chapter 14 **Image Replacement** **223**
How can I use CSS to replace text with images? 224
    No perfect solution 224
    Use, but with caution. 224
Method A: Fahrner Image Replacement (FIR). 224
    The markup 225
    The extra element 225
    The CSS 225
        Hide the text 225

Assign a background 226
Advantages. 227
Drawbacks 227
Weigh the pros and cons. 227
Method B: Leahy/Langridge Image Replacement (LIR). 228
The markup and CSS 228
Box model woes. 229
Drawbacks 229
Method C: The Phark Method. 229
The markup and CSS 230
Still not perfect 230
Method D: sIFR. 230
Summary. 232
Extra credit 233
Logo swapping. 233
Hi-fi and lo-fi 233
The example. 233
A pair of logos 234
The CSS 235
Regain the hyperlink 235
The results 236
Accessible image-tab rollovers 236
The problem 237
The solution 237
The markup: One list to rule them all 237
One image, three states. 238
The CSS: This is where the magic happens. 239
The results 240
Why use it?. 240
But wait, the text doesn't scale! 240
Compatibility 241
Wrapping up 241

Chapter 15 **Styling <body>** **243**

Two and sometimes three columns. 244
Markup and style structure 246
Article page 246
Index page 247
This <body> has class 248
Not just for columns 248
"You are here" 249
The navigation list 249
Identify the parts 250
The magic CSS 251
Summary. 252

Chapter 16 **Next Steps** **255**

Where do you go from here? 256
  Organizations and publications 256
    W3C 256
    Web Standards Project 256
    A List Apart 256
    CSS Zen Garden 257
    Dive Into Accessibility 257
    css-discuss 257
    Digital Web Magazine 257
    Vitamin 257
  Influential and inspirational weblogs 258
    Jeffrey Zeldman Presents: The Daily Report 258
    Stopdesign 258
    mezzoblue 258
    meyerweb.com 258
    Tantek Çelik 259
    456 Berea Street 259
    Jason Santa Maria 259
    Jina Bolton 259
    Adactio 259
    Cameron Moll 259
    Mark Boulton 259
    Molly.com 260
    Shaun Inman 260
    Stuff and Nonsense 260
    Unstoppable Robot Ninja 260
    Subtraction 260
    Veerle's Blog 260
    D. Keith Robinson 260
    Simon Willison's Weblog 260
  Books 261
  Parting words 261

Index **263**

FOREWORD

You hold in your hands a recipe book. With clear examples and no wasted words, designer Dan Cederholm shows how to put web standards to work creating beautiful, lightweight interfaces that are accessible to all.

Dan isn't here to make the creative or business case for standards-based web design. Others (cough) have already done that. And frankly, if you've bothered to pick up this book and thumb through its pages, you probably already know the accessibility, longevity, and business benefits standards-based design provides. You don't need another overview or elevator pitch; you need a practical, roll-up-your-sleeves, component view, and that's what this book delivers.

In down-to-earth, natural language—the same kind of language that's found on good websites—Dan examines universal site elements such as page divisions and navigation. Using a teaching method he pioneered at SimpleBits.com, Dan shows how web standards make these universal page components easier to create, easier to modify when your boss or client requests last-minute changes, and most important of all, easier for people to use.

Here's one simple example of how this book works and why it is worth your time and your dime:

The site you're designing requires a three-column layout on its primary landing pages, and a two-column layout on inner content pages. The old-school approach is to build two unrelated HTML formatting tables as master templates. The new-school approach, recommended by the World Wide Web Consortium (W3C) and practiced by standards-based designers, is to structure the content with minimal, semantic XHTML markup and use Cascading Style Sheets (CSS) for layout.

As an experienced web designer, you might naturally assume that you'll have to craft two different XHTML templates and two different style sheets to generate your two- and three-column master layouts. But as this book shows, a single XHTML structure and just one style sheet can create both layouts. Switching from one master layout to the other is as simple as applying a class attribute to the <body> tag.

This book is filled with insights and methods like that one—methods that can boost your output and simplify your job while stimulating your creativity. Some of these Dan has invented; others come from an emerging body of modern best practices developed by a vanguard of standards-based web designers. You need to know this stuff. And the best way to start mastering it is right in your hands. Enjoy.

—Jeffrey Zeldman,
author of *Designing With Web Standards*

xvii

ABOUT THE AUTHOR

Dan Cederholm is a web designer, author, and founder of SimpleBits, a tiny design studio.

A recognized expert in the field of standards-based web design, Dan has worked with Google, MTV, ESPN, Fast Company, Blogger, Yahoo! (and others), also collaborating with Happy Cog on selected projects. He embraces flexible, adaptable design using web standards through his client work, writing, and speaking.

Dan is the author of two best-selling books: *Bulletproof Web Design, Second Edition* (New Riders, 2007) and *Web Standards Solutions* (Apress/friends of ED, 2004). Dan also runs a popular blog where he writes articles and commentary on the Web, technology, and life. And he plays a mean ukulele.

He lives in Salem, Massachusetts, with his wife Kerry and two kids, Jack and Tenley.

ABOUT THE TECHNICAL REVIEWER

Drew McLellan (first-edition technical reviewer) is a web application developer and author from just west of London. He spends his days heading up web development for a successful creative agency and his nights writing and editing technical books. He maintains a personal website on topics relating to his work at www.allinthehead.com.

Drew is the author of *Dreamweaver MX Web Development* (New Riders, 2002) and has published technical articles on sites such as A List Apart (www.alistapart.com) and Macromedia (www.macromedia.com). He is a member of the Web Standards Project (www.webstandards.org) and helps out with public relations and various other duties.

When he grows up, he'd like to be a spaceman.

Matt Heerema (special edition technical reviewer) is a designer and developer who has been making web pages since 1999. He currently works as principal designer for Weblogs, Inc. at AOL MediaGlow and on occasion consults on web standards, usability, accessibility, and optimization issues. Matt works out of his home in Iowa, where he lives with his wife, two daughters, and a cat. In his spare time he enjoys music, reading, outdoor sports, and the fellowship of his church. You can find out way more than you want to know about him at www.mattheerema.com.

ACKNOWLEDGMENTS

I'm entirely grateful to the following people who helped make this book possible:

To Chris Mills, for being in on this from the very beginning, guiding me through and making sure the whole thing came together.

To Drew McLellan, for his jolly good advice, guidance, and hard work, and Matt Heerema, for his hard work on this edition.

To Jeffrey Zeldman, without whom I wouldn't be writing this book and who has done more for web standards than anyone else.

To Douglas Bowman, for providing impeccable design inspiration and proving that CSS layouts can work beautifully on large-scale commercial sites.

To Dave Shea, for planting the garden and proving that CSS-based design can do just about anything we want it to.

To Jason Kottke, for posing the question (the spark).

To the readers of SimpleBits, for providing valuable discussions that fueled the idea for this book.

To Eric Meyer, Christopher Schmitt, Tantek Çelik, Molly Holzschlag, Todd Dominey, Mike Davidson, Ryan Carver, Dan Rubin, D. Keith Robinson, Mark Pilgrim, Joe Clark, Craig Saila, Nick Finck, Owen Briggs, Simon Willison, Ian Lloyd, Dan Benjamin, and many others, whose online and offline efforts within the web standards community have helped thousands like myself.

To the members of the Web Standards Project, whose education continues to benefit web designers and developers from all over.

To my former web team colleagues at Fast Company and Inc.—especially Rob Roesler, who gave me a great opportunity and support; David Searson, whom I've learned more from than he'll ever know; ditto Bob Joyal; Paul Maiorana for putting up with my Journey obsession; Daigo Fujiwara; Paul Cabana; Nick Colletta; Heath Row; Irina Lodkin; Carole Matthews; Becca Rees; Alex Ashton; Peter Wilkinson—and Linda Tischler for bringing me to FC.

To my family and friends and, most importantly, my wife Kerry—for her relentless support no matter what we're up to.

And to you, for reading.

INTRODUCTION

Welcome to the second edition of *Web Standards Solutions*. Why do we need an updated book? Well, while the rules have remained the same, the game has changed. We've had a full suite of new browsers since the first edition of this book (Internet Explorer 7 and 8, Chrome, Firefox 3, Safari 4, Opera 9), and their adoption of present (and evolving) standards is moving ahead at a rapid pace. The good news is that all of the main browser vendors have focused on standards compliance, so things are getting easier. The bad news is that there are still a lot of legacy browsers in the wild to account for, and many of the hoops we've had to jump through remain.

This book is designed to give you ammunition—ammunition to bring web standards solutions to your own projects and the ability to make better choices with markup and style. Throughout each chapter, we'll be comparing common web design methods, trying to answer why one way may be better than the other. By examining that comparison, we'll be able to apply the best tool for the job in our own projects.

But first, let's make sure we're all on the same page—this book is filled with acronyms, blocks of code, and concepts that might be foreign. First, let's talk about web standards.

What are web standards?

Quoting the World Wide Web Consortium (www.w3.org/Consortium/):

> *"The World Wide Web Consortium was created in October 1994 to lead the World Wide Web to its full potential by developing common protocols that promote its evolution and ensure its interoperability. W3C has around 400 member organizations from all over the world and has earned international recognition for its contributions to the growth of the Web."*

Founded by Tim Berners-Lee, the W3C is responsible for the web standards specifications that make up the Web today. We'll be concerning ourselves primarily with two of the standards: eXtensible HyperText Markup Language (XHTML), which features the semantics of HTML 4.01 with the syntax of XML; and Cascading Style Sheets (CSS), used for styling web pages.

Why web standards?

I bought a window shade yesterday. I measured the window. I went to the store. I pulled a 23-inch shade off the shelf and brought it home. It fits perfectly.

Last year, my wife and I bought a new dishwasher. We pulled the old one out and ordered a new one. When the new model arrived, it fit—perfectly.

I'm merely making a point here: that home improvement is made easier by standards. Someone like me can walk into a store, buy a garbage disposal hose, and more than likely it'll fit just right. I can also purchase a new doorknob, and nine times out of ten it'll fit the door without any major adjustments.

Predetermined, standard measurements make life easy for people who build and maintain houses. When new owners need to update or maintain their home, standards make it easier to fix or improve it.

This wasn't always the case, of course. Not all houses built prior to the twentieth century utilized standards. This didn't mean that houses built without standards were bad houses—it just meant that updating, fixing, or maintaining these houses required extra work.

Often, people buy old houses and renovate them. Once the hard work in renovating a house is complete, the owner can take advantage of standard sizes and measurements to make maintaining the house easier.

This book isn't about houses. Yet the preceding analogy can be applied to the Web—that by using standards in our web pages, maintaining them becomes far easier. Fellow web designers and developers can more easily jump in and understand how pages are structured and styled.

Historically, designers and developers have relied on bloated markup to achieve the designs that still flood the Web today. Nesting tables three levels deep while using transparent GIF images for pixel-precise layouts has been the norm for years. But as the support for standards has increased in the popular browsers, the ability to combine lean, structured markup and CSS has reached a threshold where being standards-compliant doesn't have to mean boring design.

The trend is shifting, and those who become aware of the benefits of web standards now will gain a jump on the rest of the web design and development community. This is the way things will be going.

By understanding and using web standards, the following benefits are there for the taking:

- *Reduced markup*: Less code means faster pages. Less code also means more server capacity, which in turn means less money needed for server space and bandwidth.
- *Increased separation of content and presentation*: By using CSS to control a site's design, updates and redesigns become easier. Site-wide changes can be made instantly through the update of a single style sheet.
- *Improved accessibility*: Web standards enable us to reach the highest possible number of browsers and devices. Content can be easily read in any browser, phone, PDA, or by those using assistive software.
- *Forward compatibility*: By authoring pages using web standards, you are ensuring that they will still be readable in the future.

Any one of the preceding benefits would be reason enough to use web standards, and this book will show you how to shake those bad habits as well as tips and tricks for creating attractive standards-based designs.

Why XHTML?

This book's markup examples are written in XHTML, or eXtensible HyperText Markup Language. Technically speaking, XHTML is the reformulation of HTML 4 in XML. What does that mean? Well, you're familiar with HTML, right? XHTML is just like that—with a few extra rules.

To once again quote the W3C (www.w3.org/TR/xhtml1/#xhtml):

> *"The XHTML family is the next step in the evolution of the Internet. By migrating to XHTML today, content developers can enter the XML world with all of its attendant benefits, while still remaining confident in their content's backward and future compatibility."*

That's a good place to start—future compatibility. By authoring web pages now using XHTML, we're taking steps to ensure these pages will work with future browsers and devices.

XHTML is also designed to be readable by the highest number of browsers, devices, and software. Markup that is written in XHTML stands a better chance of being properly understood no matter what is reading it.

But there are rules.

In the world of XHTML, stricter rules exist for what is considered valid markup. All tags and attributes must be in lowercase, attributes must be enclosed with double quotes, and all tags must eventually close. These are a few of the rules inherited from XML. But these rules are good for you.

In addition to future compatibility, by adhering to the stricter rules that govern proper and valid XHTML, designers and developers can more easily debug code (especially helpful when multiple authors are working on the same markup), and their pages have a better chance of rendering properly on browsers that understand standards as well. Throughout this book, we'll be using XHTML for all of our examples.

Structured markup

You may hear me use the word "semantic" quite a bit throughout this book. I may also use the term "structured markup" at times as well. They are interchangeable. What I mean when I talk about semantics is that we're striving to use tags that imply meaning, rather than a presentational instruction. Are you dealing with a list of items? Then mark it up as such. Is this a table of data? Then structure it that way.

By structuring web pages with semantic markup, we'll move closer to separating content from presentation and, in turn, our pages will have a better chance of being understood properly—the way you intend them to be—by a wider variety of browsers and devices.

As I had mentioned earlier, historically web designers have relied on nesting tables with spacer graphics to achieve pixel-precise layouts. The <table> element was used to map out every component of a web page, adding an enormous amount of unnecessary code—not to mention resulting pages that are practically unreadable for those browsing with text browsers, small-screened devices, or assistive software. The bloat was (and is) choking the Web.

Throughout the chapters of this book, I'll explain how semantic markup helps pages become leaner, more accessible, and easily styled with CSS.

Origins of this book

It started innocently enough. I thought I'd pose a simple quiz on my personal website. A multiple-choice question, where each of the answers achieved the same or similar results. Why is one method better than the other? That was to be the real answer to the quiz question.

The goal of the quiz was to show the pros and cons over each method, noting that even multiple methods that are valid markup aren't always necessarily the best solutions. Readers could comment and leave their opinions, and through the discussion came that ammunition I was talking about earlier. If we can understand why it's important to use page headings and proper lists, then we can take that information and apply it to our everyday projects.

It's also important to mention that I'm not trying to dictate singular ways of marking up certain components of a page—like everything in web design, there are multiple ways to achieve the same or similar results. Use what's best for the task at hand—but by understanding the pros and cons of the multiple methods, you can make better choices when the right time comes.

About the format

This book is separated into two parts, the first covering markup topics, the second covering CSS. Each chapter answers a specific question, often presenting multiple methods to achieve the same results. We'll look closely at each method, noting the good and bad of each. At the end of many of the chapters are additional "Extra credit" sections that delve further into more advanced markup and CSS topics relating to the chapter.

I hope you enjoy it—now let's get started.

GET DOWN WITH MARKUP

Spaghetti	Green Beans	Milk
Spaghetti	Green Beans	Milk
Spaghetti	Green Beans	Milk
Spaghetti	Green Beans	Milk
Spaghetti	Green Beans	Milk
Spaghetti	Green Beans	Milk

Spaghetti	Green Beans	Milk
Spaghetti	Green Beans	Milk
Spaghetti	Green Beans	Milk
Spaghetti	Green Beans	Milk
Spaghetti	Green Beans	Milk
Spaghetti	Green Beans	Milk

Spaghetti	Green Beans	Milk
Spaghetti	Green Beans	Milk
Spaghetti	Green Beans	Milk
Spaghetti	Green Beans	Milk
Spaghetti	Green Beans	Milk
Spaghetti	Green Beans	Milk

CHAPTER 1
LISTS

Apples	**Spaghetti**	Green Beans	Apples	**Spaghetti**	Green Beans	Apples	**Spaghetti**	Green Beans
Apples	**Spaghetti**	Green Beans	Apples	**Spaghetti**	Green Beans	Apples	**Spaghetti**	Green Beans
Apples	**Spaghetti**	Green Beans	Apples	**Spaghetti**	Green Beans	Apples	**Spaghetti**	Green Beans
Apples	**Spaghetti**	Green Beans	Apples	**Spaghetti**	Green Beans	Apples	**Spaghetti**	Green Beans
Apples	**Spaghetti**	Green Beans	Apples	**Spaghetti**	Green Beans	Apples	**Spaghetti**	Green Beans
Apples	**Spaghetti**	Green Beans	Apples	**Spaghetti**	Green Beans	Apples	**Spaghetti**	Green Beans

Lists. They're found in just about any page on the Web. Lists of hyperlinks, lists of items in a shopping cart, lists of your favorite movies—even lists for the navigation of an entire website. While it might seem arbitrary to some, *how* we mark up these lists is what we'll explore, discovering the advantages (and disadvantages) of a few common methods. Later, we'll put those advantages to the test with several examples on how to style an ordinary list.

Let's go shopping

Initially, I thought about using a laundry list as the example for the chapter, but then quickly realized that I have no idea what items would be included in such a list. So for this example's sake, groceries it is....

Let's imagine that you needed to mark up a simple grocery list for inclusion on your personal website. You may be wondering what place a grocery list has on any website, but that's beside the point. We just need a reason to start thinking about lists.

On the page, say we'd like the grocery list to look like... well, a list—a vertical series of items, each on its own line:

Apples

Spaghetti

Green Beans

Milk

A seemingly simple task, right? Now, like all facets of web design and development, there are a variety of ways we could attack this to achieve the same (or similar) results. As in all examples found throughout this book, I'll be presenting things from an e**X**tensible **H**yper**T**ext **M**arkup **L**anguage (**XHTML**) point of view—making sure that the methods chosen are valid markup and adhere to the standards outlined by the **W**orld **W**ide **W**eb Consortium (**W3C**, www.w3.org/).

We could simply add a `<br />` element after each item and be done with it, or we could tap into various list elements to get the job done. Let's look at three different possibilities, and the consequences of using each of them.

Quiz time

Which of the following would be best for marking up a grocery list?

Method A: The <br /> breakdown

```
Apples<br />
Spaghetti<br />
Green Beans<br />
Milk<br />
```

Method A is certainly one that's been used for years, heavily, on perhaps millions of web pages. In fact, I'm sure we're all guilty of using this approach at one time or another, right? We'd like each item in the list to be on its own line, and by inserting a break element (using the valid XHTML, self-closing version here, `<br />`) a line break will be added after each item. That's about all it does, and it *seems* to work.

However, what if we wanted to style the grocery list differently from other elements on the page? For instance, what if we would like this list to have red links instead of the default blue, or a different font size from the rest of the text on the page? We really can't. We're stuck with whatever default font styles we've set for the entire document (if there are any at all), and since there's no surrounding element for the list, we can't assign it any unique CSS rules.

It's a wrap

Let's also say that we added a particularly long grocery item to the list: "Five Foot Loaf of Anthony's Italian Bread." Depending on where this list is placed in the layout of the page, long items may run the risk of wrapping to the next line if there isn't enough horizontal space, or if the user's browser window width is narrow.

It would also be nice to take into account the possibility of low-vision users increasing their default text size to gain readability. Line items that we thought fit just great in a narrow column, as in Figure 1-1, now break in unpredictable places, as in Figure 1-2, throwing off the design when the text size is increased by the user.

Apples
Spaghetti
Green Beans
Milk
Five Foot Loaf of Anthony's Italian Bread

Apples
Spaghetti
Green Beans
Milk
Five Foot Loaf of
Anthony's Italian
Bread

Figure 1-1. An example with default text size

Figure 1-2. The same example with increased text size

Hmm. Now, I know I'm supposed to buy bread, but the two lines that precede it in Figure 1-2 are a bit confusing.

A similar wrapping dilemma rears its ugly head when long lines are viewed on the small screen of a device such as a phone or Blackberry. The ultimate technophile may stroll into the supermarket with small-screened device in hand, rather than the traditional sheet of paper for their shopping list, yet they eventually wander aimlessly, looking up and down the aisles for "Anthony's Italian."

I'm essentially proving a point here—that using Method A doesn't take into account the fluidity that web pages can have depending on variables that are outside the designer's control.

Method B: The bullet that bites

```
<li>Apples<br />
<li>Spaghetti<br />
<li>Green Beans<br />
<li>Milk<br />
```

Most competent browsers will insert a bullet to the left of a list item when the `<li>` element is used. One might use Method B to achieve those results, adding the `<li>` by itself when a bullet is desired. However, some of those same competent browsers won't display the bullet when an `<li>` element isn't contained within one of its proper parents, the mighty `<ul>`. The `<li>`'s other parent is the `<ol>` element, for "ordered lists," which I'll discuss later in this book.

The bullet *does* help the wrapping issue to a certain extent. A new grocery item would be signified by a bullet, to its left. If an item wraps to the next line, the absence of a bullet should be enough to distinguish itself from being a whole new item. But there is something else wrong with Method B, aside from its resulting display: it's not valid.

Validation, please

According to the W3C's XHTML 1.0 specification, all elements must eventually close—and if we were to go ahead and open an `<li>` for each grocery item, without closing it at the other end as in the example, shame on us!

We've mimicked the automatic line-breaking that occurs when a proper unordered list is used by adding the `<br />` element at the end. But there's a better way.

It's valuable to get used to the idea of writing valid markup, consistently. By ensuring our markup is valid, we'll worry less about problems that may occur because of unclosed or improperly nested elements in the future. Not to mention that if anyone else is looking at our code, it's easier for everyone involved to dive in and understand exactly what's going on.

Be sure to use the W3C's online validation tool (http://validator.w3.org/) to validate your files by URI or file upload. You'll be happy you did in the long run.

Method C: Getting closer

```
<li>Apples</li>
<li>Spaghetti</li>
<li>Green Beans</li>
<li>Milk</li>
```

Method C brings us closer to a preferable solution, but fails miserably in one potentially obvious way: it's *still* not valid markup.

We've closed each <li> element properly, and since they are **block-level** elements, using them eliminates the need for a <br /> element, putting each list item on its own line. But we're missing an outer layer of structure, lacking a containing element that denotes "This group of items is a list!"

It's important to view this from a semantic angle as well—that the list is a group of items that *belong* together, and therefore they should be denoted as such. Furthermore, using proper list elements says very clearly to the browser, software, or device, "This group of items is a list!" This is a good example of how semantic markup is about structuring items for what they *are*.

> ***Block level vs. inline***: *HTML elements can inherently be either block level or inline. Block-level elements begin on their own line, followed by a line break, while inline elements are rendered on the same line as other inline elements. Block-level elements can contain other block-level or inline elements, while inline elements can't contain block-level elements.*
>
> *Some examples of block-level elements include* <div>, <h1>–<h6>, *and* <form>. *Some examples of inline elements include* <span>, <strong>, <em>, *and* <q>.

If we were to look at our grocery list in purely an XML sort of way, we might choose to mark it up as shown in this example:

```
<grocerylist>
  <item>Apples</item>
  <item>Spaghetti</item>
  <item>Green Beans</item>
  <item>Milk</item>
</grocerylist>
```

The entire list has a containing element, <grocerylist>, that all of the grocery items belong to. Grouping the items in this manner will make life easier for XML-based applications that may want to extract the items from the list.

For instance, a developer could author an XSLT style sheet that would transform this list of items into XHTML, plain text, or even a PDF document. Because of the predictable nature of a group of list items, software will have an easy time taking the information and doing something useful with it.

While I'm not dealing with XML in this book directly, the principles are carried over to the world of XHTML. Providing a meaningful structure to our markup gains flexibility later on. Whether it be the increased ease of adding CSS to properly structured documents or the improved manageability of making changes to markup that is easy to understand—providing that structure will make for less work later on down the road.

Let's take a close look at Method D and see how this all fits together—providing a structure that most browsers and devices can read, while also allowing us to style our list in several different ways.

Method D: Wrapper's delight

```
<ul>
  <li>Apples</li>
  <li>Spaghetti</li>
  <li>Green Beans</li>
  <li>Milk</li>
</ul>
```

So what makes Method D so special? First and foremost, it's completely valid. A proper unordered list has a containing <ul> element, with each item within wrapped in opening and closing <li> elements. Now just when you think all we're going for here is demonstrating how to be valid for validity's sake, we'll take a look at it in action.

Because we've properly marked up our grocery list, each item will be on a separate line (due to the block-level nature of the <li>) and most visual browsers will render a bullet next to each item, as well as indent any wrapping lines that may occur (see Figure 1-3).

- Apples
- Spaghetti
- Green Beans
- Milk

Figure 1-3. Default rendering of an unordered list

Users of Blackberrys, phones, or other small-screened devices will also be able to view the list in a similar, clearly organized fashion. Because we've told the device what the data is (a list in this case), it can best decide how to display it according to its capabilities.

If a long line wraps due to increased text size or a narrow browsing window, the wrapped line will appear indented to line up with the text above it. It'll be darn clear to distinguish between items no matter what the browsing circumstances.

Summary

Now that I've picked each possible method apart, let's quickly review what I've covered about each:

Method A:

- Leaves out the possibility for styling the list uniquely.
- Could create confusion when longer lines wrap in a narrow column or small-screened device.
- Lacks semantic meaning.

Method B:

- Adding a bullet helps for signifying a new item, but some browsers may choose not to show it without its parent `<ul>` element.
- No containing `<ul>` element or closing `</li>` elements means difficult to style.
- Invalid.

Method C:

- Closing the `</li>` element eliminates the need for `<br />` elements.
- Omitting the `<ul>` element makes it difficult to style this particular list differently.
- Invalid.

Method D:

- Valid!
- Provides semantic meaning and structure.
- Bullets will render to the left of each item on most browsers.
- Wrapping lines will indent on most browsers.
- It can be easily styled uniquely with CSS.

As you can see, you can learn a lot from a seemingly innocent little question. Even if you're already using Method D exclusively on all of your pages, it's nice to know *why* you do things the way you do. We'll continue to explore such "why" questions throughout the book, giving you more ammunition to make the best choice at the right time.

Extra credit

For extra credit, let's look at a few different ways we can take advantage of our marked-up grocery list, using CSS to style it several different ways. We'll throw away defaults, add custom bullets, and then turn it horizontal for a few navigation bar ideas.

Bite the bullet

"But I hate the way the bullets look on my grocery list, so I should just keep using those `<br />` elements."

No need to revert to old habits—we can continue to use our structured unordered list and let CSS turn off the bullets and indenting (if that sort of thing floats your boat). The key here is to keep our list structured, and then let CSS handle presentation details.

First add a CSS rule that will turn off the bullets:

```
ul {
  list-style: none;
  }
```

the results of which can be seen in Figure 1-4.

Apples
Spaghetti
Green Beans
Milk

Figure 1-4. A list with
bullets turned off

Now, we'll turn off indenting. By default, there is a certain amount of padding added to
the left side of any unordered list. But don't worry—we can just chop it off if we'd like:

```
ul {
   list-style: none;
   padding-left: 0;
   }
```

The results are seen in Figure 1-5.

Apples
Spaghetti
Green Beans
Milk

Figure 1-5. A list with
bullets and indenting
turned off

While the example in Figure 1-5 *looks* like we've just marked it up with a few <br /> elements, it's still the same structured, valid, unordered list—ready to be viewed in any
browser or device and styled differently with the update of a few CSS rules, if so desired.

Getting fancier with custom bullets

Perhaps you *would* like bullets for your list but want to use your own bullet image rather
than letting the browser use its boring defaults. There are two ways to do this—I prefer
the second due to its more consistent results across various browsers.

The first option is to use the list-style-image property to assign an image to use in place
of the default bullet:

```
ul {
   list-style-image: url(fancybullet.gif);
   }
```

This is the simplest method; however, it renders somewhat inconsistent results in some browsers in respect to the vertical positioning of the image. Some browsers will line it up directly in
the middle of list item text; others may position it slightly higher. It's a bit inconsistent.

To get around the vertical placement issue that list-style-image reveals on a few popular browsers, I like to use an alternative method, which is to set the image as a background for each <li> element.

First we'll turn off the default bulleting, and then add our own background image:

```
ul {
  list-style: none;
  }

li {
  background: url(fancybullet.gif) no-repeat 0 50%;
  padding-left: 17px;
  }
```

no-repeat tells the browser not to tile the image (which it does by default), while the 0 50% tells the browser to place the background 0 pixels from the left and 50 percent down from the top, essentially vertically centering the fancybullet.gif. We could have also used exact pixel locations from left and top the same way. 0 6px would have placed the bullet 0 pixels from the left and 6 pixels from the top.

We also add 17 pixels of padding to the left of the list item so that our 15-pixel-wide by 5-pixel-high image will show through completely, and with a little whitespace, without any overlapping of the text. This value would be adjusted depending on the width of the bullet image you were using (see Figure 1-6).

Figure 1-6. A list with custom bullets

Lists that navigate

I've shared a few methods of turning unordered lists into horizontal navigation on my personal site (www.simplebits.com), creating tab-like effects using ordinary, structured XHTML—just like the example grocery list.

For instance, here we'll take the grocery list and turn it into a navigation bar for an online supermarket (that happens to only sell a handful of items).

We'd like the navigation in this case to be horizontal and also have some way of highlighting an item when it's hovered over or selected, creating a tab-like effect.

First, we'll add an id to our list so that we can apply specific CSS styles to it. We'll also make each grocery item a link.

```
<ul id="minitabs">
  <li><a href="/apples/">Apples</a></li>
  <li><a href="/spaghetti/">Spaghetti</a></li>
  <li><a href="/greenbeans/">Green Beans</a></li>
  <li><a href="/milk/">Milk</a></li>
</ul>
```

Now, start to add the accompanying CSS:

```
#minitabs {
  margin: 0;
  padding: 0 0 20px 10px;
  border-bottom: 1px solid #696;
  }

#minitabs li {
  margin: 0;
  padding: 0;
  display: inline;
  list-style: none;
  }
```

What we've done here is essentially turn off bullets and default indenting. We've also taken the first step in making the list horizontal, rather than vertical, by setting the display to inline. A bottom border has been added as well to help define the group of links.

The second step in making the navigation bar horizontal is to float our links to the left. We'll also style the hyperlinks a little and adjust some padding and margins:

```
#minitabs {
  margin: 0;
  padding: 0 0 20px 10px;
  border-bottom: 1px solid #696;
  }


#minitabs li {
  margin: 0;
  padding: 0;
  display: inline;
  list-style-type: none;
  }

#minitabs a {
  float: left;
  line-height: 14px;
  font-weight: bold;
  margin: 0 10px 4px 10px;
  text-decoration: none;
  color: #9c9;
  }
```

Here we've told all a elements within our list to float: left, essentially forcing them all to line up horizontally in a row. We've also added some color, made the links bold, and turned off underlines.

Next, create a tab-like border below the links that is activated when hovered or selected:

```
#minitabs {
  margin: 0;
  padding: 0 0 20px 10px;
  border-bottom: 1px solid #696;
  }

#minitabs li {
  margin: 0;
  padding: 0;
  display: inline;
  list-style-type: none;
  }

#minitabs a {
  float: left;
  line-height: 14px;
  font-weight: bold;
  margin: 0 10px 4px 10px;
  text-decoration: none;
  color: #9c9;
  }

#minitabs a.active, #minitabs a:hover {
  border-bottom: 4px solid #696;
  padding-bottom: 2px;
  color: #363;
  }

#minitabs a:hover {
  color: #696;
  }
```

For highlighting and hovering, we've added a 4-pixel-tall bottom border to the selected or hovered <li> elements to create a tab-like effect. Highlighted tabs can also be "kept lit" by adding class="active" to the href of our choice:

```
<li><a href="/spaghetti/" class="active">spaghetti</a></li>
```

This active class shares identical CSS rules with a:hover.

Figure 1-7 shows the resulting navigation bar.

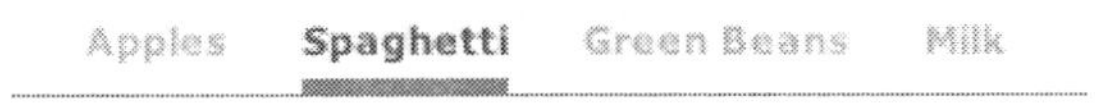

Apples   **Spaghetti**   Green Beans   Milk

Figure 1-7. The resulting mini-tab navigation bar

I've used this method of navigation for a previous incarnation of my own personal site (www.simplebits.com), but you can also see them in action (along with the code) at *Listamatic*, a resource for lists styled with CSS (http://css.maxdesign.com.au/ listamatic/horizontal06.htm).

With some padding and border width adjustments, a variety of tab-like effects can be achieved, and we've done all of this so far using zero images or JavaScript and our basic XHTML-structured grocery list. Hooray for us!

Mini-tab shapes

For something a little different than your average, boxy CSS border, with a few slight modifications we can add fun shapes to the mix to create some interesting navigational effects.

We can use the same unordered list, building on similar CSS from the previous mini-tab example:

```
#minitabs {
  margin: 0;
  padding: 0 0 20px 10px;
  border-bottom: 1px solid #9FB1BC;
  }

#minitabs li {
  margin: 0;
  padding: 0;
  display: inline;
  list-style-type: none;
  }


#minitabs a {
  float: left;
  line-height: 14px;
  font-weight: bold;
  padding: 0 12px 6px 12px;
  text-decoration: none;
  color: #708491;
  }

#minitabs a.active, #minitabs a:hover {
  color: #000;
  background: url(tab_pyra.gif) no-repeat bottom center;
  }
```

This CSS will probably look similar to the previous example. The main difference here is the absence of a border-bottom that created the 4-pixel-tall tab and the addition of a single background-image set to sit bottom center for all hover and selected states (see Figure 1-8).

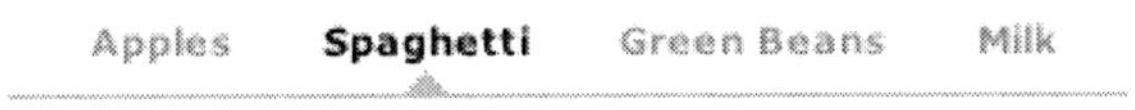

Apples   **Spaghetti**   Green Beans   Milk

Figure 1-8. A mini-tab navigation bar with shaped background images

The trick here is to choose an image that is narrow enough to fit under your smallest navigation item. This ensures you'll only need **one single image** to use for highlighting all of your navigational links, regardless of varying character widths. There are, of course, unlimited possibilities in regard to the shapes you could use on your own projects (see Figure 1-9).

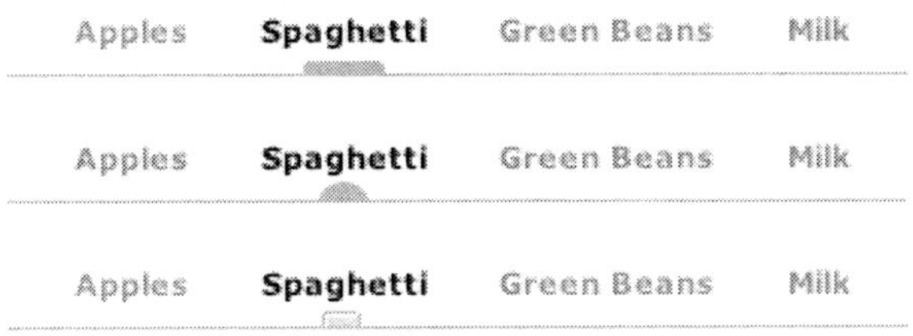

Apples   **Spaghetti**   Green Beans   Milk

Apples   **Spaghetti**   Green Beans   Milk

Apples   **Spaghetti**   Green Beans   Milk

Figure 1-9. A few other shape possibilities

For source code and working examples of these mini-tabs, see www.simplebits.com/publications/tips/. And for more creative ways to style lists, check out Mark Newhouse's "Taming Lists" article at *A List Apart* magazine (www.alistapart.com/stories/taminglists/).

CHAPTER 2
HEADINGS

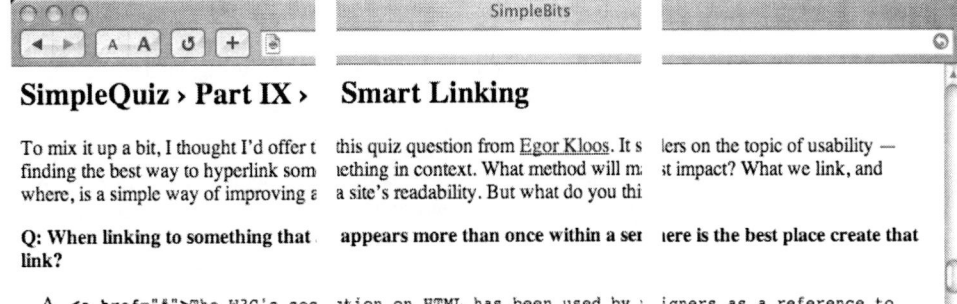

SimpleQuiz › Part IX ›   Smart Linking

To mix it up a bit, I thought I'd offer t   this quiz question from Egor Kloos. It s   lers on the topic of usability —
finding the best way to hyperlink som   iething in context. What method will m: st impact? What we link, and
where, is a simple way of improving ɛ   a site's readability. But what do you thi

**Q: When linking to something that   appears more than once within a sei   iere is the best place create that
link?**

    A. `<a href="#">`The W3C's sec   :tion on HTML has been used by :   igners as a reference to

Not only are page headings necessary for just about any web page, but when marked up properly, they can be powerful both to the design and accessibility of a site.

Visually, a page heading is commonly treated with a larger font size and maybe a different color or typeface than the normal flow of body text. A page heading "briefly describes the topic of the section it introduces," so says the W3C, delineating the various sections that may appear on a page.

So how should we mark up a page heading to get the most out of the information we're presenting? In this chapter, we'll get a chance to investigate a few familiar ways of dealing with headings, trying to find the one that will give us the most bang for our buck. Later, we'll take the best method and style it up a bit with a few CSS tricks and techniques.

What is the best way to mark up the title of a document?

To answer the preceding question, let's imagine that we were placing the title of the document at the top of the page. We'll then look at three ways of achieving similar results.

Method A: Meaningful?

```
<span class="heading">Super Cool Page Title</span>
```

Although <span> can be a handy element in some circumstances, it doesn't make a whole lot of sense for page headings. One benefit to using this method is that we could add a CSS rule for the heading class that's been assigned to make the text appear *like* a heading.

```
.heading {
  font-size: 24px;
  font-weight: bold;
  color: blue;
  }
```

Now all headings marked up with the heading class will be big, bold, and blue. Great, right? But what if someone views the page using a browser or device that doesn't support CSS?

For instance, what if we were putting this particular CSS rule in an external style sheet that was being hidden from older browsers—or if a screen reader was reading the page to a visually impaired person? A user visiting our page by these means would see (or hear) nothing different from normal text on the page.

While class="heading" adds a bit of meaning to the element, <span> is just a generic wrapper, free from default styling in most browsers.

Search engines that crawl this page would gloss over the <span> element as if it wasn't even there, unwilling to give extra weight to any keywords that might be contained within. We'll talk more about the search engine/header relationship further on in the chapter.

Finally, since the <span> element is an inline element, we would most likely need to wrap Method A in an extra element that is block-level, like a <p> or <div> element, in order to make it live on its own line, further mucking up the markup with unnecessary code. So even by adding the extra, necessary markup, browsers that lack CSS support would still display the text no differently from any other on the page.

Method B: The p and b combo

```
<p><b>Super Cool Page Title</b></p>
```

Using a paragraph element, as Method B does, will get us the block-level display that we'd like and the <b> element will render the text in bold (on most browsers)—but we're faced with the same meaningless results when marking up an important heading this way.

Unlike Method A, the presence of the <b> element will most likely render the text in bold in visual browsers—even with the absence of CSS. But as with the <span> element, search engines won't place a higher priority on something that is simply bold in its own paragraph.

Difficult to style

Using the plain Jane combination of <p> and <b> elements also leaves out the possibility of later styling this heading differently from any other paragraph on the page. We'd probably want to call out headings in a unique way, adding definition and structure to the page content—but we're stuck with just having it appear bold using this method.

Method C: Style and substance

```
<h1>Super Cool Page Title</h1>
```

Ah, good ol' heading elements. They've been around this whole time, but plenty of web designers have yet to fully embrace them in a consistent manner. When used properly, page headings can anchor a page's content, providing flexible, indexable, and stylable structure.

Markup-wise, you have to love their simplicity. There is no need for adding extra elements, and you could even argue that you're saving a few bytes by using them as opposed to the other two options. Negligible maybe, but every little bit counts.

<h1> through <h6> denote the six levels of headings, from most important (<h1>) to least important (<h6>). They are block-level in nature and don't need an additional element to put them on their own line. Simple, and effective—the right tool for the job.

Easily styled

Because the <h1> element we're using is unique, rather than <b> or <p> elements that are likely to be used throughout the page, we can then style it in a variety of ways using CSS (which we'll get a chance to explore later in the "Extra credit" section of this chapter).

More importantly, though, is that without any styling at all, a heading element is obviously a heading! Visual browsers will render an <h1> in a larger, bold font. An unstyled view of the page will show the document structure as it was intended, with the proper heading element conveying *meaning* rather than just presentational instructions (see Figure 2-1).

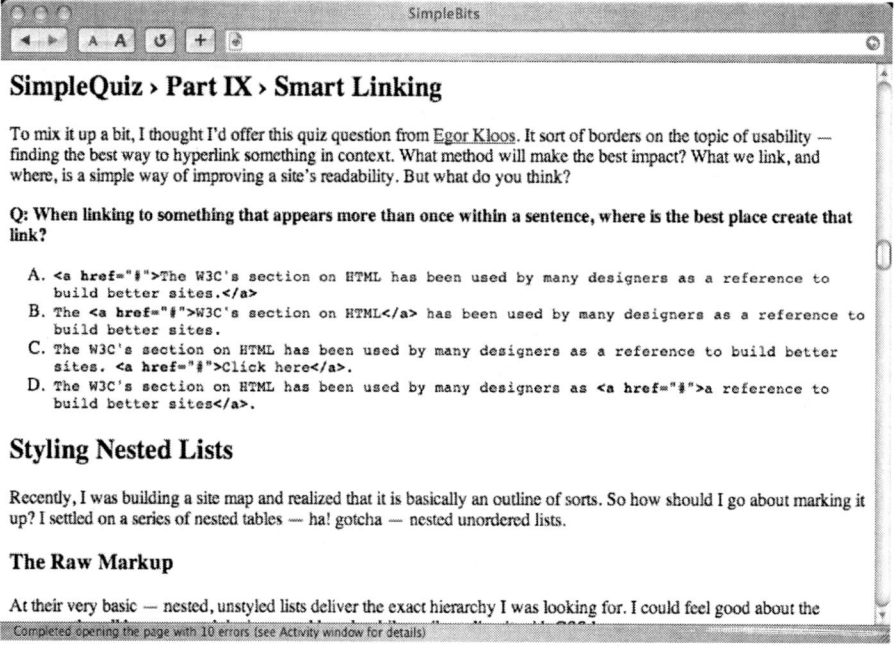

Figure 2-1. An example of an unstyled view of a page that uses heading elements

Screen readers, handheld devices, phones, and other visual and nonvisual browsers will also know what to do with a heading element, handling it correctly and treating it with importance over normal text on the page. Use a <span> element, and browsers that don't (or can't) handle CSS will present it as if it were nothing particularly special.

Default distaste

Historically, designers may have avoided using heading elements altogether due to their beastly appearance when viewed unstyled with default settings. Alternatively, some may have avoided <h1> or <h2> because of their larger size by default, instead opting to use a higher heading number to achieve a smaller text size.

It's important to stress, however, that by using CSS we can easily alter the appearance of these headings in any manner we wish—an <h1>, for instance, doesn't have to be a gigantic billboard, engulfing half of the user's screen. Later in this chapter, I'll demonstrate how easy it is to style headings with CSS, hopefully helping to alleviate the fear of the mighty <h1>.

Search engine friendly

This is a huge one. Search engines love heading elements. A <span> element or plain paragraph that is bold, on the other hand, means less to them. Properly marking up your headings with <h1> through <h6> elements takes little effort, yet can make it easier for search engines to index your pages, and ultimately for people to find them as well.

Search engine robots place special importance on heading elements—a place where you're likely to have some keywords sprinkled about. Just as they index <title> and <meta>, they'll set their sights next on any heading elements you may have down the page. If you don't use them, those keywords contained within them won't be as valuable and could get overlooked.

So with very little effort, you'll be increasing the likelihood of someone finding your site based on its *content*. Sounds good, doesn't it?

An aside on heading order

In the example, this particular heading is the most important on the page because it's the title of the document. Therefore, we'll use the most important heading element, <h1>. According to the W3C, some believe it to be bad practice to skip heading levels. For instance, imagine we have the following on the page:

```
<h1>Super Cool Page Title</h1>
```

As mentioned previously, designers might have used an <h4> for the most important heading on the page, simply because the default font size wasn't as honking large as it would be if they used an <h1>. But remember, structure now, style later. We can always style the heading to whatever text size we'd like using CSS.

Summary

Let's recap why, in general, it's best to use heading elements (<h1> through <h6>) to introduce different sections on a page.

Method A:

- Visual browsers (e.g., Firefox, Safari, and Internet Explorer) will render the heading the same as normal text on the page when CSS is disabled or unavailable. Nonvisual browsers won't know the difference between the heading and normal text.
- Search engines won't place greater importance over headings that are marked up with <span>.
- We can style it uniquely, but we're locked into the heading class when adding similar headings in the future.

Method B:

- Visual browsers will render the text only in bold and the same size as the default.
- We can't style this heading uniquely from other text on the page.
- Search engines won't place greater importance over headings that are marked up with <p> and <b> elements.

Method C:

- Conveys meaning to the text contained within.
- Visual and nonvisual browsers will treat the heading correctly regardless of any style that is associated with it.
- Easily styled uniquely with CSS.
- Search engines will place importance on keywords contained within heading elements.

Extra credit

So here we'll take Method C and put it to the test with some simple CSS styling. We'll take full advantage of the heading element's uniqueness, sleeping well at night because we know the underlying structure is solid for whatever browser or device that may read it. Then we'll dress it up and take it out on the town (if you could actually take an HTML *element out* anywhere . . . and I've tried).

Simple styling

Using CSS, the simplest and easiest thing we can do is give our heading different font styles. We can create a CSS rule that will apply those styles to all <h1> elements that appear on the page (or an entire site, when using an external style sheet). If later we wanted to change the color, size, or font face of all <h1> elements that appear on an entire site, then all we need to do is change a few CSS rules, and they'll be instantly changed. Sounds pretty enticing, doesn't it?

Let's reacquaint ourselves with our super cool heading:

```
<h1>Super Cool Page Title</h1>
```

Let's change the color, font face, and size of it with CSS:

```
h1 {
   font-family: Arial, sans-serif;
   font-size: 24px;
   color: #369;
   }
```

We've just said, rather simply, that any <h1> found throughout the page should be treated in Arial (or default sans-serif) typeface at 24 pixels and blue, as demonstrated in Figure 2-2.

Super Cool Page Title

Figure 2-2. An example of a styled heading

Next, let's add a 1-pixel gray border underneath the text for added definition (see also Figure 2-3):

```
h1 {
    font-family: Arial, sans-serif;
    font-size: 24px;
    color: #369;
    padding-bottom: 4px;
    border-bottom: 1px solid #999;
    }
```

Super Cool Page Title

Figure 2-3. A styled heading with a gray bottom border

We've added a bit of padding under the text to let the line underneath breathe a little. The border will extend not only under the text, but because a heading is a block-level element, it will stretch across as wide as it can horizontally on the page.

It's also worth pointing out that we're using the shorthand method for creating a border by specifying the three parts in one statement: width, style, and color. Play around with these values to see different results.

Adding backgrounds

Backgrounds can add neat effects to page headings. Add a little padding and a background color, and we'll have image-free but stylish titles, as shown in this example:

```
h1 {
    font-family: Arial, sans-serif;
    font-size: 24px;
    color: #fff;
    padding: 4px;
    background-color: #696;
    }
```

We've turned the text white, adding 4 pixels of padding all the way around, and changed the background to green. As Figure 2-4 shows, this will create a nice, fat, pool-table green bar that'll extend across the page, dividing the section.

Super Cool Page Title

Figure 2-4. A heading example with background color and padding

Backgrounds and borders

By adding a thin border to the bottom of the heading, coupled with a light background color, you can create a three-dimensional effect without the need for a single image.

The CSS is similar to the previous example, with a few color changes and the addition of a 2-pixel border to the bottom.

```
h1 {
    font-family: Arial, sans-serif;
    font-size: 24px;
    color: #666;
    padding: 4px;
    background-color: #ddd;
    border-bottom: 2px solid #ccc;
    }
```

By playing around with different shades of the same color, the dimensional effect comes to life, as shown in Figure 2-5.

Super Cool Page Title

Figure 2-5. A heading with background and border bottom

Tiled backgrounds

The possibilities become far more creative when background images are added to the mix. Let's create a small, 10×10-pixel image in Photoshop or your favorite image editor that has a black border on top, with a gray gradient flowing down to the bottom, as shown in Figure 2-6.

Figure 2-6. A 10×10-pixel image created in Photoshop (magnified)

We can take this tiny image and tile it along the bottom of our <h1> using CSS:

```
h1 {
    font-family: Arial, sans-serif;
    font-size: 24px;
    color: #369;
    padding-bottom: 14px;
    background: url(10x10.gif) repeat-x  bottom;
    }
```

By telling the browser to repeat-x the background image, we ensure that it will tile only horizontally (repeat-y will tile vertically). We're also setting the image to the bottom of the element, and by adding a little extra padding-bottom, we can adjust the space between the tiled image and the text above (see Figure 2-7).

Super Cool Page Title

Figure 2-7. A heading with tiled background image

Swappable icons

Instead of hard-coding decorative bullets and icons on the page as inline images, we can continue to use the background property to set icons to the left of the text using CSS. This method makes changing the look and feel of a site a snap—with the update of that one CSS file instantly changing all the pages of an entire site.

The code is much like the preceding tiled example:

```
h1 {
    font-family: Arial, sans-serif;
    font-size: 24px;
    color: #369;
    padding-left: 30px;
    background: url(icon.gif) no-repeat 0 50%;
    }
```

Here we're giving extra space to the left (where we'd like the icon to show through), and we're saying no-repeat so that the background image displays only once (see Figure 2-8). We'd like it to line up 0 pixels from the left and halfway (50%) from the top.

Super Cool Page Title

Figure 2-8. A heading with a background image icon

Easy updates

Think about a scenario where, instead of using the preceding example, we've coded these icons with <img> elements right in the page on a site that contains 100 documents. Perhaps the icon matches a theme that's found throughout the site. Fast-forward a few weeks when the site's owner decides to change the site's look and feel. The new icon is a different dimension than the old one. Uh-oh. We'll need to go back into **all 100 documents** to change each <img> element and update it with the new image path. Yuck. And just imagine what the extra time can do to a project's budget, pushing a deadline further out than would be needed otherwise. Time is money.

Additionally, by keeping those nonessential, decorative images in one CSS file, it's possible to change the background image in a matter of minutes rather than days, while the site will instantly be updated. You can start to see the power of separating your structured markup from the presentation.

The chameleon effect

I'm going to go ahead and contradict myself here for a minute, but I think this next trick can be useful in some circumstances. It's a method I used heavily in the standards-compliant redesign of *Fast Company* magazine's website (www.fastcompany.com) in April 2003.

We were using small, 13×13-pixel icons within most of the <h3> headings that were used throughout the site like this:

```
<h3><img src="http://images.fastcompany.com/icon/first_imp.gif"➥
width="13" height="13" alt="*" /> FIRST IMPRESSION</h3>
```

We had decided on coding them right in the page for two reasons. There were a variety of icons, depending on the topic of the heading (a book for the Book Club, quote marks for the daily quote, etc.). The second reason we coded them in the page was because, at the time, we swapped the color scheme of the entire site each month to coincide with the current issue's magazine cover. This swapping was made possible by using CSS.

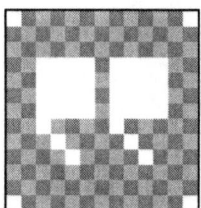

To allow the icons to swap color along with other elements on the page without having to continually create new images for each new color, we created one set using only two colors: white and transparent (where the swapped color would show through). Figure 2-9 shows an example of one of the icons that was used to call out the home page's daily quote.

Figure 2-9. A 13×13-pixel transparent icon (zoomed)

To fill in the transparent portion of the icon, we used the handy CSS background property yet again to specify the color we'd like to shine through. We wanted this color to appear *only* behind the image and not the associated text in the heading. We achieved this by using a contextual selector to apply rules to the images that are contained only *within* <h3> elements.

```
h3 img {
  background: #696;
}
```

The preceding code states that all img elements that are contained within <h3> elements should have a background of green. That color shows through in the transparent spots of the image, while the white portions stay white. Each month, we could update this one CSS rule with a different color value to magically change the color of every heading and icon combination that we had throughout the site. Like magic.

Aligning the <img> element

To help the icon line up with the text correctly (we want it to be centered vertically), we add the following CSS rule:

```
h3 img {
  background: #696;
  vertical-align: middle;
}
```

That ensures the image will align to the middle of the text contained within the <h3>. Figure 2-10 shows the resulting heading.

☐ FIRST IMPRESSION

Figure 2-10. The resulting transparent image with CSS background applied

I bring up this particular solution for another notable reason—background colors that are specified in CSS show up *behind* any images that are either coded inline on the page *or* also specified in CSS.

For instance, let's go back to the previous "Swappable Icons" example and add some background color:

```
h1 {
    font-family: Arial, sans-serif;
    font-size: 24px;
    color: #fff;
    padding-left: 30px;
    background: #696 url(transparent_icon.gif) no-repeat 0 50%;
}
```

The transparent_icon.gif will sit above the color we specified before it in the same rule (see Figure 2-11)—in this case #696, a lovely shade of pool-table green.

→ Super Cool Page Title

Figure 2-11. A heading with background image and color applied

This trick becomes especially handy when placing little rounded corners or decorative images on a page where color is concerned. These nonessential images are then completely contained in the CSS file and are easily swappable if an update happens in the future. Easy work now, less work later.

I liked the idea so much, I ended up creating a customizable icon set based on this concept, where the purchaser can enter an HTML hex color code, creating a set of stock icons that will fit their own site's palette. Check them out at http://www.iconshoppe.com/families/chameleon.

Wrapping up

I hope that by comparing a few common methods of markup, it's easy to see the value in using proper heading elements. Visual and nonvisual browsers and devices will understand and display them accordingly, search engines will index them properly, and styles can be easily applied and maintained using CSS.

CHAPTER 3
TABLES ARE EVIL?

Boston Red Sox World S

Year	Opponent
1918	Chicago Cubs
1916	Brooklyn Robins
1915	Philadelphia Phillies
1912	New York Giants

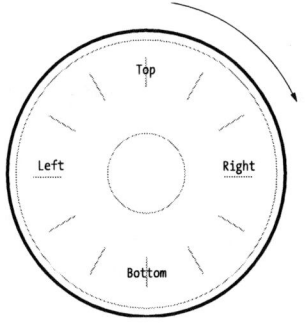

Boston Red Sox World

▦ Year	▨ Opponent
1918	Chicago Cubs
1916	Brooklyn Robins
1915	Philadelphia Phillie
1912	New York Giants

Say what? When did using tables become an act of pure evil? Certainly one of the biggest myths of building a site with web standards is that you should never use a table. Ever. That you should avoid them like the plague, seal them up, and place them on a dusty shelf like an artifact of the web development days of old.

Where did the distaste come from? It probably began innocently enough, with at least good intentions from the start. Many have been rightfully preaching the benefits of tossing out conventional nested table and spacer GIF layouts and replacing them with lean, structured markup and CSS for presentation. We may have tossed out the peeler with the peelings, though, with some touting the banishment of tables in general—for *any* situation.

We'll tackle CSS layouts and all the benefits they produce later on in the book, but let's focus right now on using tables for situations where they *are* appropriate—namely for marking up *tabular data*. We'll figure out a few simple things we can do to make our data tables more accessible and stylish.

Totally tabular

There is absolutely no reason not to use a table for marking up tabular data. But wait, what is tabular data? Here are just a few examples:

- Calendars
- Spreadsheets
- Charts
- Schedules

For these examples and many others, it would take some severe CSS acrobatics to mark the data up to appear visually *like* a table. You could imagine trying to float and position all of the items with crafty CSS rules, only to end up with frustratingly inconsistent results. Not to mention that accurately reading the data *without* CSS would be nightmarish. The fact is, we shouldn't be afraid of tables—and we should use them for what they were designed for.

A table that everyone can sit at

One of the reasons that tables get a bad rap is due to the accessibility problems they can cause if not carefully used. For instance, screen readers can have difficulty reading them properly, and small-screened devices are often hindered by tables when they are used for layout. But there are a few simple things we can do to increase the accessibility of a *data* table, while at the same time creating a lean structure that will be easy to style later on with CSS.

Let's take a look at the simple table example found in Figure 3-1, illustrating one of American baseball's longest droughts. (A drought no more, with the Red Sox victories of 2004 and 2007. I'm convinced this chapter had everything to do with it.)

Boston Red Sox World Series Championships

Year	Opponent	Season Record (W-L)
1918	Chicago Cubs	75-51
1916	Brooklyn Robins	91-63
1915	Philadelphia Phillies	101-50
1912	New York Giants	105-47

Figure 3-1. Example of a typical data table

Although at one time an extremely depressing set of statistics for a Red Sox fan to look at, Figure 3-1 is a perfect example of tabular data. There are three table **headers** (Year, Opponent, and Season Record (W-L)) followed by the **data** for each of the four years presented. Above the table is a **caption**, defining what is contained below.

Marking up this data table is relatively straightforward, and we might do something like the following:

```
<p align="center">Boston Red Sox World Series Championships</p>
<table>
  <tr>
    <td align="center"><b>Year</b></td>
    <td align="center"><b>Opponent</b></td>
    <td align="center"><b>Season Record (W-L)</b></td>
  </tr>
  <tr>
    <td>1918</td>
    <td>Chicago Cubs</td>
    <td>75-51</td>
  </tr>
  <tr>
    <td>1916</td>
    <td>Brooklyn Robins</td>
    <td>91-63</td>
  </tr>
  <tr>
    <td>1915</td>
    <td>Philadelphia Phillies</td>
    <td>101-50</td>
  </tr>
  <tr>
    <td>1912</td>
    <td>New York Giants</td>
    <td>105-47</td>
  </tr>
</table>
```

That should render close to what we see in Figure 3-1; however, there are a few improvements we can make here.

First off, we can treat the title of the table, "Boston Red Sox World Series Championships," a little more semantically correct by using the <caption> element. The <caption> is required to immediately follow the opening <table> element and usually holds the title and/or nature of what's contained within the table.

Visually, it will be easy for sighted people to understand the table's purpose, while assisting those browsing by nonvisual means as well.

Let's replace the opening paragraph and add in a proper <caption>:

```
<table>
  <caption>Boston Red Sox World Series Championships</caption>
  <tr>
    <td align="center"><b>Year</b></td>
    <td align="center"><b>Opponent</b></td>
    <td align="center"><b>Season Record (W-L)</b></td>
  </tr>
  <tr>
    <td>1918</td>
    <td>Chicago Cubs</td>
    <td>75-51</td>
  </tr>
  <tr>
    <td>1916</td>
    <td>Brooklyn Robins</td>
    <td>91-63</td>
  </tr>
  <tr>
    <td>1915</td>
    <td>Philadelphia Phillies</td>
    <td>101-50</td>
  </tr>
  <tr>
    <td>1912</td>
    <td>New York Giants</td>
    <td>105-47</td>
  </tr>
</table>
```

It's important for captions to quickly convey what the data is that follows. By default, most visual browsers will place text that's contained within <caption> elements centered and just above the very top of the table. We could, of course, alter the default styling of the caption after the fact using CSS if we wished—and we'll do just that later in the "Extra credit" section of this chapter. The fact that it's now in its own unique element makes this nice and easy.

Adding a summary

Additionally, we could add the summary attribute to the <table> element, further explaining the purpose and contents of what is contained in our table. The summary is especially helpful for those using nonvisual means to read the information.

The following shows the summary attribute and value added to our table example:

```
<table summary="This table is a chart of all Boston Red Sox World
Series wins.">
  <caption>Boston Red Sox World Series Championships</caption>
  <tr>
    <td align="center"><b>Year</b></td>
    <td align="center"><b>Opponent</b></td>
    <td align="center"><b>Season Record (W-L)</b></td>
  </tr>
  <tr>
    <td>1918</td>
    <td>Chicago Cubs</td>
    <td>75-51</td>
  </tr>
  <tr>
    <td>1916</td>
    <td>Brooklyn Robins</td>
    <td>91-63</td>
  </tr>
  <tr>
    <td>1915</td>
    <td>Philadelphia Phillies</td>
    <td>101-50</td>
  </tr>
  <tr>
    <td>1912</td>
    <td>New York Giants</td>
    <td>105-47</td>
  </tr>
</table>
```

The head(s) of the table

Table headers are important to make use of when building data tables. Instead of using a presentational element like <b> to visually cue the user that the cell is of importance in grouping the data that follows, we can take advantage of the <th> element, much like we used proper heading elements for section page content in Chapter 2.

Visual browsers might render information contained in <th> elements as bold and centered by default, but again we can use the uniqueness of the <th> element to style these important cells differently from the rest of the table data that's contained in a <td>.

In addition to their presentational advantages, using <th> elements can be beneficial to nonvisual browsers as well—as we'll dive into further on.

The headers in our example table are found in the top row: **Year**, **Opponent**, and **Season Record (W-L)**. Let's replace our previous, presentational markup with proper headers:

```
<table summary="This table is a chart of all Boston Red Sox World
Series wins.">
  <caption>Boston Red Sox World Series Championships</caption>
  <tr>
     <th>Year</th>
     <th>Opponent</th>
     <th>Season Record (W-L)</th>
  </tr>
  <tr>
     <td>1918</td>
     <td>Chicago Cubs</td>
     <td>75-51</td>
  </tr>
  <tr>
     <td>1916</td>
     <td>Brooklyn Robins</td>
     <td>91-63</td>
  </tr>
  <tr>
     <td>1915</td>
     <td>Philadelphia Phillies</td>
     <td>101-50</td>
  </tr>
  <tr>
     <td>1912</td>
     <td>New York Giants</td>
     <td>105-47</td>
  </tr>
</table>
```

Using <th> elements to mark up the header cells will give us the same visual results shown in Figure 3-1. Let's review why this is a preferred way:

- We eliminate the need for extra presentational markup to differentiate the header cells from normal ones.
- By default, most visual browsers will render text within <th> elements bold and centered—making it easier to see the difference between headers and data.
- Because of their uniqueness from normal <td> elements, we can later style table headers differently from other cells in the table.

There is also an additional reason for using table headers that we'll discuss next.

Header and data relationships

To make things a bit more organized for people using a screen reader to read the information from our table, we can utilize the headers attribute to associate header cells with the corresponding data found in <td> elements. Doing this will allow the screen reader to read the header and data information in a more logical order, rather than strictly reading each row left to right as it normally might.

Let's again use our Red Sox table as an example on how to achieve this. First, we'll need to add a unique id to each <th> in our table. We can then add the headers attribute to each data cell to match the two up accordingly.

Adding the id to each header is as simple as this:

```
<table summary="This table is a chart of all Boston Red Sox World
Series wins.">
  <caption>Boston Red Sox World Series Championships</caption>
  <tr>
    <th id="year">Year</th>
    <th id="opponent">Opponent</th>
    <th id="record">Season  Record (W-L)</th>
  </tr>
  <tr>
    <td>1918</td>
    <td>Chicago Cubs</td>
    <td>75-51</td>
  </tr>
  <tr>
    <td>1916</td>
    <td>Brooklyn Robins</td>
    <td>91-63</td>
  </tr>
  <tr>
    <td>1915</td>
    <td>Philadelphia Phillies</td>
    <td>101-50</td>
  </tr>
  <tr>
    <td>1912</td>
    <td>New York Giants</td>
    <td>105-47</td>
  </tr>
</table>
```

We've used short, descriptive names for each header id. Now we can add the appropriate headers attribute to each data cell—with its value corresponding to the id that it's associated with.

```
<table summary="This table is a chart of all Boston Red Sox World
Series wins.">
  <caption>Boston Red Sox World Series Championships</caption>
  <tr>
    <th id="year">Year</th>
    <th id="opponent">Opponent</th>
    <th id="record">Season  Record (W-L)</th>
  </tr>
  <tr>
    <td headers="year">1918</td>
    <td headers="opponent">Chicago Cubs</td>
    <td headers="record">75-51</td>
  </tr>
  <tr>
    <td headers="year">1916</td>
    <td headers="opponent">Brooklyn Robins</td>
    <td headers="record">91-63</td>
  </tr>
  <tr>
    <td headers="year">1915</td>
    <td headers="opponent">Philadelphia Phillies</td>
    <td headers="record">101-50</td>
  </tr>
  <tr>
    <td headers="year">1912</td>
    <td headers="opponent">New York Giants</td>
    <td headers="record">105-47</td>
  </tr>
</table>
```

When we create relationships between our header and data information, a screen reader might read this table as follows: "Year: 1918, Opponent: Chicago Cubs, Season Record (W-L): 75-51," and so on for each table row. This makes a little more sense than hearing each row read left to right.

It also doesn't hurt for us to have those unique ids for each <th> in our table. We could later take advantage of that identification with exclusive CSS rules. And we'll do just that in the "Extra credit" section later in this chapter.

Using the abbr attribute

In the preceding example, let's say that you thought the header "Season Record (W-L)" was a bit too long for a speech synthesizer to read out. By adding the abbr attribute, we can shorten what is read to whatever we'd like, while keeping the original text in the <th> cell for visual browsers.

```
<table summary="This table is a chart of all Boston Red Sox World
Series wins.">
  <caption>Boston Red Sox World Series Championships</caption>
  <tr>
    <th id="year">Year</th>
    <th id="opponent">Opponent</th>
    <th id="record" abbr="Record">Season  Record (W-L)</th>
  </tr>
  <tr>
    <td>1918</td>
    <td>Chicago Cubs</td>
    <td>75-51</td>
  </tr>
  <tr>
    <td>1916</td>
    <td>Brooklyn Robins</td>
    <td>91-63</td>
  </tr>
  <tr>
    <td>1915</td>
    <td>Philadelphia Phillies</td>
    <td>101-50</td>
  </tr>
  <tr>
    <td>1912</td>
    <td>New York Giants</td>
    <td>105-47</td>
  </tr>
</table>
```

We've added abbr="Record" so that screen readers will use that shortened version ("Record") of the table header when reading out the data of that particular cell.

<thead>, <tfoot>, and <tbody>

There are three additional elements related to tables that I'd like to mention. Not only do they provide extra semantic meaning to the structure of a table, but they also provide additional elements for CSS rules to take advantage of, avoiding the need to add extra classes to <tr> elements for styling table rows.

To quote the W3C's HTML 4.01 specification on these elements (http://www.w3.org/TR/html4/struct/tables.html#h-11.2.3):

"Table rows may be grouped into a table head, table foot, and one or more table body sections, using the THEAD, TFOOT, and TBODY elements, respectively. This division enables user agents to support scrolling of table bodies independently of the table head and foot. When long tables are printed, the table head and foot information may be repeated on each page that contains table data."

So you can see that organizing a table this way can also be useful for browsing software that supports independent scrolling of <tbody> sections—and especially helpful for longer tables.

<thead> and <tfoot> elements must appear above <tbody> sections to allow for browsers and devices to load that content first. An example of a table marked up with grouped table rows may go something like this:

```
<table>
  <thead>
    <tr>
      ...table header content...
    </tr>
  </thead>
  <tfoot>
    <tr>
      ...table footer content...
    </tr>
  </tfoot>
  <tbody>
    <tr>
      ...table data row...
    </tr>
    <tr>
      ...table data row...
    </tr>
    <tr>
      ...table data row...
    </tr>
  </tbody>
</table>
```

You can see that both the header and footer information gets placed *before* the data rows when using <thead> and <tfoot>.

As I mentioned earlier, not only do these elements provide extra meaning to a table, but they also give us a few more "style hooks" to apply CSS to, without adding extraneous classes to any of the <tr> elements.

For instance, if we wished to give only the data sections (marked up with <tbody>) a different background color than the other sections, we could write one CSS rule to handle this:

```
tbody {
  background-color: gray;
  }
```

Without the <tbody> element, we would've had to add a class attribute to each <tr> element that we wished to have a gray background. A fine example of how meaningful markup can oftentimes lead to easier styling with CSS later on.

Are tables evil?

I think the answer to this question is a resounding "no," as long as tables are used for their intended purpose. While tables rightfully get a bad rap when abused in creating complex, nested layouts, they provide the necessary structure for blocks of data and information.

We could've filled an entire book with all of the various techniques you can employ to build great tables, but hopefully we've gotten you off on the right foot for creating simple tables that are accessible to all and easily styled using CSS.

Speaking of style, let's spruce up our example table with a few CSS tricks.

3

Extra credit

As with the previous examples, we're going to take our lean, mean, structured markup and apply some CSS rules to add bits of style.

First, we'll go over a simple border trick to create a single-pixel grid on our example, and then we'll uniquely style the table's caption and headers.

Creating a grid

Tired of the three-dimensional look that the good ol' border attribute brings to the table? Me too. Typically, adding border="1" to the <table> element would get you an effect similar to what's found in Figure 3-1. But alternatively, here's a cool trick for getting a nice, neat grid using CSS instead. We'll start by adding a 1-pixel border to two sides (right and bottom) of each <th> and <td> cell:

```
th, td {
  border-right: 1px solid #999;
  border-bottom: 1px solid #999;
  }
```

Adding the border to only two sides is key for creating a grid that has equally sized borders all the way around that still looks correct in all modern browsers. If we added the same border to all four sides, they would double up on the top and left, where the cells meet. There is an alternate way of achieving the grid using a single border rule that I'll explain following this example.

You'll notice in Figure 3-2 that we're only missing borders on the extreme top and left of the entire table. To complete the grid, we'll add a border-top and border-left to the table element using the same color and style (see Figure 3-3).

```
table {
  border-top: 1px solid #999;
  border-left: 1px solid #999;
  }
```

```
th, td {
    border-right: 1px solid #999;
    border-bottom: 1px solid #999;
    }
```

Boston Red Sox World Series Championships

Year	Opponent	Season Record (W-L)
1918	Chicago Cubs	75-51
1916	Brooklyn Robins	91-63
1915	Philadelphia Phillies	101-50
1912	New York Giants	105-47

Figure 3-2. Table example with borders added to right and bottom of `<th>` and `<td>`

Boston Red Sox World Series Championships

Year	Opponent	Season Record (W-L)
1918	Chicago Cubs	75-51
1916	Brooklyn Robins	91-63
1915	Philadelphia Phillies	101-50
1912	New York Giants	105-47

Figure 3-3. Table example with top and left borders added

Collapsing the gaps

Now we have a complete grid, but what's with the little gaps between the borders? Unfortunately, most browsers will reveal these pesky gaps because they add slight margins by default.

What we can do is use the border-collapse property on the table element to close the gaps and get the resulting grid we're looking for:

```
table {
    border-collapse: collapse;
    }
th, td {
    border: 1px solid #999;
    }
```

Adding the value collapse to the border-collapse property ensures that precise, single-pixel look we're going for here. Let's take a look at the results shown in Figure 3-4.

Boston Red Sox World Series Championships

Year	Opponent	Season Record (W-L)
1918	Chicago Cubs	75-51
1916	Brooklyn Robins	91-63
1915	Philadelphia Phillies	101-50
1912	New York Giants	105-47

Figure 3-4. A perfect grid using the border-collapse property

An IE/Mac note

While Internet Explorer for the Mac is no longer being developed, it's worth pointing out that it handles the border-collapse property poorly, doubling up some of the borders we've added.

The table will still function normally, but in the rare event that you need IE/Mac to *render* identically to other modern browsers, here's the CSS that's needed to make that happen:

```
table {
  border-top: 1px solid #999;
  border-left: 1px solid #999;
  border-collapse: collapse;
  }
th, td {
  border-right: 1px solid #999;
  border-bottom: 1px solid #999;
  }
```

For the remainder of the exercise, we'll stick to the simpler version that looks slightly off in IE/Mac only.

Spaced out

We now have a perfect grid on our hands. But it's looking a little cramped. Let's allow it to breathe a bit more, as shown in Figure 3-5, by simply adding a little padding to our combined th, td rule:

```
table {
  border-collapse: collapse;
  }
th, td {
  padding: 10px;
  border: 1px solid #999;
  }
```

Boston Red Sox World Series Championships

Year	Opponent	Season Record (W-L)
1918	Chicago Cubs	75-51
1916	Brooklyn Robins	91-63
1915	Philadelphia Phillies	101-50
1912	New York Giants	105-47

Figure 3-5. 10 pixels of padding added

Did you know? Setting padding with one value (in this case 10 pixels) will add that value amount to all four sides of the element. You can also set the value for each side separately by following the order like a clock (top, right, bottom, left). A handy mnemonic device to remember this is to think of the word "trouble." So, including padding: 10px 5px 2px 10px; *will add 10 pixels of padding to the top, 5 on the right, 2 on the bottom, and 10 to the left (see Figure 3-6).*

Another shortcut: if your top and bottom values are the same and also if your left and right values match up, you need only set each value once. So, including padding: 10px 5px; *will add 10 pixels of padding to the top and bottom, while adding only 5 pixels for both the right and left sides.*

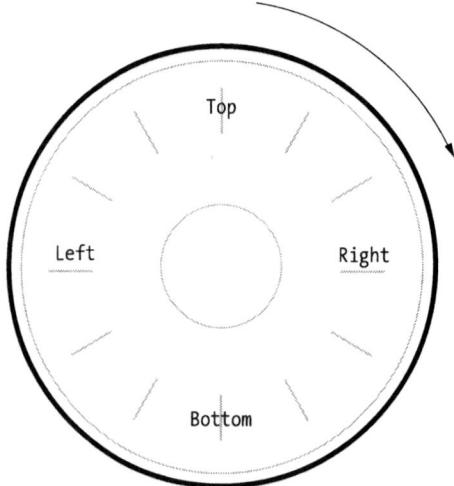

Figure 3-6. The face of a clock represents the order of margin or padding values.

Customizing the headers

To make the table headers stand out even more, we can easily add a background color and different font to those particular cells. Because we're using <th> elements, rather than making their text bold inline, we don't have to add any additional markup to call the headers out uniquely.

Let's also add a little padding to the bottom of the caption as well as a different font and color (red, of course) to make it stand out from the rest of the table (see Figure 3-7):

```
table {

  border-collapse: collapse;
  }
caption {
```

```
      font-family: Arial, sans-serif;
      color: #993333;
      padding-bottom: 6px;
      }
th, td {
   padding: 10px;
      border: 1px solid #999;
   }
th {
   font-family: Verdana, sans-serif;
   background: #ccc;
   }
```

3

Boston Red Sox World Series Championships		
Year	**Opponent**	**Season Record (W-L)**
1918	Chicago Cubs	75-51
1916	Brooklyn Robins	91-63
1915	Philadelphia Phillies	101-50
1912	New York Giants	105-47

Figure 3-7. Caption and <th> styled

Headers with background images

We've added a gray background color to the <th> elements in our table, but we could go a step further and instead create a stylish background image that would tile within those cells—for instance, a subtle gray striped pattern similar to that found in the first releases of Mac OS X.

Tiny tile

First, let's create the one tiny image that's necessary in Photoshop or your favorite image editor. The image need only be 4 pixels tall since for this example we'd like the stripes to have 2-pixel gray lines alternate with 2 pixels of white. We could make the width of the image whatever we'd like since it will tile in the <th> cell to create the stripe effect. For bandwidth's sake, we'll only make the width 1 pixel (see Figure 3-8).

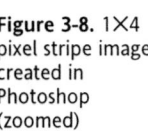

Figure 3-8. 1×4 pixel stripe image created in Photoshop (zoomed)

The CSS

All we really needed to do differently from the previous example is replace the background color we were using with the path to the tiny image we created earlier. Unless otherwise specified, a background image will tile and repeat automatically in every direction, by default.

43

```
table {
    border-collapse: collapse;
  }

caption {
    font-family: Arial, sans-serif;
    color: #993333;
    padding-bottom: 6px;
  }

th, td {
    padding: 10px;
    border: 1px solid #999;
  }

th {
    font-family: Verdana, sans-serif;
    background: url(th_stripe.gif);
  }
```

Figure 3-9 shows the resulting styled table—this time with a striped background for the table headers only. You could easily experiment with other tiled shapes to create varied effects for the headers and/or normal data cells. Have fun with it.

Boston Red Sox World Series Championships

Year	Opponent	Season Record (W-L)
1918	Chicago Cubs	75-51
1916	Brooklyn Robins	91-63
1915	Philadelphia Phillies	101-50
1912	New York Giants	105-47

Figure 3-9. An example of a tiled image background applied to table header cells

Assigning icons to IDs

Remember earlier in the chapter when we assigned a unique id to each <th> in our table? We coupled those ids with headers attributes in the data cells to help those browsing by nonvisual means. We can now take advantage of the ids in another way—by assigning a specific icon to each <th> as a background image.

The icon images themselves will be kept entirely within the CSS, allowing for easy swap-out in the event of a site redesign or update. The markup will stay exactly the same.

The icons

I've created three unique icons in Photoshop—one for each table heading in our example:
Year, Opponent, and Season Record (W-L). Figure 3-10 shows the three icons.

Figure 3-10. Three table
header icons created in
Photoshop

The CSS

Adding the CSS is simple. Because we've assigned an id to each <th>, we can specify the
correct icon using the background property:

```
table {

  border-collapse: collapse;
  }

caption {
  font-family: Arial, sans-serif;
  color: #993333;
  padding-bottom: 6px;
  }

th, td {
  padding: 10px;
    border: 1px solid #999;
  }

th {
  font-family: Verdana, sans-serif;
  }

#year {
  padding-left: 26px;
  background: #ccc url(icon_year.gif) no-repeat 10px 50%;
  }

#opponent {
  padding-left: 26px;
  background: #ccc url(icon_opp.gif) no-repeat 10px 50%;
  }

#record {
  padding-left: 26px;
  background: #ccc url(icon_rec.gif) no-repeat 10px 50%;
  }
```

You'll notice that, because we're using the **shorthand** method for declaring backgrounds, we've taken the background:#ccc; rule out of the th declaration and have added it instead for each header along with the appropriate icon image. This will allow the image to "sit" on top of the gray color that we've specified. We've given enough padding on the left of each header to let the icon have enough room to be seen without any text overlap. Figure 3-11 shows the results found in the browser.

Boston Red Sox World Series Championships

⊞ Year	▨ Opponent	▨ Season Record (W-L)
1918	Chicago Cubs	75-51
1916	Brooklyn Robins	91-63
1915	Philadelphia Phillies	101-50
1912	New York Giants	105-47

Figure 3-11. An example of unique icons assigned to each <th>

> *Using the shorthand method has its obvious advantages; however, if we had declared the image only, without the color, using the* background *property, we'll have overridden any default color we had previously set using* background *on the* <th> *element.*

Combining rules for simpler bits

An alternate method that achieves the same results would be to write the rules that get duplicated for each separate header (in this case padding, background color, and position) **once** in the th declaration (because they are indeed *all* <th>s), and save the unique bits (the image path) for the #year, #opponent, and #record declarations.

```
table {
    border-collapse: collapse;
  }

caption {
  font-family: Arial, sans-serif;
  color: #993333;
  padding-bottom: 6px;
  }

th, td {
  padding: 10px;
    border: 1px solid #999;
  }
```

```
th {
  font-family: Verdana, sans-serif;
  padding-left: 26px;
  background-color: #ccc;
  background-repeat: no-repeat;
  background-position: 10px 50%;
  }

#year {
  background-image: url(icon_year.gif);
  }

#opponent {
  background-image: url(icon_opp.gif);
  }

#record {
  background: url(icon_rec.gif);
  }
```

A little more compact, isn't it? By combining those common rules into one, we save repeating ourselves over and over. For this particular example, it may seem like six and a half of one, half a baker's dozen of the other—but for larger style sheets it can save quite a few bytes when those repeated rules are combined into one declaration.

More table style examples

For more inspiration in the various ways data tables can be styled with CSS, check out these resources:

- http://www.smashingmagazine.com/2008/08/13/top-10-css-table-designs/
  A great tutorial on taking a semantically marked-up table and applying 10 unique designs to it using CSS
- http://veerle.duoh.com/blog/comments/a_css_styled_table/
  Veerle Pieters' tutorial on creating a stylish data table
- http://icant.co.uk/csstablegallery/
  An ongoing showcase of table designs from submitted CSS files

Wrapping up

What we've discovered throughout this chapter is that not only are tables not evil, but by understanding them better, we see that they are appropriate for marking up tabular data—and can still be accessible all the while.

We also found that with a little bit of style, we can take control of tabular markup and make it look attractive. Fear not the table.

CHAPTER 4
QUOTATIONS

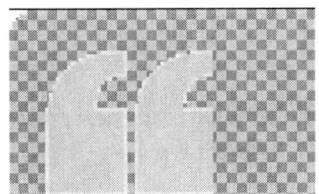

Misquotations are the
only quotations that are
never misquoted.

—Hesketh Pearson

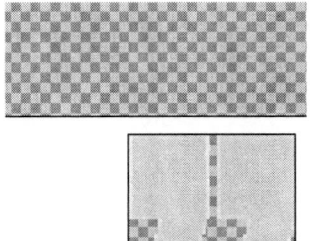

"Misquotations are the only quotations that are never misquoted."

—Hesketh Pearson

Quotations are used frequently on all types of websites. Whether quoting another web page, author, or publication, there are advantages to be had by marking quotations up in defined ways. Once structured, quotations can become a stylish design element when spiced up with some simple CSS.

Let's take a look at three different ways a quotation might be marked up, noting the pros and cons of each method. Once we've settled on the best, we'll talk about a few related elements and add a few bits of style. When marking up a long quotation, which method is best?

Let's look closely at each of these methods, striving to find the best tool for job—and more importantly, *why* it's the best tool.

Method A: Lacks meaning

```
<p>Misquotations are the only quotations that are never misquoted.</p>
<p>&mdash; Hesketh Pearson</p>
```

When calling it out on the page, often it's desirable to have the quotation appear different from the rest of the text on the page. It's helpful to cue the reader into knowing that this portion of the page is from a different source, breaking (in a good way) the normal flow of content.

Method A is marked up no differently from any other paragraph on the page, so unfortunately we have no easy way to style it differently. The double quotation marks themselves are the only visual cue that this is indeed a quotation.

Method B: A class act?

```
<div class="quotation">
  <p>Misquotations are the only quotations that are never misquoted.</p>
  <p>&mdash; Hesketh Pearson </p>
</div>
```

Because of the class="quotation" that is added to the <div> element that surrounds the quotation, we could style it uniquely with CSS, after the fact. But it seems a bit unnecessary to create this extra class when there's a perfectly good HTML element that exists for this purpose. And we'll reveal that perfectly good HTML element in just a minute.

Once we start using a <div> with a class attached, we're also locked into coding all quotations throughout an entire site this way if we'd like the style to be consistent. We must also remember this particular syntax for marking up quotations in the future. This is especially a bummer if we're dealing with a large site with multiple <div> and class combinations for various structural elements throughout the page. It can easily start to get messy, and you'd need a roadmap to keep track of all the custom class names you've created.

There is also the issue of viewing a quotation marked up this way without CSS, whether it be unavailable or unsupported. Since the <div> is just a generic container, no default styling is applied to content placed within them. This is important for people using old browser versions, text browsers, or screen readers. Take a look at the quotation sans CSS, and it would appear just like everything else on the page.

Method C: <blockquote> is best

```
<blockquote>
  <p>Misquotations are the only quotations that are never misquoted.</p>
  <p>&mdash; Hesketh Pearson </p>
</blockquote>
```

The W3C recommends using the <blockquote> element for long quotations (block-level content), and it's the element that was designed to handle the exact situation that we're discussing. By using it, we're giving structural meaning to the content, while at the same time providing a unique label for adding style for visual browsers. You'll notice we're also wrapping lines inside of the <blockquote> with paragraph elements. This is also good practice, adding the appropriate semantic value to those pieces of content. In other words, we wouldn't use a <br /> to separate paragraphs within a <blockquote>. The <p> elements here provide the proper structure, as well as making them easily styled with CSS.

Without any styling added, content within <blockquote> elements will be indented. This is a minimal, but sufficient, visual cue for separating the quotation from normal text. This default indenting, however, has given birth to a nasty habit, which we'll discuss next.

Using a screwdriver to hammer a nail

You may remember using <blockquote> in the past because it was like a paragraph that was indented. If you needed to indent a block of text, you wrapped it in <blockquote> and that was that.

Unfortunately, it was a bad habit to get into, and one that's remedied by instead applying padding-left or margin-left values to the proper elements using CSS. Historically, <blockquote> has been abused in this way, being exploited more for presentational reasons than for structural circumstances.

Because of this bad habit, the W3C has recommended that the rendering of quotation marks be left to the style sheet and not the default styling of the browser. We'll look at a neat way of inserting stylish quotation marks in the "Extra credit" section of this chapter.

51

Summary

Let's briefly review why we think using Method C is the better choice over the other two for marking up a long quotation.

Method A:

- The paragraph can't be easily styled separately to distinguish itself from the rest of the page.
- This method doesn't provide any meaning or structure to the quotation.

Method B:

- Adding the unique class makes for easy styling, but is unnecessary when `<block-quote>` is available.
- We're locked into marking up future quotations using this method if we'd like consistent styles throughout the page and/or entire site.

Method C:

- It's the element that was designed by the W3C for this purpose, providing meaning and structure to the content.
- It's easy to style quotations uniquely using CSS rules on the `<blockquote>` element.
- In the absence of CSS, the default rendering of `<blockquote>` will be a sufficient cue for visual and nonvisual browsers.

It's now time to kick the tires on our `<blockquote>` and find some creative ways to add style.

Extra credit

For extra credit, we'll be looking at a few creative ways to style quotations marked up with `<blockquote>`, but before that, let's talk a little about the cite attribute as well as *inline quotations*.

A cite for curious eyes

Getting tired of the corny headings yet? Oh, good. Neither am I. It's important to mention the cite attribute when discussing quotations. According to the W3C's specification, cite gives the designer a place to reference the source from which the quotation was borrowed—meaning if the quotation comes from another web page, we can add the URL of that page as the value of the cite attribute.

Let's take a look at how this works in the code.

```
<blockquote cite="http://www.somewebsite.com/path/to/page.html">
  <p>Misquotations are the only quotations that are never misquoted.</p>
  <p>&mdash; Hesketh Pearson </p>
</blockquote>
```

At the time of this writing, most browsers aren't going to do anything particularly special with the cite attribute that we've just added. But things start to get interesting when advanced CSS techniques or scripting applications are used to display or index the information contained within the cite attribute. The location of the quotation is an additional nugget of information that helps describe the content it contains—and that can be very valuable in the future.

Think of adding cite information as you would putting pennies in a piggy bank. The pennies aren't worth much today, but you'll be happy later on down the road that you saved them all.

> *For inline citations, the* <cite> *element is available to wrap references to other sources (e.g.,* <p>The following material is an excerpt from the <cite>New York Times</cite>.</p>*).*

Inline quotations

What about quotations that are short and meant to be referenced inline? For instance, if you're quoting someone within a sentence, use the <q> element demonstrated here:

```
I said, <q>Herman, do you like bubblegum?</q> And he said,➥
<q>Yes, the kind that comes with a comic.</q>
```

which, in a visual browser, would most likely appear like this:

I said, "Herman, do you like bubblegum?" And he said, "Yes, the kind that comes with a comic."

Just as we did with <blockquote>, we could also add the cite attribute to the <q> element, referencing the source of the quote:

```
<q cite="http://bubblegumcomicfans.com/manifesto.html">Yes, the kind
that comes with a comic.</q>
```

No need for marks

Most visual browsers will insert quotation marks where <q> and </q> elements are used, so there's no need to type them in. The W3C also recommends adding the lang attribute with whatever language the quotation is in, as the value. Certain languages may display the quotation marks differently, depending on the language.

```
I said, <q lang="en-us">Herman, do you like bubblegum? </q> And he ➥
said, <q lang="en-us">Yes, the kind that comes with a comic.</q>
```

A full listing of possible language codes is available at the W3C site (www.w3.org/TR/html4/struct/dirlang.html#langcodes).

Nesting inline quotations

You can also nest inline quotations when you're quoting someone *within* a quotation. Confused? Me too. Let's take a look at an example:

```
I said, <q lang="en-us">Herman, do you like bubblegum? </q> And he ➥
 said, <q lang="en-us">Yes. Bubblegum is what Harry calls ➥
<q lang="en-us">delicious</q>.</q>
```

Double and single quotation marks would be used in the appropriate places like this:

I said, "Herman, do you like bubblegum?" And he said, "Yes. Bubblegum is what Harry calls 'delicious'."

Styling <blockquote>

For a few years now, Fast Company has been running a daily quotation from the magazine's archives on its home page. To preserve FC's typographic style and emphasis, the quote had, for a long while, been created as a GIF image, with the ability to manipulate the font any which way the designer wished.

In the early fall of 2003, right about the time I was watching my beloved Red Sox come oh-so-close to a historic World Series berth, I decided to toss out the GIFs and use a styled <blockquote> instead.

From an accessibility angle, it sure made sense to have the quotation as text rather than an image, and while we couldn't reproduce the flexibility in typography of the GIF, we had the challenge of making the quote stylish in some fashion. CSS to the rescue, of course.

Background quote marks

The idea is pretty simple, and involves creating opening and closing quote marks as two separate images, light enough in shade to be sitting *behind* the text of the quote that will overlap a bit on top of them. The quote also lives in a 270-pixel-wide, light gray box that has rounded corners to match the rest of the look and feel of the website. A third image is used to complete the rounded effect along with the quotation marks. All three images are contained entirely within CSS using the background property on the various elements that are available.

Let's first create those quotation mark and rounded-corner images in Adobe Photoshop or your favorite image editor. Here is the opportunity to use a custom font that would normally be unavailable to the everyday browser. In the case of Fast Company, I was able to use a font for the quotation marks that was found throughout the magazine.

Three images

Figure 4-1 shows the three images created, one that handles both the opening quotation mark and top rounded corners, one for the closing quotation mark, and one for the two bottom rounded corners.

The images are transparent to let the gray background that we'll specify in CSS show through: white where we can create the rounded corners and gray for the quotation marks.

Figure 4-1. Three images created in Photoshop to create quotation marks and rounded corners

Tagging the elements

At present, you can only assign one background image to an element using the background or background-image property. So, we'll add an id to each of the paragraphs within our <blockquote>.

One paragraph we'll tag as #quote and the other as #author so that in the end, we'll have three unique elements to assign background images to.

Take a look at the modified markup that we'll be using for the rest of this exercise:

```
<blockquote cite="http://www.somesite.com/path/to/page.html">
  <p id="quote"><strong>Misquotations</strong> are the only quotations ➡
that are <strong>never</strong> misquoted.</p>
  <p id="author">&mdash;Hesketh Pearson</p>
</blockquote>
```

Now we're ready to assign the images.

Three elements, three backgrounds

As mentioned previously, at present, you can specify just *one* background image for an element using the background or background-image property. So we'll take advantage of the three available elements in our example—the <blockquote>, the #quote paragraph, and the #author paragraph—in order to assign the three images needed to complete the effect we're after.

It's always a good idea to take a look at what elements you have available before adding new ones. Often, it's possible to get the CSS styling you need with elements that are already in place from writing good, structured markup.

To begin, we'll write the CSS rules for the <blockquote> element:

```
blockquote {
    width: 270px;
    margin: 0;
    padding: 0;
    font-family: georgia, serif;
    font-size: 150%;
    letter-spacing: -1px;
    line-height: 1em;
    text-align: center;
    color: #555;
    background: #eee url(top.gif) no-repeat top left;
    }
```

We've given the entire package a width of 270 pixels, the same width as the top.gif image that's creating the rounded borders as well as the opening quotation mark. We're also giving the text some love by specifying font, size, and color. Lastly, we're centering all of the text and have assigned the background color, image, and position in the last rule.

Turning off margins and padding for the <blockquote> is important as well. We'll be adding padding to each of the paragraph elements instead. This will allow us to work around Internet Explorer version 5 in Windows' misinterpretation of the CSS *box model*. We'll discuss in detail the box model further on in Part Two of the book.

Next, let's set up the rules for the #quote paragraph:

```
blockquote {
    width: 270px;
    text-align: center;
    margin: 0;
    padding: 0;
    font-family: georgia, serif;
    font-size: 150%;
    letter-spacing: -1px;
    line-height: 1em;
    color: #555;
    background: #eee url(top.gif) no-repeat top left;
    }

#quote {
    margin: 0 10px 0 0;
    padding: 20px 10px 10px 20px;
    background: url(end_quote.gif) no-repeat right bottom;
    }
```

By setting margin: 0 10px 0 0;, we'll collapse the browser's default spacing for the paragraph on top and bottom, instead using a bit of precise padding to get the layout just right. We're adding a 10-pixel margin to the right side, however, effectively offsetting the quote mark background image by exactly that amount to match the left side. If we leave those 10 pixels out, the image would sit flush to the right edge of the entire box. Another option is to add that 10 pixels of padding to the right of the image itself.

Also note that background image (the closing quotation mark) is specified to sit at the bottom and right of the <blockquote>.

Lastly, we'll use the author paragraph (#author) element to add the last background image—the rounded corners for the bottom of the box.

```
blockquote {
  width: 270px;
  text-align: center;
  margin: 0;
  padding: 0;
  font-family: georgia, serif;
  font-size: 150%;
  letter-spacing: -1px;
  line-height: 1em;
  color: #555;
  background: #eee url(top.gif) no-repeat top left;
  }

#quote {
  margin: 0 10px 0 0;
  padding: 20px 20px 10px 20px;
  background: url(end_quote.gif) no-repeat right bottom;
  }

#author {
  margin: 0 10px 0 0;
  padding: 0 0 10px 0;
  color: #999;
  font-size: 60%;
  background: url(bottom.gif) no-repeat bottom;
  }
```

Again, we've collapsed the default margin of the paragraph, opting instead to use a bit of padding on the bottom to get things lined up. The third image is in place now, and adds the bottom left and right rounded corners to the box. By using padding instead of margin to set spacing for the author, we ensure that the rounded-corner image can sit where it needs to—precisely at the bottom.

The results

Figure 4-2 shows the results as seen in a typical, modern graphical browser. The rounded box is complete and quotation marks are tucked in nicely behind the quotation text. What's especially nice about this method is that the entire box is scalable—meaning you can drop in a quote of any length, and the box will expand or contract perfectly, with the quotation marks and rounded corners lining up in the right spots. This also means the design of the quote and containing box will be maintained if a user with low vision increases the text size.

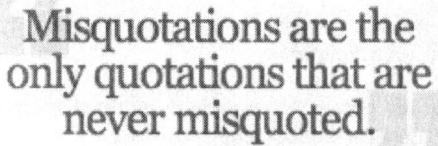

Figure 4-2. Resulting styled block quote using three background images and text

Calling out special words

One additional design touch that I added to the Fast Company quote was to use the <strong> element to call out certain important words within the quotation, to further mimic the typography that was used throughout the magazine.

By using <strong>, I could ensure that most unstyled viewers and nonvisual visitors of the quote would still receive a bold or strongly emphasized word (which makes perfect sense in this case), while at the same time, I could treat <strong> elements within the <block-quote> with a darker color as well, in the CSS.

The markup would change slightly, with the addition of selected words wrapped in <strong> elements:

```
<blockquote cite="http://www.somesite.com/path/to/page.html">
  <p id="quote"><strong>Misquotations</strong> are the only quotations ➥
that are <strong>never</strong>  misquoted.</p>
  <p id="author">&mdash;Hesketh Pearson</p>
</blockquote>
```

And here's the one additional CSS declaration that needs to be added:

```
#quote strong {
  color: #000;
  font-weight: normal;
  }
```

Now, any <strong> elements that are within our quotation will be black (none more black) and since the rest of the quote is of normal font-weight, we'll override the default bold that occurs with <strong> with a value of normal.

You can see the results of the <strong> elements in Figure 4-3, where we've called out the words "Misquotations" and "never."

> **Misquotations** are the only quotations that are **never** misquoted.
>
> —Hesketh Pearson

Figure 4-3. The styled `<blockquote>` with `<strong>` elments added for calling out certain words

How does it degrade?

We've seen how stylish our `<blockquote>` can be with just a few background images and CSS rules, but what about browsers and devices that don't handle CSS well? How well does this method degrade?

Well, fortunately because we're using the `<blockquote>` element as it was meant to be used, unstyled viewers, old browsers, phones, PDAs, and screen readers will treat it appropriately. For instance, Figure 4-4 demonstrates how our lean markup will look without the fancy CSS applied. I've added a bit of dummy text around the quotation to give the complete effect.

Lorem ipsum dolor sit amet, consectetuer adipiscing elit. Suspendisse commodo adipiscing augue. Fusce eu lectus. Integer pulvinar ipsum ut enim elementum eleifend. In et est at libero rhoncus tempor. Etiam tincidunt lorem in lacus. Nullam nonummy cursus sem. Sed vel augue ut sapien eleifend sagittis. Nulla semper metus id mauris. Sed eleifend odio ac purus. Duis quis felis.

Misquotations are the only quotations that are **never** misquoted.

—Hesketh Pearson

Etiam bibendum. Sed eu sapien. Donec est nulla, gravida a, euismod id, viverra non, nisl. Donec diam mauris, pellentesque sed, aliquet at, eleifend in, dui. Pellentesque ut mauris. Aliquam erat volutpat. Nullam quis magna nec ante tempus eleifend. Nulla augue eros, tempus quis, sollicitudin a, tempus eu, nibh. Suspendisse imperdiet fringilla tellus. Vivamus non wisi.

Figure 4-4. An unstyled view of our `<blockquote>` example

Wrapping up

After looking closely at a few different methods for marking up quotations, it was easy to find the right tool for the job in the `<blockquote>` element. Gone are the days of using `<blockquote>` simply to indent text; now we can now employ its intended use: quoting a source with a long quotation.

Once that structure is in place, stylish design can be easily applied to `<blockquote>` elements, making them stand out from the normal flow of text—all the while being still properly read by non–CSS-enabled browsers or other devices.

CHAPTER 5
FORMS

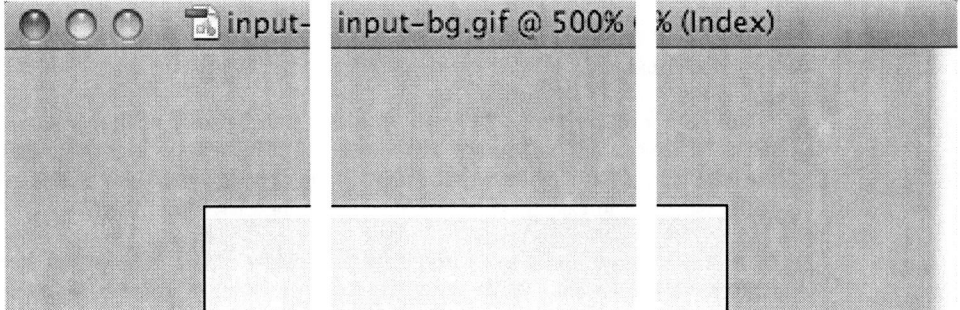

Interactivity has always been an integral part of the Web, letting the user and site communicate through the exchange of information. Forms allow us to collect input from users in an organized, predetermined fashion, and have always been sort of an "anything goes" area when building websites. For instance, we'll discover that marking up a form can be handled in approximately 10,000 different ways. OK, perhaps not that many, but there are several options to consider as well as steps that we can take to ensure our forms are structured in a way that'll benefit both the user and site owner.

What are our options when marking up a form?

Let's take a look at four different ways to mark up the same, simple form—all of which achieve similar results. We'll go over each method and talk about the pros and cons that are involved.

Method A: Using a table

```
<form action="/path/to/script" method="post">
  <table>
    <tr>
      <th>Name:</th>
      <td><input type="text" name="name" /></td>
    </tr>
    <tr>
      <th>Email:</th>
      <td><input type="text" name="email" /></td>
    </tr>
    <tr>
      <th> </th>
      <td><input type="submit" value="submit" /></td>
    </tr>
  </table>
</form>
```

Tables have long been used to mark up forms, and because of that frequent use, seeing forms laid out in this particular way has become familiar to us: right-aligned text labels in the left column, left-aligned form controls in the right column. Using a simple, two-column table is one of the easiest ways to achieve a usable form layout.

Some could argue that a table isn't necessary, while others believe that forms could be considered tabular data. We're not going to argue either side, but instead state that using a table is sometimes the best way to achieve *certain* form layouts—especially complex forms that involve multiple controls like radio buttons, select boxes, and so forth. Relying solely on CSS to control the layout of complex forms can be frustrating, and often involves adding extraneous <span> and <div> elements, with more code bloat than that of a table.

Let's take a look at Figure 5-1 to see how Method A would appear in a typical visual browser.

Name:
Email:
submit

Figure 5-1. Method A as rendered
in a browser

You can see that by using a table, the labels and form elements line up nicely. For such a simple form, though, I would probably opt to avoid the table altogether in favor of something that requires less markup. Unless this particular layout is crucial to the visual design of the form, using a table here isn't *necessary*. There are also a few accessibility concerns we could address—and we will, while looking over the next two methods.

Method B: Tableless, but cramped

```
<form action="/path/to/script" method="post">
  <p>
    Name: <input type="text" name="name" /><br />
    Email: <input type="text" name="email" /><br />
    <input type="submit" value="submit" />
  </p>
</form>
```

Using a single paragraph and a few <br /> elements to separate the items is a passable solution—but could visually render a bit on the cramped side. Figure 5-2 shows how this would typically appear in a browser.

Name:
Email:
submit

Figure 5-2. Method B as rendered
in a browser

You can see that while we got away without using a table, it looks rather cramped and ugly. We also run into the problem of the form controls not lining up perfectly, as seen in Figure 5-2.

We could alleviate some of the crowding by adding some margins to the <input> elements using CSS like this:

```
input {
  margin: 6px 0;
  }
```

The preceding would add a 6-pixel margin to both the top and bottom of each <input> element (the name, e-mail, and submit controls), spacing out the elements as shown in Figure 5-3.

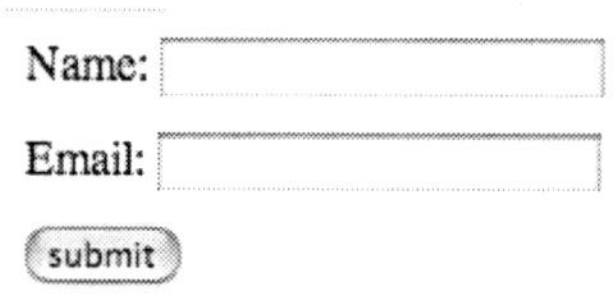

Name: [   ]

Email: [   ]

(submit)

Figure 5-3. Method B with padding added to the input elements

While there's nothing particularly *wrong* with Method B, there are a few adjustments we can make to build a better form. And those adjustments are evident in Method C. So let's take a look.

Method C: Simple and more accessible

```
<form action="/path/to/script" id="thisform" method="post">
  <divlabel for="name">Name:</label><br />
  <input type="text" id="name" name="name" /></div>
  <div><label for="email">Email:</label><br />
  <input type="text" id="email" name="email" /></div>
  <div><input type="submit" value="submit" /></div>
</form>
```

I like Method C for several reasons. First, for a simple form like this example, I find it convenient to contain each label and control in its own <div>. When viewed unstyled, the default behavior of a <div> (each on its own line) should be enough to set the items apart in a readable way. Later, we could control precise spacing with CSS on <div> elements that are contained within our form.

We've even gone a step further and have given this form a unique, but boring, id="thisform". So, that precise spacing I was just referring to could go something like this:

```
#thisform div {
  margin: 6px 0;
  }
```

Essentially, we're saying that all <div> elements in this form should have top and bottom margins of 6 pixels.

Another advantage that Method C has over the previous two is that while each group (label and field) is wrapped in <div> elements, a <br /> puts each on its own line. Using a <br /> to separate the items gets around the issue of fields not lining up perfectly due to text labels of different lengths.

Figure 5-4 shows how Method C would appear in a visual browser, with the CSS applied to each <div> element as mentioned earlier.

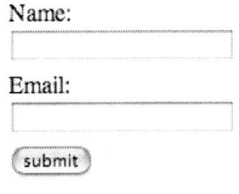

Figure 5-4. Method C as viewed in a browser, with CSS applied to <p> elements

Aside from the visual aspects of Method C, let's take a look at the most important advantages it has: in particular, an accessibility improvement.

The <label> element

There are two steps to utilizing the <label> element for making your forms more accessible, and both are in place in Method C. The first step is to use <label> elements to associate the label text with its corresponding form control, whether it be a text field, text area, radio button, check box, or another control. Method C uses <label> on the "Name:" and "Email:" headers to couple it with text input boxes that will contain that information.

The second step is adding the for attribute to the <label> element as well as a matching id attribute to the form control it belongs to.

For instance, in Method C we wrap the <label> element around Name: with the value of the for attribute that matches the value of the id for the text field that follows.

```
<form action="/path/to/script" id="thisform" method="post">
  <p><label for="name">Name:</label> <br />
  <input type="text" id="name" name="name" /></p>
  <p><label for="email">Email:</label><br />
  <input type="text" id="email" name="email" /></p>
  <p><input type="submit" value="submit" /></p>
</form>
```

Why <label>?

Perhaps you've heard others tell you that you should always add <label> elements to your forms. The important question to ask (always) is *why* you should use <label> elements.

Creating label/ID relationships allows screen readers to properly read the correct label for each form control—regardless of where each falls within the layout. That's a good thing. Also, the <label> element was *created* to mark up form labels, and by utilizing it we're adding structure to the form by adding *meaning* to these components.

An additional benefit to using <label> elements when dealing with radio button or check box controls is that most browsers will toggle the control on or off when the user clicks the text contained within the <label>. This in turn creates a *larger clickable area* for the control, making it easier for mobility-impaired users to interact with the form (see Mark Pilgrim, "*Dive Into Accessibility*," http://diveintoaccessibility.org/day_28_labeling_form_elements.html).

For example, if we add a check box option to our form that gives the user the option to "Remember this info," we can use the <label> element like this:

```
<form action="/path/to/script" id="thisform" method="post">
  <p><label for="name">Name:</label><br />
  <input type="text" id="name" name="name" /></p>
  <p><label for="email">Email:</label><br />
  <input type="text" id="email" name="email" /></p>
  <p><input type="checkbox" id="remember" name="remember" />
  <label for="remember">Remember this info?</label></p>
  <p><input type="submit" value="submit" /></p>
</form>
```

By marking the check box option up this way, we've gained two things: screen readers will read out the form control with the correct label (even though in this case, the label comes *after* the control), and the target for toggling the check box becomes larger, which now includes the text as well as the check box itself (in most browsers).

Figure 5-5 demonstrates how the form would appear in a browser, with the increased clickable area for the check box highlighted.

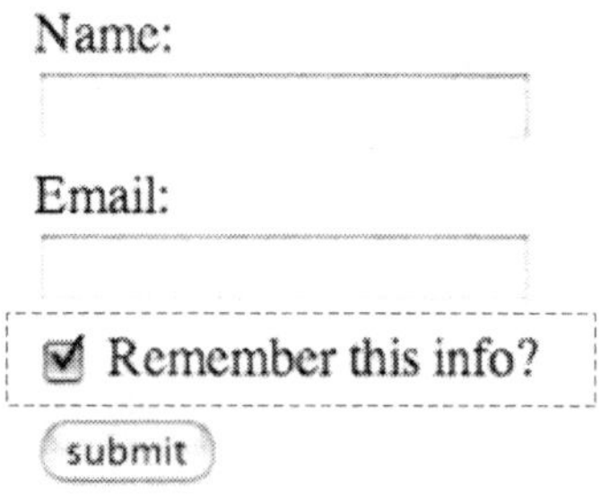

Figure 5-5. Example of a check box option added with clickable text

Apart from tables and paragraphs, I'd like to show you one last method for marking forms—using a definition list.

Method D: Defining a form

```
<form action="/path/to/script" id="thisform" method="post">
  <dl>
    <dt><label for="name">Name:</label></dt>
    <dd><input type="text" id"name" name="name" /></dd>
    <dt><label for="email">Email:</label></dt>
    <dd><input type="text" id="email" name="email" /></dd>
    <dt><label for="remember">Remember this info?</label></dt>
    <dd><input type="checkbox" id="remember" name="remember" /></dd>
    <dt><input type="submit" value="submit" /></dt>
  </dl>
</form>
```

The last method we'll look at in regard to form layout involves the use of a definition list to define label and form control pairs. It's a somewhat controversial move—skirting the fringe of what a definition list is designed to do. But it's also a method that's gaining in widespread use, and one worthy of mention in this book.

Further ahead, in Chapter 8, we'll talk in more detail regarding definition lists—and the fact that they certainly are capable of more uses than most designers are aware of. Using a <dl> to mark up a form is a perfect example.

You'll notice in the code example that each form label is wrapped in a definition term element (<dt>) followed by its associated form control wrapped in a definition description element (<dd>). Doing this creates a pairing of label to form control, which when viewed in a browser without any style applied looks like Figure 5-6.

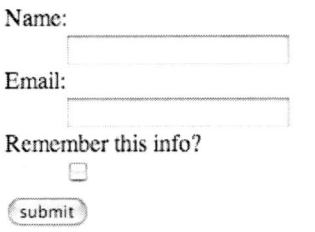

Figure 5-6. Default form layout using a definition list

By default, most visual browsers indent the <dd> element on its own line. Fantastic. Without adding any additional <p> or <br /> elements, we have a readable form layout for those browsing without CSS.

Defining style

The simplest style we could add would be to easily remove the default indenting of <dd> elements within our form:

```
form dd {
  margin: 0;
  }
```

The preceding snippet of CSS would render our Method D example as viewed in Figure 5-7.

Name:

Email:

Remember this info?

submit

Figure 5-7. Definition list form example with <dd> margins removed

The table-like format of Method A could also be achieved by floating `<dt>` elements in our form:

```
form dd {
  margin: 0;
  }

form dt {
  float: left;
  padding-right: 10px;
  }
```

By floating the `<dt>` elements to the left, the form controls contained in `<dd>` elements will align themselves to the right, as seen in Figure 5-8. You'll notice that the form controls don't line up with each other *perfectly*—but at the very least this illustrates that while it's possible to use a `<dl>` element to lay out a form, the layout doesn't have to put each element on its own line.

In fact, because of the presence of the `<dl>`, `<dt>`, and `<dd>` elements—which are in addition to the form `<label>` and `<input>` elements—you'll have plenty to work with in the way of elements that can be styled with CSS.

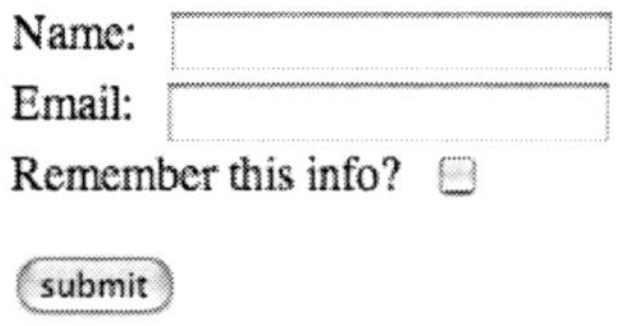

Name:

Email:

Remember this info?

submit

Figure 5-8. Form layout with floated `<dt>` elements

Summary

We've looked at four different ways to mark up the same simple form, noting the pros and cons of each. It's important to point out that the accessibility features that we added to Methods C and D could, of course, be easily added to the first two methods as well—and those methods would be better because of those added features.

Neither one of the methods that we've looked at here are necessarily miles ahead of the others in terms of a "best solution." But it's valuable to know your options—and what you can combine from all four to create better forms in your own projects.

Let's recap the differences between the methods presented.

Method A:

- Visually, it's a nice, neat way to organize form controls and labels—especially for larger complex forms.

- However, using a table for such a simple form seems a bit unnecessary.

Method B:

- Simple markup will degrade nicely in text browsers and small-screened devices.
- Visually, just using `<br />` elements results in a cramped layout.

Method C:

- Simple markup will degrade nicely in text browsers and small-screened devices.
- This method allows for labels and controls of different lengths without any "lining up" issues.
- This method contains an important accessibility feature (that could also be applied to the previous methods).

Method D:

- Structured markup will degrade nicely in text browsers and small-screened devices.
- This method contains an important accessibility feature (that could also be applied to the previous methods).
- Labels and form controls could be placed on the same line or separate lines using CSS.

While you wouldn't be guilty of web design crimes if you were to use Method A or B, taking what we know that is good from Method C and applying it to the previous examples would be a step in the right direction.

There is also room for improvement on Method C as well, and we'll take a look at a few additional features we can add in the "Extra credit" section that follows. We'll also talk about some simple CSS that we can apply to make our form more visually appealing.

Extra credit

For this extra credit session, we'll discuss the tabindex and accesskey attributes and how they can do wonders to make our form more navigable. We'll also explore the `<fieldset>` element, which can help in organizing form sections. Finally, we'll cover CSS as it relates to spicing up our form's appearance.

The fabulous tabindex

A feature that we can easily add to our form is the tabindex attribute. Adding tabindex, and a numerical value, enables users to navigate the focus of form controls with the keyboard (typically using the Tab key). Repeatedly hitting the Tab key will change the focus to the next form control, in an order that we can specify. By default, every interactive element has an implied "tab order," but using the tabindex attribute takes that ordering away from the browser, putting you in full control.

For instance, let's add the tabindex attribute to the form controls in our example (Method C):

```
<form action="/path/to/script" id="thisform" method="post">
  <p><label for="name">Name:</label><br />
  <input type="text" id="name" name="name" tabindex="1" /></p>
  <p><label for="email">Email:</label><br />
  <input type="text" id="email" name="email" tabindex="2" /></p>
  <p><input type="checkbox" id="remember" name="remember" tabindex="3" />
  <label for="remember">Remember this info?</label></p>
  <p><input type="submit" value="submit" tabindex="4" /></p>
</form>
```

Now, when the user tabs through the form, we'll be ensuring the focus of the cursor follows the exact order we intended: Name:, Email:, Remember this info?, and the submit button.

Using tabindex to set focus order becomes even more useful for complex forms and those where there might be multiple input boxes or other form controls for a single label.

Why tabindex?

Aside from being simple to implement on our form, we'll again be helping mobility-impaired users by letting them navigate the form entirely with the keyboard. Rather than grabbing the mouse to enter each form item, the user will be able to tab through each control, in the correct order. Think about those who, for whatever reason, are unable to use both hands to navigate the Web. This will help.

accesskey for frequented forms

Similar to tabindex, the accesskey attribute is another easily added feature that can be useful for mobility-impaired users—and just darn convenient for others.

For instance, if we add the accesskey attribute to the <label> element that surrounds the Name: text of our form, when the user presses the key we specify the focus of the cursor will change to the field that's associated with the label.

Let's take a look at the code that'll make this happen:

```
<form action="/path/to/script" id="thisform" method="post">
  <p><label for="name" accesskey="9" >Name:</label><br />
  <input type="text" id="name" name="name" tabindex="1" /></p>
  <p><label for="email">Email:</label><br />
  <input type="text" id="email" name="email" tabindex="2" /></p>
  <p><input type="checkbox" id="remember" name="remember"        ➥
tabindex="3" />
  <label for="remember">Remember this info?</label></p>
  <p><input type="submit" value="submit" tabindex="4" /></p>
</form>
```

Depending on the system, the user will either use the Alt or Ctrl key in conjunction with the 9 key that we've specified in the markup. Focus will immediately shift to the Name: field in our form.

Easily accessed search

Adding the accesskey attribute can be especially helpful when used on frequently used forms such as a search box or membership login. Without having to reach for the mouse, users can instantly change focus and start their query or input using only the keyboard.

> *It's important to note that, while not all browsers handle* accesskey, *it's an added benefit for those that do. For instance, to access the search form field where we've added* accesskey="9", *Windows users would press Alt+9, while Mac users would press Command+9 to shift the focus to the search field.*

Styling forms

Now that we have a nicely structured form, let's uncover a few CSS techniques we can use to customize it visually.

Setting the width of text inputs

Form controls can be tricky to deal with in their varying widths and heights that are dependent on browser type. In our form example, we haven't specified a size for the text inputs and have left the width of these up to the browser's defaults. Typically, a designer might specify a width using the size attribute, adding it to the <input> element like this:

```
<input type="text" id="name" name="name" tabindex="1" size="20" />
```

Setting a size of "20" specifies the width of the text input box at 20 *characters* (and not pixels). Depending on the browser's default font for form controls, the actual *pixel* width of the box could vary. This makes fitting forms into precise layouts a tad difficult.

Using CSS, we can control the width of input boxes (and other form controls) by the pixel if we wish. For instance, let's assign a width of 200 pixels to all <input> elements in our form example. We'll take advantage of the id that is assigned to the form, in this case thisform.

```
#thisform input {
  width: 200px;
  }
```

Now, all <input> elements within #thisform will be 200 pixels wide. Figure 5-9 shows the results in a visual browser.

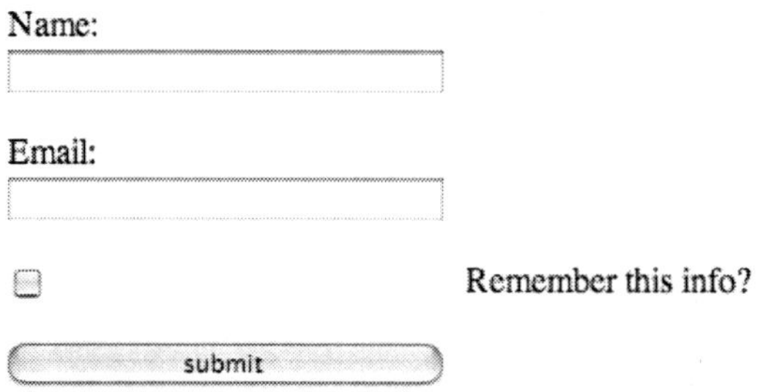

Name:

Email:

Remember this info?

submit

Figure 5-9. Our example form with 200 pixel width applied to all `<input>` elements

Oops. The check box and submit button are also an `<input>` element, and therefore receive that same value. So instead of applying the width to *all* `<input>` elements, let's use the IDs that we set for the "Name" and "Email" controls only.

```
#name, #email {
  width: 200px;
  }
```

Figure 5-10 shows the corrected results in a browser, with only the two text input boxes at 200 pixels wide.

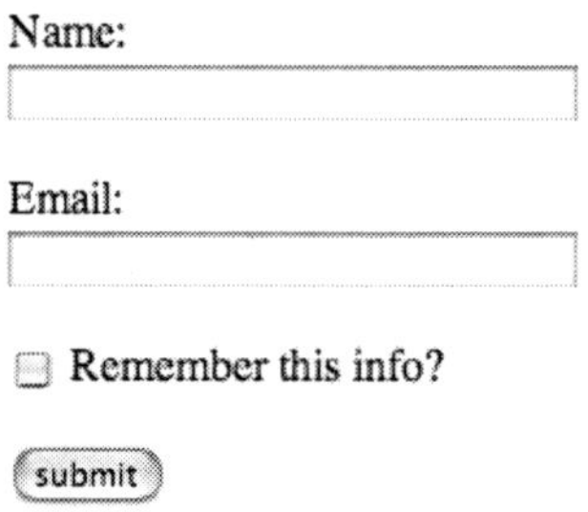

Name:

Email:

Remember this info?

submit

Figure 5-10. Our form example with only text inputs at 200 pixels wide

Using <label> to customize fonts

We have a few different options for customizing the size, face, and color of text that's contained within our form. And in another example of "using the markup you've been given," we'll utilize the `<label>` element to dress up the text.

I like the idea of using the `<label>` element to specifically style form text, primarily for one reason. I can see scenarios where we'd like the label to be called out differently from other text that may be included within the `<form>` element. For instance, alternatively we could add styles to all paragraph elements that fall within our form with a unique style.

```
#thisform p {
  font-family: Verdana, sans-serif;
  font-size: 12px;
  font-weight: bold;
  color: #66000;
  }
```

This would style all text contained in paragraphs within our form with a bold, burgundy, Verdana 12-pixel font. But the same results can be achieved by applying those same rules to just <label> elements within our form like this:

```
#thisform label {
  font-family: Verdana, sans-serif;
  font-size: 12px;
  font-weight: bold;
  color: #66000;
  }
```

5

The results of this styling can be seen in Figure 5-11.

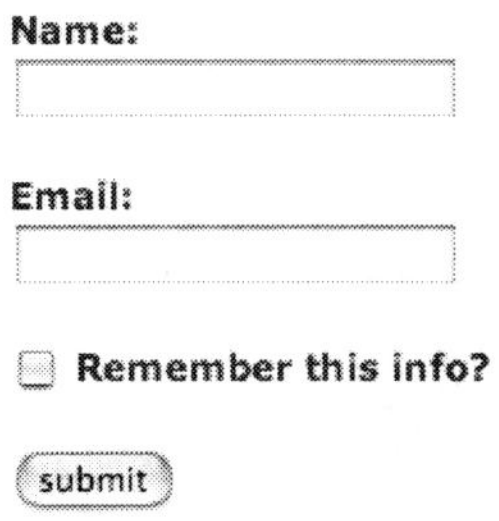

Name:

Email:

☐ **Remember this info?**

(submit)

Figure 5-11. Our example form with styled <label> elements

Why do I like this better? Let's say that aside from labels, the form has additional instructions or text contained within <p> elements. This additional text would inherit the same styles if we applied them to <p> elements within our form.

We could instead apply a generic style to all text within our form, and then use the label styling specifically for customizing form controls uniquely.

The CSS would go something like this:

```
#thisform {
  font-family: Georgia, serif;
  font-size: 12px;
  color: #999;
  }
```

```
#thisform label {
  font-family: Verdana, sans-serif;
  font-weight: bold;
  color: #660000;
  }
```

No need to be redundant

You'll notice that we don't have to repeat the font-size: 12px; rule in the #thisform label declaration. Since <label> elements are contained within #thisform, they will inherit that property. It's always good practice to set shared rules at a high level, then override *only* those that are unique and necessary further down the element tree. This will save bytes of code, which, besides being a good thing, also makes for easier updates later on. If you wish to change the font-family for the entire form, you need only update one rule, rather than each place that the rule is repeated.

Imagine you've built an entire site that uses the Georgia font face exclusively. You've added the identical rule, font-face: Georgia, serif;, to 20 different CSS declarations. Your boss comes to you a week later and says, "The CEO hates serif fonts now. Change the site to Verdana." Now you have to dig through all 20 rules and make your updates.

Alternatively, you could set the rule at a high level, say the <body> element—once. The entire document would inherit the Georgia font face, unless otherwise specified. Now, when your boss asks you to make the change, you can say, "No problem, it'll be done in 2 minutes." Or, you could keep the simplicity to yourself, tell him it'll take you 2 hours, and then spend the extra time bidding on eBay items.

OK, of course, you should tell your boss the truth—your boss should know how valuable you are, saving their company time and code with your newfound solutions.

Use <fieldset> to group form sections

Using the <fieldset> element is a handy way of grouping form controls into sections. Additionally, including a descriptive <legend> will, in most browsers, add a stylish border around the form controls that you're grouping. Did I say stylish? Well, I happen to like the border, and with a little CSS, we can make it even more attractive.

First, though, let's take a look at what the markup looks like when creating field sets. We'll add one to our example form:

```
<form action="/path/to/script" id="thisform" method="post">
  <fieldset>
    <legend>Sign In</legend>
    <p><label for="name" accesskey="9" >Name:</label><br />
    <input type="text" id="name" name="name" tabindex="1" /></p>
    <p><label for="email">Email:</label><br />
    <input type="text" id="email" name="email" tabindex="2" /></p>
    <p><input type="checkbox" id="remember" name="remember" ➥
    tabindex="3" />
```

```
    <label for="remember">Remember this info?</label></p>
    <p><input type="submit" value="submit" tabindex="4" /></p>
  </fieldset>
</form>
```

Figure 5-12 shows us how our form appears in a typical browser with the <fieldset> and <legend> elements added, along with the CSS that we're applying to the <label> elements. You'll notice the stylish border that surrounds the form controls that fall within the <fieldset> elements, with the <legend> breaking the border at the top left of the box.

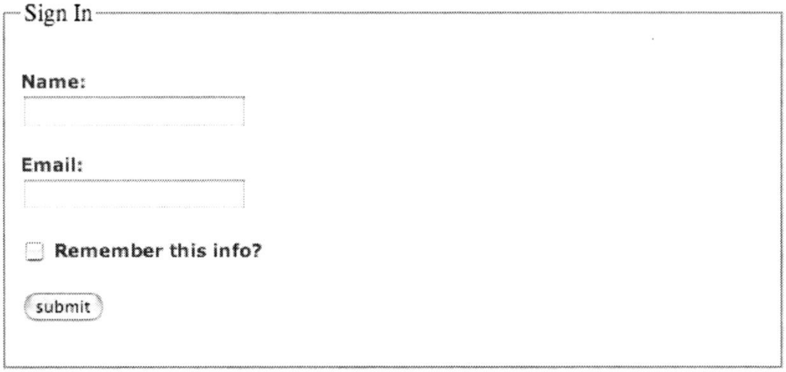

Figure 5-12. Our form example with <fieldset> and <legend> added

The reason I call it "stylish" is because, for a default rendering, with no CSS added at all, it's rather impressive. And it can get even more interesting when we choose to add a bit more customization, which we'll do next.

You may also begin to see how useful <fieldset> could be for grouping different sections of a form together. For instance, if our example form was the first part of a larger form that had other groups contained in it, using <fieldset> to visually box those sections off is a semantically rich way to make our forms more organized and readable.

Adding style to <fieldset> and <legend>

We can customize the appearance of the default <fieldset> border and <legend> text with CSS just as easily as with any other element. First, let's change the border's color and width, and then we'll modify the text itself.

To stylize <fieldset>'s border, making it a bit more subtle, we'll use the following CSS:

```
#thisform {
  font-family: Georgia, serif;
  font-size: 12px;
  color: #999;
  }
```

```
#thisform label {
  font-family: Verdana, sans-serif;
  font-weight: bold;
  color: #660000;
  }

#thisform fieldset {
  border: 1px solid #ccc;
  padding: 0 20px;
  }
```

We also specify a 20-pixel margin on both the right and left, with zero margins on both top and bottom. Why zero margins? Because our form labels and controls are wrapped in <p> elements, there's already enough padding at both the top and bottom.

Figure 5-13 shows how our slightly styled form looks in a browser.

Figure 5-13. Our form example with <fieldset> styled

Three-dimensional <legend>

Finally, let's apply some CSS to the <legend> element, creating a three-dimensional box effect that appears connected to the border created by the <fieldset> element.

```
#thisform {
  font-family: Georgia, serif;
  font-size: 12px;
  color: #999;
  }

#thisform label {
  font-family: Verdana, sans-serif;
  font-weight: bold;
  color: #660000;
  }
```

```
#thisform fieldset {
  border: 1px solid #ccc;
  padding: 0 20px;
  }

#thisform legend {
  font-family: arial, sans-serif;
  font-weight: bold;
  font-size: 90%;
  color: #666;
  background: #eee;
  border: 1px solid #ccc;
  border-bottom-color: #999;
  border-right-color: #999;
  padding: 4px 8px;
  }
```

As you can see, we're doing several things here. First, we're customizing the font, weight, and size of the <legend>. Second, for the 3-D effect, we've set the background to a light gray, and then we've added a single-pixel border around the whole <legend> that matches the border that we've used for the <fieldset> element. For the shading effect, we've over-ridden the border's color on the bottom and right sides only, with a slightly darker gray.

Since we've previously set font-size: 12px; *for the entirety of* #thisform, *to make the* <legend> *text smaller, we'll just use a percentage. Setting a font size at a high level and then using percentages further down the hierarchy makes for easier maintenance later on. Need to bump up the whole site's font size? Just make a single update, and the percentages will change accordingly. In fact, ideally we'd set that initial size on the* <body> *element, and use percentages everywhere else. For this example, though, we've chosen to set it at the* <form> *level.*

Padding was also adjusted to give the text in the box some breathing room. That's it! Figure 5-14 shows the finished results with all of the CSS we've been adding throughout the chapter—all the while using our lean, mean, marked-up form.

Sign in

Name:

Email:

☐ **Remember this info?**

(submit)

Figure 5-14. Our completed form example, styled with CSS

Borders and backgrounds on form elements

It didn't used to be the case, but browsers are getting better and better about enabling us to *style* form elements. You should certainly use caution, of course, as in the end, a form element should still look like a form element, and it should be obvious to users where they're able to interact with the form.

That said, there's nothing wrong with *subtly* styling form elements by altering their default borders and backgrounds, for example.

Let's first add a 1-pixel gray border around each of the Name and Email input fields in our example form, overriding the usual beveled shadow that most browsers apply.

```
#name,
#email {
  padding: 5px;
  font-size: 16px;
  border: 1px solid #ccc;
  }
```

You'll notice we've also added a little padding and increased the font-size to make the inputs a little easier to read and use, as Figure 5-15 shows.

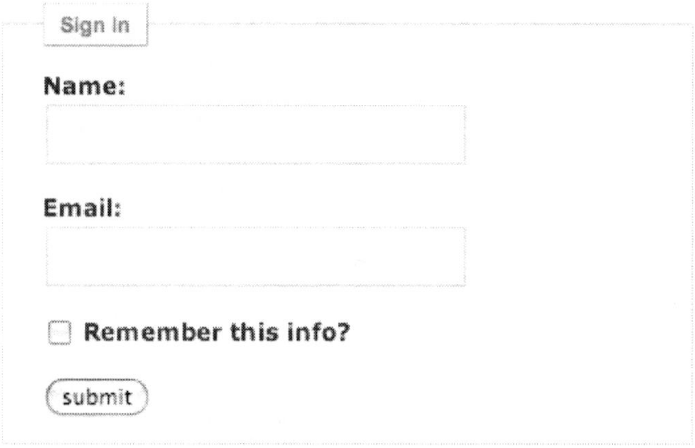

Figure 5-15. Form input boxes with 1-pixel gray borders

Next, let's add a background gradient image that tiles horizontally to give a custom 3-D look to the inputs. Figure 5-16 shows the image that we'll use to tile—a gray shadow, fading downward to white.

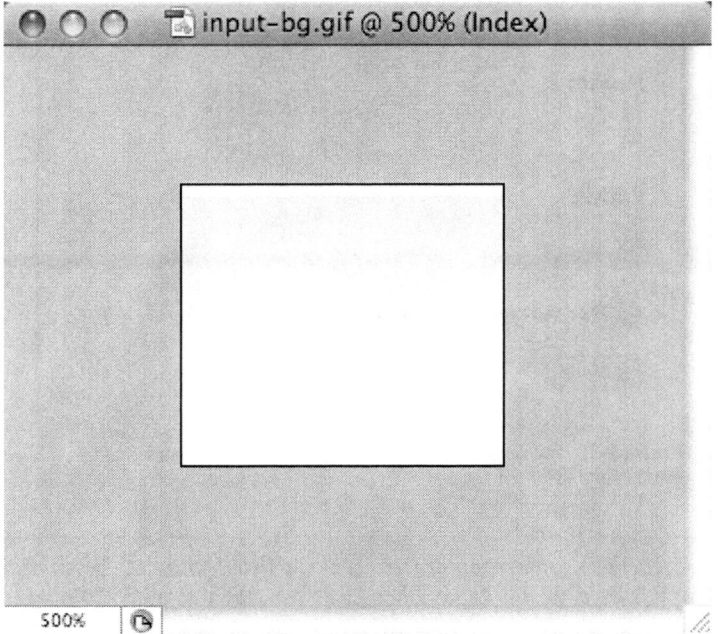

Figure 5-16. The input-bg.gif image, zoomed at 500 percent in order to see detail

And here's the CSS rule that'll add that tiled gradient to the inputs:

```
#name,
#email {
    padding: 5px;
    font-size: 16px;
    border: 1px solid #ccc;
    background: #fff url(input-bg.gif) repeat-x top left;
    }
```

Figure 5-17 shows the finished styled form, just scratching the surface of what can be achieved in styling form elements themselves. Just remember it's often best to be conservative so as not to throw off the user. Familiarity in form controls is important! But altering a form control's font, border, background, padding, and so forth can make an immense difference in the appearance of a well-designed form.

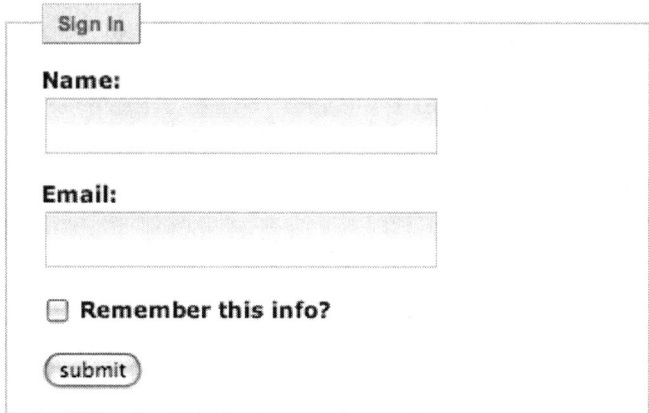

Figure 5-17. The completed form, with custom borders and background gradient

> For a comprehensive comparison of form controls styled with CSS, based on browser and platform, take a look a Roger Johansson's collection of over 200 screenshots at http://www.456bereastreet.com/archive/200701/styling_form_controls_with_css_revisited/. Very helpful in determining which CSS properties will work when styling form controls and which ones will fail. Roger correctly states that consistent form styling across all browsers and platforms is impossible—but that shouldn't stop you from experimenting, making trade-off decisions based on your site's browser/platform statistics.

Wrapping up

There are many ways to mark up forms—whether you use a table, a definition list, or simple paragraph elements to structure your form labels and controls, keep in mind the accessibility features that can easily be applied to any of the methods we've looked at in this chapter.

Attributes such as tabindex and accesskey can improve your form's navigation. <label> elements with corresponding id attributes can ensure those browsing with assistive software can still interact with your forms. You can even subtly style your forms to make them more usable and appealing.

Small, simple additions. Improved results.

CHAPTER 6

<STRONG>, <EM>, AND OTHER PHRASE ELEMENTS

Breadcrumb navigation. This is a
Baekdal. Breadcrumb navigation is
the user where they are within the
easy way of getting back.

Marking up a breadcrumb trail of li
and I'm interested in hearing
presented structurally, keeping in n

In addition to the four methods b
scenarios. Don't be afraid to sugges

**Q: Which is the best method f
links?**

We've talked a little about semantic markup in the Introduction as well as in previous chapters—using elements that apply meaning to the document, rather than using elements purely for presentational purposes. While constructing *purely* semantic web pages is a nice idea, I see it more as an ideal and a target to strive for. Not hitting the bull's-eye doesn't mean all is for naught; rather, getting close to the mark is, at the very least, a worthy effort.

Often in real-world situations, adding nonsemantic markup in order to fulfill a certain design requirement becomes necessary. This is primarily due to the lack of 100 percent standards support from the current crop of popular browsers. Certain CSS rules fall short of working properly in some modern browsers, and that can lead to the unfortunate peppering of extraneous elements to make certain designs work.

The important thing to keep in mind is that there are real benefits to be had by trying your best to use semantic structure—whenever possible. And that standards support, while not 100 percent, has reached a threshold where we can start building our sites *now*, using web standards methods. Sometimes, a compromise is necessary, but the more structure we can adhere to, the easier our jobs will become in the future.

Presentational vs. structural

This chapter covers the difference between *presentational* and *structural* markup—but more specifically the difference between using <strong> instead of <b>, and likewise, <em> instead of <i>. Later in the chapter, we'll also talk about a few other *phrase elements* and their importance in the world of standards-compliant, structured markup.

You may have heard others telling you to swap out <strong> for <b> when bold text is desired, but with no further explanation as to *why* you should make the switch. And without the "why," it's hard to expect other designers to change their markup habits just because they are being told to.

Why are <strong> and <em> better than <b> and <i>?

What's all this hoo-ha about tossing out the <b> and <i> elements in favor of <strong> and <em>? Well, it's all about conveying *meaning* and *structure*, rather than giving a *presentational instruction*. And it's that same structure that we're striving for in the examples throughout the book.

Check in with the experts

First, let's hear what the W3C says about <strong> and <em> as part of the HTML 4.01 Specification on Phrase Elements (www.w3.org/TR/html4/struct/text.html#h-9.2.1):

"Phrase elements add structural information to text fragments. The usual meanings of phrase elements are [the] following:

> `<em>`

indicates emphasis.

> `<strong>`

indicates stronger emphasis."

So we're talking two levels of emphasis here—for instance, a word or phrase that is intended to be louder, higher in pitch, faster or, well . . . *emphasized* more than normal text.

The W3C goes on to say the following:

"The presentation of phrase elements depends on the user agent. Generally, visual user agents present `<em>` text in italics and `<strong>` text in bold font. Speech synthesizer user agents may change the synthesis parameters, such as volume, pitch, and rate accordingly."

Aha, that last sentence is of particular interest. Speech synthesizer user agents (what we've been calling "screen readers") will treat emphasized words and phrases the way they were intended, and that is surely a good thing.

Alternatively, using `<b>` or `<i>` is simply a visual presentation instruction. If our goal is to separate structure from presentation as much as possible, then we'll be right on track when we use `<strong>` and `<em>`, saving instances where you simply want bold or italicized text, visually, for CSS. And we'll talk more about those instances later in the chapter.

Let's look at two markup examples to help us figure out the difference.

Method A

> `Your order number for future reference is: <b>6474-82071</b>.`

Method B

> `Your order number for future reference is: <strong>6474-82071</strong>.`

Bold and beautiful

Here's a perfect example of a situation where using `<strong>` over `<b>` is appropriate— where we're looking to give greater importance over the rest of text in the sentence. In addition to visually rendering the order number in bold text, we'd also like screen readers to change the way they present that particular bit as well—increasing the volume, or changing the pitch or rate. Using Method B does both of these for us.

What about \<em\>?

Similarly, by using `<em>` over `<i>`, we can convey emphasis rather than just making the text italic. Let's look at two examples.

Method A

> `It took me not one, but <i>three</i> hours to shovel my driveway this ➡`
> `morning.`

Method B

It took me not one, but three hours to shovel my driveway this ➡ morning.

Emphasis mine

In the preceding example (a true statement at the time of this writing), my intention is that the word "three" be spoken with emphasis over the rest of the text, as if I was reading it aloud. Visually, Method B will be rendered as italicized text in most browsers, and speech synthesizers will adjust the tone, speed, or pitch accordingly.

Just bold or italic, please

It's important to note that there may be plenty of scenarios where you'd like bold or italic text for the visual effect only. In other words, let's say you had a list of links contained in a sidebar, and you're fond of the way all of the links look—in bold text (see Figure 6-1, for example).

Figure 6-1. An example of a list of bold links contained within a sidebar

There is no intention of a strong emphasis on the links, other than a visual characteristic. This is where it's best to let CSS handle the visual change in the link's appearance, so as *not* to convey emphasis for screen readers and other nonvisual browsers.

For instance, do you really intend to have the list of bold links read faster, louder, or higher in pitch? Probably not. The bold intention is purely presentational.

Worth its (font-)weight in bold

To demonstrate in code what Figure 6-1 illustrates, let's say the column of links is a <div> with an id of sidebar. We could simply state in CSS that all links *within* #sidebar be bold like this:

```
#sidebar a {
  font-weight: bold;
  }
```

Extremely simple, and I feel sort of silly making a point out of it—yet it's a perfectly easy way to continue to help separate content from presentation.

That's italic!

Likewise, the same can be applied when thinking about italic text—for instances where you're not intending emphasis, but rather you're simply intending to render text in italics. CSS can again be used for such cases through the font-style property.

Let's use the same #sidebar column as an example; for instance, if we'd like all of the links within #sidebar to be italic, the CSS would go like this:

```
#sidebar a {
  font-style: italic;
  }
```

Again, an absurdly simply concept, yet I think it's important to talk about in the realm of structured markup—instances where instead of using presentational markup, we allow CSS to handle the styling. Sometimes, the simplest solutions are the easiest to overlook.

Both bold and italic

For scenarios where you're intending to render text both in bold *and* italics, then I feel a decision would first need to be made. What level of emphasis are you trying to convey? Based on your answer, I would choose the correct element: <em> (for emphasis) or <strong> (for stronger emphasis) and mark up the text with that element.

For instance, for the following example, I'd like the word "fun" to appear both bold *and* in italics. I've chosen to use the <em> element to emphasize the text as well.

```
Building sites with web standards can be <em>fun</em>!
```

Most browsers will render the preceding only in italics. To achieve both bold *and* italics, we have a few different options. Oh, and I sincerely hope that you agree with the preceding statement.

Generic <span>

One option would be to nest a generic <span> element around "fun" as well and use CSS to render all <span> elements within <em> elements in bold text. The markup would look like this:

```
Building sites with web standards can be <em><span>fun</span></em>!
```

while the CSS would go like this:

```
em span {
  font-weight: bold;
  }
```

Obviously, not ideal in the semantic department because of the extraneous element we're adding—but one that will work nonetheless.

Emphasis with class

Another option would be to create a class for <em> elements that triggered the bold with CSS. The markup would look like this:

```
Building sites with web standards can be <em class="bold">fun</em>!
```

while the CSS would go like this:

```
em.bold {
  font-weight: bold;
  }
```

The presence of the <em> element would handle our italicizing (and implied emphasis), while adding the class bold would also make the text within the <em> element, well... bold.

A similar setup could be used in reverse for <strong> elements, where an italic class could be written to render text in italics in addition to the bold that comes with the <strong> element when used for stronger emphasis.

The markup would go like this:

```
Building sites with web standards can be ➡
<strong class="italic">fun</strong>!
```

while the CSS would go like this:

```
strong.italic {
  font-style: italic;
  }
```

Summary

I thought it was important to talk about this topic, as it's a nice example of one of the core themes of the book: that separating content from presentation is important, and beneficial, and swapping out <b> and <i> elements for their structural equivalents (when conveying emphasis) can be a simple way of helping to achieve that separation.

So, the next time you hear someone announce, "Yes, you should always use <strong> instead of <b>," you'll now have some reasoning to back that statement up.

In most cases, it's appropriate to use <strong> or <em> when conveying emphasis. And when a visual bold or italic is all that you're after, use CSS.

Extra credit

So far in this chapter, we've focused on <strong> and <em>, which are part of a larger group of elements that the W3C likes to call "phrase elements." For extra credit, let's take a look at a few more of these phrase elements, and how they relate to the web standards world.

6

The phrase elements

In addition to <strong> and <em>, the entire list of phrase elements as outlined by the W3C's HTML 4.01 Specification contains the following:

- <cite>: Contains a citation or a reference to other sources
- <dfn>: Indicates that this is the defining instance of the enclosed term
- <code>: Designates a fragment of computer code
- <samp>: Designates sample output from programs, scripts, etc.
- <kbd>: Indicates text to be entered by the user
- <var>: Indicates an instance of a variable or program argument
- <abbr>: Indicates an abbreviated form (e.g., WWW, HTTP, URI, Mass., etc.)
- <acronym>: Indicates an acronym (e.g., WAC, radar, etc.)

Let's take a deeper look at a few of these, beginning with <cite>.

<cite> design

<cite> is an interesting element to discuss—especially when talking about substituting the <i> element due to its purely presentational nature. <cite> is used to reference a citation of a source: an author or publication. Historically, designers may have used the <i> element to render a book title in italics, but we've learned earlier in the chapter that CSS is the best tool for styling text this way.

You may suggest marking up a publication's title with <em> instead—but when referencing a book or other publication, we're not intending to add emphasis; we're merely trying to set it apart from normal text. We're also trying to stay in line with conventional typography practices, where titles are often shown in italics (underlining is also common in the print world, but would create obvious confusion for a hyperlink).

Here enters the <cite> element, specifically created for the job. Most browsers will even render text contained within <cite> elements in italics by default, and we can support that by adding a general CSS declaration that will do the same.

The specification

The W3C is somewhat brief regarding the <cite> element, simply saying in the HTML 4.01 Specification (www.w3.org/TR/html4/struct/text.html#h-9.2.1)

"<cite>: Contains a citation or a reference to other sources."

That's about all we have to go on, and it's unclear exactly what types of data we can wrap <cite> around. But by "sources," we can take it to mean at least people and publications.

Let's take a look at <cite> in action:

```
The novel, <cite>The Scarlet Letter</cite> is set in Puritan Boston➥
   and like this book, was written in Salem, Massachusetts.
```

From the use of <cite>, the title *The Scarlet Letter* will, in most browsers, be rendered in italics. To be sure, we'll add the following, utterly simplistic, CSS rule—for cases where the browser doesn't:

```
cite {
  font-style: italic;
  }
```

To recap, we've replaced the <i> element for instances where we're marking up book titles and other publications with <cite>. What we get is italic text in most visual browsers, and once again, we get more structure and meaning added to our pages. That structure can, as always, be harnessed fully by the use of CSS. Let's take a look.

A change in <cite> style

When we talk about building pages with structure and meaning, it goes hand in hand with a page that becomes easier to style (and restyle) using CSS. Take, for instance, the <cite> element. If we become consistent in marking up titles of publications with this element, we then have full control over the style presented—to be changed at any time that we wish.

Let's say that we've authored an entire site, all the while using the <cite> element to mark up references to book and publication titles. We've added the global CSS rule to render all <cite> elements in italics, but a few months later decide that we'd like all book and publication titles to be not only in italics, but also bold and red in color with a light gray background.

We can, of course, do this quickly and easily with a few CSS rules—instantly changing all references that we've previously marked up with the <cite> element—something we couldn't specifically target if we had used <i> or <em> to simply render publication titles in italics.

```
cite {
  font-style: italic;
  font-weight: bold;
  color: red;
  background-color: #ddd;
  }
```

Figure 6-2 shows how this would appear in most browsers, and it's another nice example of the power of writing structural markup first—allowing you to make easy, site-wide design changes later.

The novel, *The Scarlet Letter* is set in Puritan Boston and like this book, was written in Salem, Massachusetts.

Figure 6-2. A book title marked up with <cite> and styled with CSS

Leveraging the structure

In addition to being easily styled, using structured markup can lead to interesting things when server-side software takes advantage of it.

Take for instance, what author and accessibility advocate Mark Pilgrim did a few years ago with the <cite> element on his personal site, "dive into mark" (www.diveintomark.org/). By marking up citations to people and publications on his weblog with the <cite> element, Mark was able to write software that would create a database from a parsing of all of his posts—organized then by the person or publication that was referenced.

Figure 6-3 shows the results of searching for "Dan Cederholm." Two posts were found on Mark's weblog—all thanks to the power of marking up the reference to "Dan Cederholm" with the <cite> element.

6

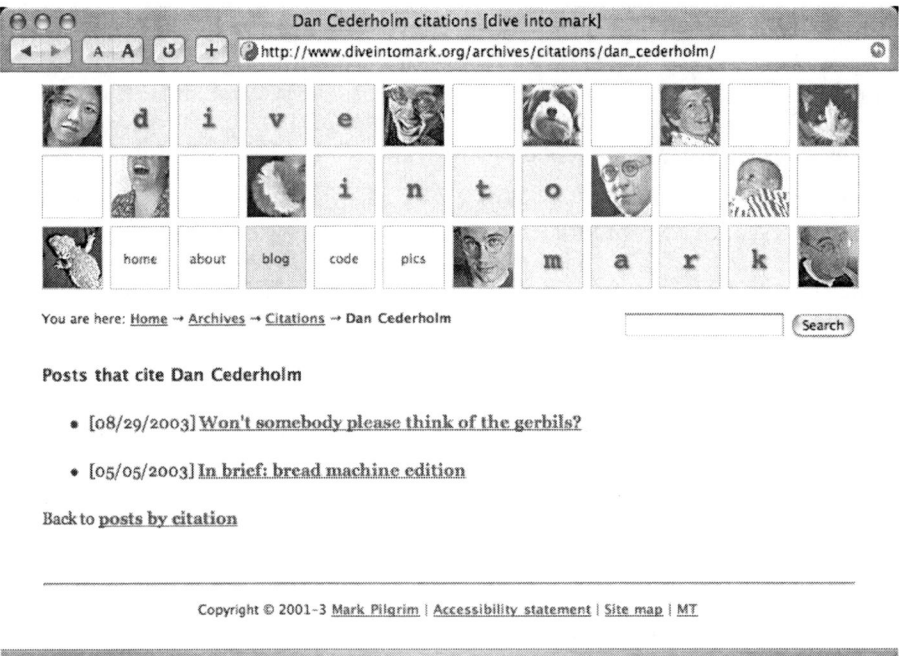

Figure 6-3. Mark Pilgrim's "posts by citation" results on a previous incarnation of "dive into mark"

<abbr> and <acronym>

Two other phrase elements that I'd like to note are <abbr> (for abbreviations) and <acronym> (for... you guessed it, acronyms). Using these elements can improve the accessibility of web pages by giving definitions to abbreviations and acronyms, so that all users are informed.

Let's reacquaint ourselves with the W3C's HTML 4.01 Specification on what the <abbr> and <acronym> elements are used for:

- <abbr>: Indicates an abbreviated form (e.g., WWW, HTTP, URI, Mass., etc.)
- <acronym>: Indicates an acronym (e.g., WAC, radar, etc.)

Using these elements along with a suitable title attribute will help users who would be otherwise unfamiliar with the term. For instance, if we were marking up the abbreviation XHTML, we could use the <abbr> element like this:

```
<abbr title="eXtensible HyperText Markup Language">XHTML</abbr>
```

Using <abbr> in this case can provide a cue for screen readers in regard to spelling out the text (X-H-T-M-L), rather than reading it as a normal word. Conversely, the use of <acronym> provides a cue to speak the word normally, rather than spell it out.

An example of the <acronym> element could be applied to the following:

```
<acronym title="North Atlantic Treaty Organization">NATO</acronym>
```

There are also two CSS rules that could be added to an aural style sheet to further reinforce these directives:

```
abbr {
  speak:spell-out;
  }

acronym {
  speak:normal;
  }
```

> *Aural style sheets allow authors to construct CSS rules specifically for screen reader applications. Harnessing structural markup, changes in pitch, voice type, inflection, and so forth can be altered to present the page aurally, more in line with what it reads like visually.*

6

Define once

Many suggest defining an abbreviation or acronym that appears multiple times on a page only once. It's argued to be a waste of bytes to redefine a term each time it appears, and better to set the title attribute only on the *first* occurrence of the page. I tend to think this makes sense, although in the event that people are directed to a *specific* section of a page, and the abbreviation or acronym is only expanded at the top, then the user can't take advantage of the definition.

Use your best judgment on when (and how often) to define your terms contained within <abbr> and <acronym> elements.

The presentation

To cue readers on the visual side, some browsers by default will render text marked up with <abbr> or <acronym> with a 1-pixel dotted bottom border, enticing users to move their mouse over the underlined abbreviation or acronym. When moused over, the definition provided in the title attribute will show up in the browser as a tooltip.

For browsers that don't by default add that dotted line, we can easily create a CSS declaration that does essentially the same:

```
abbr, acronym {
  border-bottom: 1px dotted;
  cursor: help;
  }
```

We've also added an additional rule that will turn the cursor (in most browsers) into the "help" symbol, which will help signify that this isn't a link to be clicked on, but rather a definition to be expanded with the tooltip (see Mark Newhouse, "Real World Style: CSS Help," http://realworldstyle.com/css_help.html).

Figure 6-4 shows the results in a browser, with the abbreviation XHTML expanded with its definition—as well as a dotted border and "help" cursor.

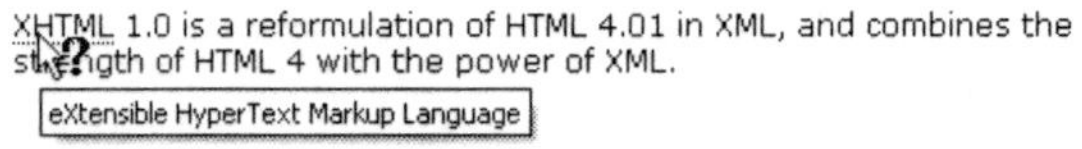

XHTML 1.0 is a reformulation of HTML 4.01 in XML, and combines the
strength of HTML 4 with the power of XML.

eXtensible HyperText Markup Language

Figure 6-4. Example of <abbr> results in a typical browser

Compatibility issues

It's important to mention that, at the time of this writing, Internet Explorer for Windows version 6 doesn't support the styling or tooltip for the <abbr> element. IE/Win does support the <acronym> element, which has encouraged some designers to use only <acronym> for both abbreviations and acronyms alike.

It might be tempting to do the same, but using the wrong element for the sake of a display issue seems like the wrong road to take. For this specific problem, I prefer marking the term up according to the specifications, and letting browsers that properly handle the <abbr> element style it accordingly.

Thankfully, support for styling the <abbr> element was added to IE7, although unlike Firefox or Safari, IE7 doesn't style <abbr> by default. Something to keep in mind.

Let's take a quick look at the remaining phrase elements that we haven't yet covered.

<code>

The <code> element is designed for demonstrating code examples within XHTML pages. For instance, if you'd like to share a CSS example, you could do something like this:

```
<code>
#content {
  width: 80%;
  padding: 20px;
  background: blue;
  }
</code>
```

Generally, visual browsers will render text held within <code> elements in a monospaced serif font, but we could, of course, style code examples any way we wish by adding a CSS rule:

```
code {
  font-family: Courier, serif;
  color: red;
  }
```

All text contained in <code> would now be rendered with the Courier typeface in red.

<samp>

The <samp> element is used to show sample output from programs and scripts. For example, if I were talking about the results of a Perl script I was working on, I may use something like

```
<p>When the script has executed, at the command line you will see the ➥
message <samp>script was successful!</samp>.</p>
```

Here, I'm essentially "quoting" the output of a script, and a similar CSS rule could be defined for styling program samples uniquely—just as we had done with <code> elements.

<var>

Related to the <samp> element, the <var> element is used to designate a program parameter or variable. For instance, if I were talking about an XSLT style sheet, I could code the following:

```
<p>I'm going to pass the parameter <var>lastUpdated</var>➥
to my main.xsl file.</p>
```

Many browsers will render text within <var> elements in italics—but feel free to write a simple rule that would override that. If you don't like italics, you could use the font-style property in CSS:

```
var {
   font-style: normal;
   font-family: Courier, serif;
   color: purple;
   }
```

Lastly, let's take a look at the <kbd> element to finish off the phrase elements.

<kbd>

The <kbd> element is used to signify text to be entered by the user. For example, if I were explaining how someone might use the accesskey we had assigned to switch focus to a search box, I might use this code:

```
<p>To quickly change focus to the search input field, Mac users type➥
<kbd>Command+9</kbd>.</p>
```

You can only guess what I'm going to say next, can't you? That's right! Through the magic of a simple CSS rule, you can customize the style of all <kbd> elements, just as we had previously with the other phrase elements.

6

Microformats

We've spent the first half of this book talking about the benefits of semantic markup—adding *meaning* to the data and content on the page. While we've focused on the appropriate elements to use according to the specs, it's a good time to talk about how we can also add valuable semantic information in the *classes* we use as well. *Microformats* offer us a perfect example of sprinkling your markup with predetermined classes, extending XHTML with a powerful, yet human-readable set of open data formats. Microformats can also enable a designer to leverage the data that already exists in the markup, exposing it to other applications and software. In short, microformats can help take the guesswork out of marking up certain sets of data, while offering some additional benefits along the way.

I feel it makes sense to talk about microformats in this chapter, as often the elements that we'll be adding semantic classes to are the very phrase elements that we've just discussed.

New growth

I had the pleasure of designing the logo and initial site design for microformats.org back in 2005, and the logo mark itself, shown in Figure 6-5, attempted to show how microformats build on existing standards (XML, XHTML) as "new growth." Instead of waiting around for standards bodies to decide on finer-grained formats for often-marked-up data (such as contact details, relationships, and reviews), the microformats community took matters into their own hands, using the tools that we already know to help enable cool stuff to happen (more on that in a bit).

Figure 6-5. The microformats logo, designed by Dan Cederholm

A simple explanation

"Dan, microformats are confusing and seem like a waste of time."

I'd hear this quite a bit from other designers and developers. And while microformats may seem a bit confusing at first, Figure 6-6 is about the simplest way I can think to explain their core value.

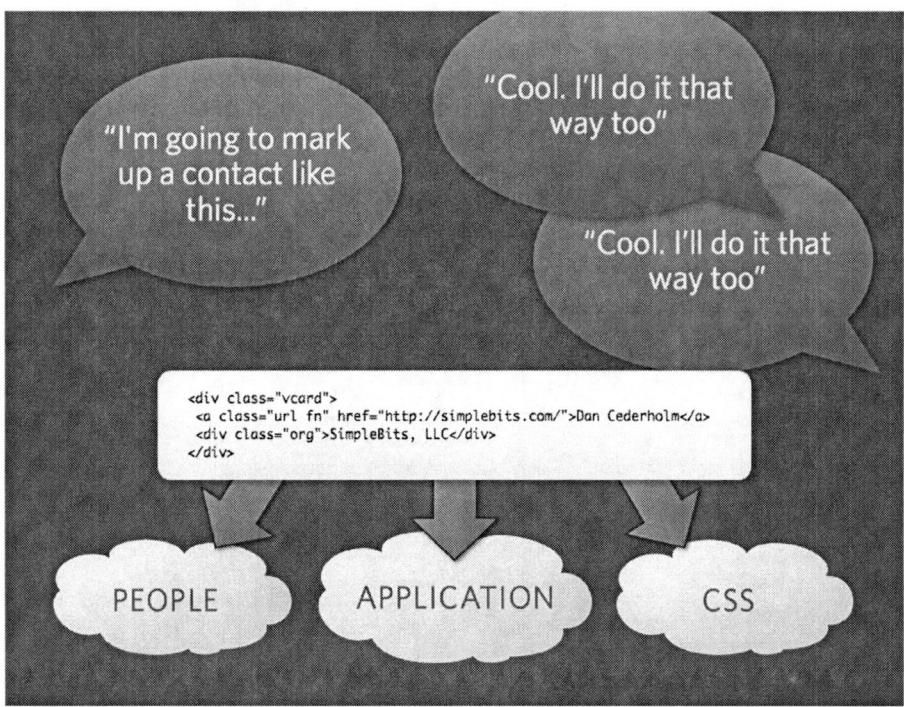

Figure 6-6. A simple illustration of why microformats are useful

Essentially, by settling on a predetermined class system for certain types of data (in this case, a person's contact details), we enable software and other web applications to easily find the data, right from the markup. It's also worth pointing out that microformats are easily read by humans (because of their simple class names) and lend themselves well to be styled uniquely with CSS due to the presence of those semantic elements and classes.

To illustrate further, let's walk through a simple scenario where microformats add value.

An hCard example

Over at my own site, SimpleBits, I have my contact details available at simplebits.com/contact. This is a pretty typical design pattern, listing name, organization, address, and phone. And this information could be marked up in a myriad of ways. I mentioned before that using microformats takes some of the guesswork out of how you might mark up these data patterns. Many smart people have thought long and hard about the best way to handle markup for contact details, and we'll take advantage by using the hCard microformat here.

Code Creator

A first step is to check out the microformats hCard Creator, which will help us build an hCard automatically, by simply filling out a form.

Figure 6-7 shows the Code Creator for hCard, which creates the markup with proper classes dynamically as you type in the contact details. This tool (and there are others for other microformats) is wonderful for learning how microformats are structured. I highly recommend that you check out these tools first if you're new to microformats or you learn better by seeing something in action (I know I do).

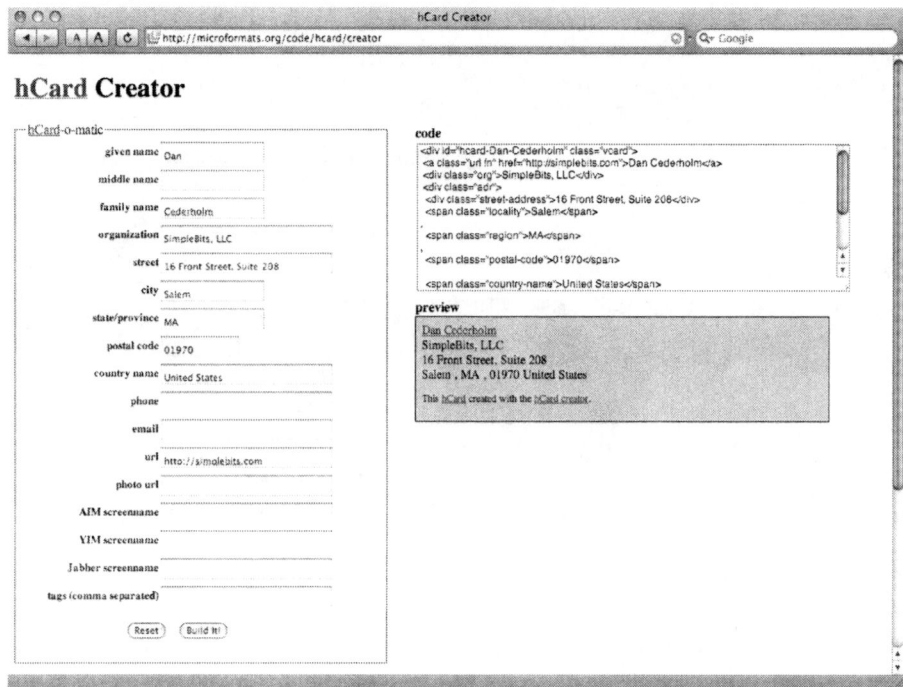

Figure 6-7. The hCard Creator tool, found at http://microformats.org/code/hcard/creator

The markup

After filling out the contact details that we want to share on the contact page (you don't need to fill out all fields), we're left with the following markup, a finished hCard:

```
<div class="vcard">
  <a class="url fn" href="http://simplebits.com">Dan Cederholm</a>
  <div class="org">SimpleBits, LLC</div>
   <div class="adr">
      <div class="street-address">16 Front Street, Suite 208</div>
      <span class="locality">Salem</span>,
      <span class="region">Massachusetts</span>
      <span class="postal-code">01970</span>
      <abbr class="country-name" ➡
title="United States of America">USA</abbr>
    </div>
```

```
    <div class="tel">
      <span class="type">Fax</span>:
      <span class="value">+1 978 744 0760</span>
    </div>
  </div>
```

You can see it's a combination of `<div>`s and `<span>`s with semantic classes added to note the various parts of the contact's details. The `<abbr>` element previously mentioned in this chapter is also used to abbreviate the country name.

While the Code Creator suggests these elements to structure the data, that doesn't mean we have to use them, as long as we assign the correct class. For example, if instead of a `<div>`, we wanted to use a heading element for the organization name, we could swap out the elements like so:

```
<h2 class="org">SimpleBits, LLC</h2>
```

In other words, you're not locked to the elements that the Code Creator suggests. Structure the data the way you'd like, then apply the classes to the appropriate bits of data.

Remember, just as with the other examples in the book, we know that regardless of the elements chosen, we can style this any way we'd like with CSS—and those extra class names added by microformats make it easy to do so.

Figure 6-8 shows how our finished hCard would appear in the browser without any CSS applied. You can see that even with default browser styling, it's a very readable address. And because it's nothing more than semantic markup and classes, it lends itself well to unique styling with CSS. All of those extra classes mean easy styling of *each* portion of the microformat.

Dan Cederholm

SimpleBits, LLC

16 Front Street, Suite 208

Salem, Massachusetts 01970 USA

Fax: +1 978 744 0760

Figure 6-8. A sample hCard, showed here unstyled

The power of microformats

Finally let's talk about the main benefit to using this hCard markup versus a format of our own choosing. Again, by using a predetermined set of classes, software and other web applications could now parse, or "scrape," your HTML and extract the contact information right from the markup.

Here's a prime example of that in practice. Often, sites offer a downloadable vCard of their contact information in addition to having it appear in the HTML of the page. This vCard file format plays nice with most operating systems' address book applications, and is a customary way of offering a "one click to add" someone to their address book. Quick and easy.

Now, because we've marked up our address using the hCard microformat, we could offer the vCard download directly from that same data instead of creating a separate file. There are various browser plug-ins and extensions that detect and consume microformats, but let's help everyone out by adding a simple "Download vCard" link to the contact page (Figure 6-9).

This link will use Technorati's Contacts Feed Service (http://technorati.com/contacts/), which offers a way of gathering up any hCards from a specified page, then spitting back a vCard file all in one click.

All we need to do is add the correct URL that specifies our contact page:

```
<a href="http://feeds.technorati.com/contact/http://simplebits.com/➡
contact">Download vCard</a>
```

Dan Cederholm

SimpleBits, LLC

16 Front Street, Suite 208

Salem, Massachusetts 01970 USA

Fax: +1 978 744 0760

Download vCard

Figure 6-9. Our microformatted hCard with added download link

Since the vCard and contact details on the website are often identical, this means we need only update the HTML to continually offer an up-to-date vCard for site visitors—all without having to separately update vCard files.

This simple example only scratches the surface of the power of microformats—providing the front-end designer with a certain amount of "oblivious development" and the power to expose data that other websites, applications, and even browsers themselves can read and reuse, all simply with XHTML. As a designer, I love that extra benefit. And really, there's no reason not to use microformats if one exists for the data set you're dealing with. It'll help you decide which markup to use, while at the same time providing that exposed data to keep websites communicating with one another using the content that's already on the page.

There are countless other (more exciting) examples of how website authors are utilizing microformats to communicate through a common language of XHTML. Be sure to check out http://microformats.org for all the info!

> *We recommend picking up a copy of John Allsopp's* Microformats: Empowering Your Markup for Web 2.0, *also published by friends of ED. It's a comprehensive reference on everything microformats.*

Final phrase

Wrapping up what we've seen from the chapter, we've gathered some ammunition for the argument of using `<strong>` and `<em>` over their presentational brethren, `<b>` and `<i>`. We've also seen how when using bold or italic for strictly presentational reasons, CSS is the way to go.

We talked about the other phrase elements as well, beginning with how the `<cite>` element can be used for people and publications—proving further the power of structural markup for both presentation and potential data parsing.

We also demonstrated how we can provide a little simple accessibility by marking up abbreviations and acronyms with their respective elements—with extra presentational and aural directives to reinforce the definitions. And we covered all the remaining phrase elements, and while each may have a default styling that is different from normal text, we can easily create simple, quick CSS rules that define our own styles for each of these elements that may appear throughout a page or entire site.

Lastly, we introduced microformats, a community-driven way to take advantage of the semantic markup we're creating in new and exciting ways.

6

CHAPTER 7
ANCHORS

I just read <u>a great article</u> that g

DownWithWallpa

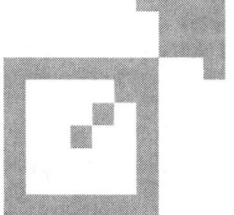

sapien. Nulla ut tortor. Nulla sol
mi. Mauris vel enim quis magna
scelerisque, egestas id, lectus. N

Oranges Are Tasty

Lorem ipsum dolor sit amet, cor
scelerisque scelerisque, massa f
eget velit ac purus ullamcorper
sapien. Nulla ut tortor. Nulla sol

HTML links, or anchors as they are properly called, enable us to point not only to files, but also to specific sections of a page, and can be a handy way of "linking with precision," narrowing the focus of a destination. In this chapter, we'll take a look at the differences between four methods of anchoring, noting what benefits either method may gain. We'll also look at the title attribute, and how it can improve a link's accessibility, as well as the styling of links using CSS.

When pointing to a specific portion of a page, what is the best way to mark up an anchor?

It's a common web design action—you'd like to link to a specific section of a web page, either within the current page that the user is on or within a separate page. You may choose to do this one of the four ways discussed in the following sections.

Let's set up the examples by saying that our intention is to link to a particular heading within the same page.

Method A: An empty name

```
<p><a href=#oranges">About Oranges</a></p>

... some text here ...

<a name="oranges"></a>
<h2>Oranges Are Tasty</h2>

... more text here ...
```

Using an empty anchor element along with the name attribute to mark a specific point will probably look familiar to you. Placing the empty <a> element and closing </a> just above the heading element and linking to it (using the # character, followed by the value matching the name attribute) will allow us to link to that specific portion of the page, which is especially helpful if the page consists of a long, scrolling list of items that we'd like to point to individually.

Figure 7-1 shows the results of clicking the "About Oranges" link, anchoring the page to where we've marked the <a name="oranges"></a>, just above the heading.

It works great, although it's a bit unsemantic to just waste an *empty* element as the marker. We can improve on that by taking a look at Method B.

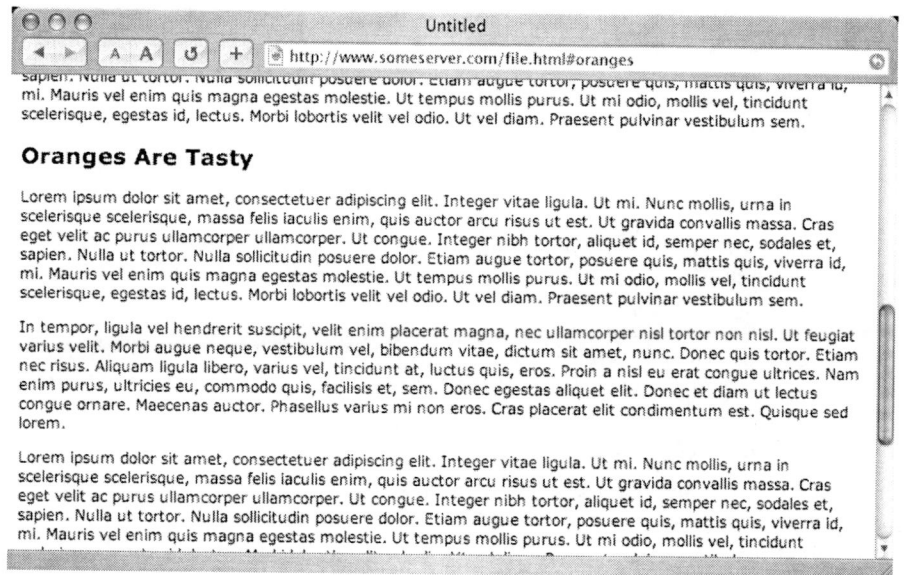

Figure 7-1. Demonstration of clicking a link to a named anchor

Method B: It's all in a name

```
<p><a href="#oranges">About Oranges</a></p>

... some text here ...

<h2><a name="oranges">Oranges Are Tasty</a></h2>

... more text here ...
```

As with Method A, we're still using the <a> element with the name attribute, yet this time we're wrapping it around the heading that we're intending to target. It does makes a little more semantic sense this way; in Method A, we're giving meaning to... well, *nothing*, whereas in Method B, we're saying that not only is this a heading element, but it's also an anchored section of the page.

Beware of global <a> styling

One thing to watch out for if using Method B is that if you're setting a global CSS style for all <a> elements (color, size, decoration, etc.), that styling would override any styles you have for <h2> elements. This would occur because the <a> element, in this example, is a child element and sits inside the <h2> that surrounds it all.

For instance, if in your CSS you had a declaration that went something like this:

```
a {
  color: green;
  font-weight: bold;
  text-decoration: underline;
}
```

using Method B along with the preceding CSS would result in the heading being green, bold, and underlined along with any other <a> elements on the page—perhaps different from the way you'd like <h2> elements to be styled.

We can avoid this (and gain some other benefits) by using the :link pseudo-class for <a> elements, which we'll go over in detail in the "Extra credit" section, later in this chapter.

Richer name attribute

One upside to using Method B, or Method A for that matter, is that the name attribute has the ability to handle richer anchor names—more specifically, the ability to use character entities in the names.

For instance, if using Method B, you could do this (where the entity é represents the "e"):

```
<p><a href="#resum&#233;">My Resum&#233;</a></p>

... some text here ...

<h2><a name="resum&#233;">Dan's Resum&#233;</a></h2>

... more text here ...
```

This becomes more important when dealing with foreign languages and the characters that stray from the English alphabet.

But there are a few more methods to investigate—the first of which eliminates completely the need for using the <a> element to set the anchor point. Let's take a close look at Method C.

Method C: Lose the name

```
<p><a href="#oranges">About Oranges</a></p>

... some text here ...

<h2 id="oranges">Oranges Are Tasty</h2>

... more text here ...
```

Aha! The id attribute acts just like the name attribute, in that it also sets an anchor point on the page. In addition, by using Method C, we can eliminate the need for the extra <a> element that's necessary when going with the name attribute in Methods A and B. We're cutting down on code, and that of course is always a good thing.

Because the id attribute can be added to any element, we can easily anchor anything we'd like on the page. In this case, we're choosing to anchor the heading, but we could also just as easily anchor a <div>, <form>, <p>, <ul>—and the list goes on.

Two birds with one stone

Another benefit to using Method C lies in the fact that, many times, we can utilize a pre-existing id attribute that we've added for the purposes of style or scripting. Because of this, we'll eliminate the need to include additional code in order to set the anchor point.

For instance, let's say you had a comments form at the bottom of a long page that you'd like to link to nearer the top. This form had an id="comments" already in place, particularly for purposes of styling it uniquely. We could link to that id as an anchor—without having to insert an <a> element with the name attribute.

The code would look something like this:

```
<p><a href="#comments">Add a Comment!</a></p>

... a lot of text here ...

<form id="comments" action="/path/to/script">
... form elements here ...
</form>
```

Also, if your page requires a long scroll, you could make it easy for users to get "back to top" by adding a link at the bottom that refers to a top-level element's id (for instance, a logo or header).

> It's a good idea to point out that, while it's the most obvious choice, it's best to avoid using the name "top" when anchoring. There are some browsers that have that particular name reserved and using it can cause mixed results. It's best to choose something similar, knowing that it won't cause problems. #genesis perhaps? #utmost? You get the idea.

Older browsers and the id attribute

An important downside to mention when using only the id attribute for anchors is that some *older* browsers don't recognize them. Ouch. This is certainly something to consider when marking up your own anchors, and an unfortunate case for backward compatibility. Let's take a look at the final example, Method D.

7

Method D: The all-in-one

```
<p><a href="#oranges">About Oranges</a></p>
```

... some text here ...

```
<h2><a id="oranges" name="oranges">Oranges Are Tasty</a></h2>
```

... more text here ...

If both forward and backward compatibility are the most important points for you when building anchors, then this method should please everyone. Older and newer browsers alike will recognize the named anchor element—but because the name attribute is deprecated by the W3C in the XHTML 1.0 recommendation (http://www.w3.org/TR/xhtml1/#C_8), you're covered for the future using the id attribute as well.

As with Method B, we'll have to beware of any global styling that may be done on the <a> element itself.

Sharing names

If choosing to go with Method D, it's perfectly acceptable (and probably convenient) to use the same value for both the id and name attributes—but only when they are contained in *a single element*. Furthermore, this is allowed only within a few *certain* elements: <a>, <applet>, <form>, <frame>, <iframe>, <img>, and <map>, to be exact. For this reason, we've moved the id="oranges" from the <h2> element to the anchor within.

Now that we've looked at four different methods to create anchors, let's summarize what each has to offer.

Summary

For this chapter, there may not be a real clear-cut winner here, although two methods rise above the others (C and D), each having its own pros and cons. Let's recap the facts regarding each:

Method A:

- This method should work across *most* browsers.
- As an empty element, it provides no structure or meaning to the markup.
- This method requires extra markup.
- With the name attribute deprecated in XHTML 1.0, forward compatibility should be a concern.

Method B:

- This method should work across all browsers.
- You must be conscious of any global <a> element styling that could override outer element styles.
- This method requires extra markup.
- With the name attribute being depreciated in XHTML 1.0, forward compatibility can be a concern.

Method C:

- This method entails less markup.
- You have the option of using an existing ID.
- This method ensures forward compatibility.
- This method requires a reasonably modern browser.

Method D:

- This method is both forward and backward compatible.
- You must be conscious of any global <a> element styling that could override outer element styles.
- This method requires extra markup.

It appears that Methods C and D are the better choices, where forward compatibility and less markup are pitched against more markup and full compatibility. My suggestion is to take into account the target audience and make an informed decision based on this.

For instance, if you're building a web-based application or intranet that you know will require a recent browser version, then going with Method C would most likely be best. Less markup is required—but this is known not to work in some version 4.x browsers. Check your site statistics to see if there is a substantial audience still using outdated ancient browsers.

Alternatively, if you're building a site that could be viewed by anyone, anytime, you may opt to go with Method D, which will ensure backward *and* forward compatibility—with the extra baggage of the anchor element added.

It's your choice, and hopefully by looking at each, you can make the right decision at the right time out in the real world.

Extra credit

For this extra credit session, we'll take a look at more things anchor related—specifically the benefits of using the title attribute as well as styling anchor links with CSS.

The title attribute

While earlier we were talking explicitly about anchors for creating page sections, let's shift gears slightly and talk about anchor links in general—when pointing to other destinations.

As an added accessibility feature, adding the title attribute to anchor links can provide a richer and more specific description of the destination that you're pointing the user to. With this added information, it becomes clearer to users as to where they are going—and they need not base their decision for clicking a link solely on just the text or image that is being anchored.

How does this added information become available to the user? We'll find that out next.

Title in action

Let's take a look at the title attribute in action. We'll mark up an ordinary hyperlink like this:

```
I just read <a href=http://www.downwithwallpaper.com/tips.html➡
title="How to Take Down Wallpaper">a great article</a> that gave me a➡
few home improvement tips.
```

Although the text is intentionally a bit vague in this example, the title attribute gives us an additional nugget of information about the link—in this case, the actual title of the article that's being pointed to.

Another common practice when inserting title attributes is to simply use the page's <title> (which is usually displayed in the browser's title bar). This, of course, should only be used if the title bar's text makes sense—ideally that includes both the site's title as well as the page-specific title.

For instance, let's say that for the preceding example, the page's title was "DownWithWallpaper.com | How to Take Down Wallpaper." Besides potentially being the *only* article necessary for the site, it could be used in the title attribute of our example as follows:

```
I just read <a href=http://www.downwithwallpaper.com/tips.html➡
title="DownWithWallpaper.com | How to Take Down Wallpaper">a great➡
article</a> that gave me a few home improvement tips.
```

We now have a richer description of what's being linked to. But how do users receive the information contained within the title attribute?

Tooltip titles

Most modern browsers support the title attribute by turning the value into a "tooltip"— a small colored box that pops up when the mouse is hovered over the link. Visually, it'll give users that extra useful bit of information just before they click the link. This has obvious benefits in letting users know *exactly where they're going*.

Figure 7-2 shows our example in a browser, with the tooltip exposed by the hovering mouse.

I just read a great article that gave me a few home improvement tips.

DownWithWallpaper.com | How to Take Down Wallpaper

Figure 7-2. An example with the `title` attribute revealed by the mouse hover

Titles are spoken

Another benefit to adding `title` attributes to links is that screen readers will read out the value along with the linked text. Sighted and nonsighted users alike will gain better understanding of the destinations you're taking them to, and that is certainly a good thing.

Styling links

Earlier in the chapter, I'd mentioned "beware of global link styling"—that there was a way to avoid unintentional styling of named anchor elements and instead narrow our focus to hyperlinks that use the `href` attribute only.

Gone are the days of defining link colors in the HTML of a document. We can separate those design details from the markup by using the pseudo-classes `:link`, `:visited`, `:active`, and `:hover` to uniquely style *hyperlinks* in a variety of ways.

Let's take a look at a few different CSS styles that we can apply to normal, everyday links:

```
a:link {
  color: green;
  text-decoration: none;
  font-weight: bold;
}
```

Quite simply, the preceding declaration will make all anchor elements that use the `href` attribute green, bold, and *not* underlined.

Instead of `text-decoration: none;`, we could've said underline (the default), overline (for the rebels out there), or a combination of the two, as shown here:

```
a:link {
  color: green;
  text-decoration: underline overline;
  font-weight: bold;
}
```

Figure 7-3 shows how the `underline overline` combination would appear in a typical browser. Sort of unconventional—but possible!

7

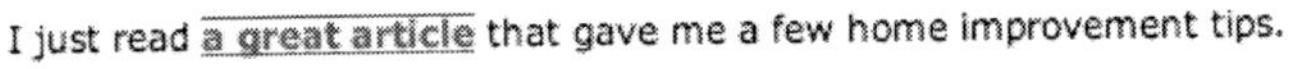

I just read a great article that gave me a few home improvement tips.

Figure 7-3. A link example with underline-overline text decoration

Backgrounds

The possibilities for uniquely styling links are just about endless. Most CSS rules that we've applied to other elements are available for anchors as well. For instance, we can apply background colors to links and/or even background images as well—perhaps a small icon, aligned to the left or right of the link text, as shown in Figure 7-4.

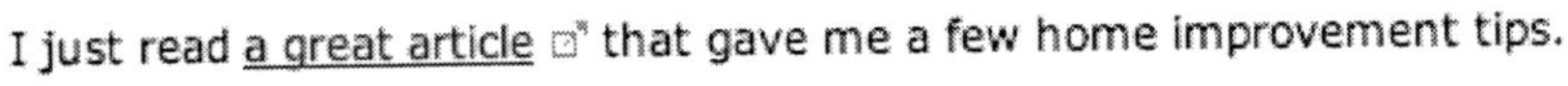

I just read a great article ⬀ that gave me a few home improvement tips.

Figure 7-4. A link with a right-aligned icon as a background image

The CSS needed for achieving Figure 7-4 goes something like this:

```
a:link {
  padding-right: 15px;
  background: url(link_icon.gif) no-repeat center right;
  }
```

We're setting the icon to align center (vertically) and to the right of the link text. Extra padding is added to the right side as well, to allow the icon to show through without any overlapping of text.

Dotted borders

Tired of the plain, solid underlines of links that we've been seeing for years now? By using the dotted or dashed value of the border property, we can create... you guessed it, dotted or dashed link borders.

First, we'll need to turn off default underlining with the text-decoration property to get it out of the way, and then we'll add a 1-pixel border-bottom that's both dotted and green.

```
a:link {
  color: green;
  text-decoration: none;
  border-bottom: 1px dotted green;
  }
```

It's important to note that, if you'd like the dotted border to be the same color as your link text, you'll need to declare that color in the border-bottom property as well. The results can be seen in Figure 7-5.

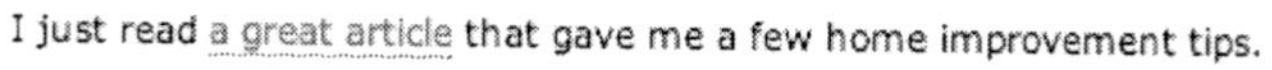

I just read a great article that gave me a few home improvement tips.

Figure 7-5. A link with a dotted border

Using the preceding method, you could also mix and match border colors, giving your link text one (with the color property) and your border another (with the border-bottom property). Furthermore, you could use the solid or dashed value for the border-bottom property.

> *Internet Explorer for Windows gets the dotted property a bit wrong when using a 1-pixel width. Using 1px as the value for a dotted border ends up looking exactly like the "dashed" style border. Fear not; it's just a small glitch.*

Where you been?

Don't forget to add an a:visited declaration to help users see where they've been before. All the usual CSS rules can be applied to this pseudo-class as well, giving visited links their own unique style, with a different color, border, background, and so forth.

The CSS goes like this:

```
a:visited {
  color: purple;
  }
```

At the very least, the preceding declaration will alert users that they've visited a link by changing its color to purple. It's very important to make even just a slight change, as the preceding one.

Hovering

Similarly, we can use the :hover pseudo-class to add powerful effects to links when they're hovered over by the mouse. This could be a color change or an addition of a border, background, or icon. The possibilities are endless.

```
a:link {
  color: green;
  text-decoration: none;
  border-bottom: 1px dotted green;
  }

a:hover {
  color: blue;
  border-bottom: 1px solid blue;
  }
```

7

113

The two preceding declarations give us links that are green with a dotted border, but then on hovering, the link turns blue, with a solid bottom border (also blue).

This is just one example of a simple hover effect. You can imagine that by trying different combinations of CSS rules on both links and hovered links, you can start to design sophisticated mouseover effects without the need for JavaScript or extra markup.

Active state

The :active pseudo-class handles the state of a link when the mouse button is clicked. The same rules can be applied here—changing the color, text decoration, background, and so on. For instance, if you had the link turn red when the mouse button is clicked, this could be an extra visual cue to users that they've chosen to head to that particular destination, and have indeed clicked.

The following declaration does just that:

```
a:active {
  color: red;
  }
```

LoVe/HAte your links

Ordering the four pseudo-classes mentioned becomes important in order for all of them to behave properly—without one overriding the other.

LoVe/HAte is a handy way to remember the correct order to place your declarations (www. mezzoblue.com/css/cribsheet/):

- a:link (L)
- a:visited (V)
- a:hover (H)
- a:active (A)

You could make up your own abbreviation for this—whatever it takes to help you remember. Love Vegetables? Have Asparagus!

To demonstrate, here are four of the preceding examples, assembled in the right order, as a complete package:

```
a:link {
  color: green;
  text-decoration: none;
  border-bottom: 1px dotted green;
  }
```

```
a:visited {
  color: purple;
  }

a:hover {
  color: blue;
  border-bottom: 1px solid blue;
  }

a:active {
  color: red;
  }
```

Fitts' Law

We can keep Fitts' Law in mind as it relates to hyperlinks and increased usability. Fitts, an American psychologist whose work is often cited by interaction design experts, says

The time to acquire a target is a function of the distance to and size of the target.

—Paul Fitts (http://www.asktog.com/basics/firstPrinciples.html#fitts's%20law)

In other words, the larger the link's target is, the quicker and easier it is to use. One easy way we can apply Fitts' Law is applying display: block; to links where appropriate. This way, not only is the link *text* clickable, but the space around the link is as well.

Take a simple unordered list of links, for example, as Figure 7-6 illustrates. By applying display: block; and a smidgen of padding to the <a> elements, we can increase the target area of the link, making it easier to scan and click the list by selecting the surrounding area (the entire row) as well as the text (see Figure 7-7). Adding a background-color to the hover state is helpful in providing feedback to the user as to the increased hotspot available.

Figure 7-6. An unordered list of links

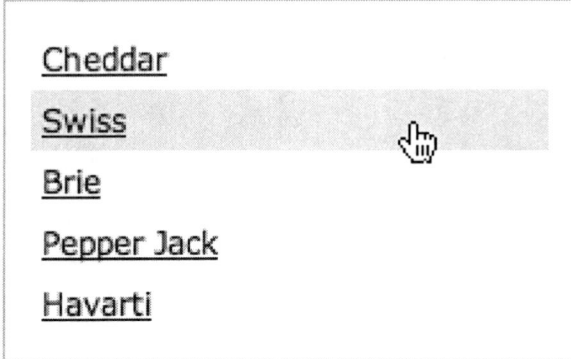

Figure 7-7. A block-level link; we've added a `background-color` to the hover state.

Here's the CSS that would enable that to happen:

```
ul li a {
  display: block;
  padding: 4px;
  }
ul li a:hover {
  background-color: #eee;
  }
```

A hack for IE6

Often, Internet Explorer version 6 adds extra vertical space to hyperlinks that are set as block-level elements. Boo. But there is a little fix for that, should you run into any rendering issues. We'll target IE6 specifically by prefacing the declaration with the `* html` hack. Only IE6 will read this declaration, and it'll be ignored by other browsers:

```
* html ul li a {
  height: 1%;
  }
```

That magic hack will make block-level links look correct in IE6. Dubbed the "Holly Hack" after its author, Holly Bergevin, `height: 1%` also fixes a plethora of related IE bugs. For more info on why it works, check out *"On having layout"* (`http://www.satzansatz.de/cssd/onhavinglayout.html`). Warning: it's not exactly light reading!

See also Dunstan Orchard's "Link Presentation and Fitts' Law" (http://www.1976design.com/blog/archive/2004/09/07/link-presentation-fitts-law/) or Dave Shea's article (http://www.mezzoblue.com/archives/2004/08/19/fitts_law/) for more information on block-level link styling.

Anchors aweigh

Before we set sail to the next chapter, let's review what we've discussed. We looked at four different ways to create anchors on a page—the last two of which we thought were more optimal. Depending on your audience, you now have the knowledge you need to make a decision on your next project.

We then talked about the title attribute and how it can improve usability by giving the user extra information about a link's destination. Visual readers and nonsighted listeners will both be able to take advantage of the title attribute's additional info.

Lastly, we looked at the styling of links using CSS's pseudo-classes. With an imagination, and a few declarations, rich, interactive effects can be achieved using zero JavaScript and no extra markup by targeting different CSS to the four different link states.

Now it's time to furl our sails and raise the anchor to the gunwale! For it's... sorry, got carried away there.

7

CHAPTER 8
MORE LISTS

Method A

- 1. Chop the onior
- 2. Saute the onio
- 3. Add 3 cloves of
  onions and the ga
- 4. Cook for anoth
- 5. Eat.

I. Chop the
II. Saute the
III. Add 3 clo
IV. Cook for
V. Eat.

1. Chop the onions.
2. Saute the onions for 3 min
3. Add 3 cloves of garlic.
4. Cook for another 3 minutes
5. Eat.

Back in Chapter 1, we talked about several ways to mark up a list of items, exploring the benefits of marking them up as an *unordered list* using the <ul> and <li> elements. This method provided structure to the list, ensuring that all browsers and devices would present it correctly, and also enabled us to style the list in a variety of ways using CSS.

In addition to unordered lists, there are two other types—and it wouldn't be difficult to fill an entire book with various methods for marking up all types of lists for various scenarios. While I'm not going to fill the entire book, I *will* devote another chapter to a few other list types, discovering a few instances where list markup makes for the best solution.

Lists can be a powerful way to structure your pages semantically, giving meaning to the separate items that can later be utilized for unique CSS styling.

Let's first take a look at a numbered list of items, with two different ways to mark them up. It may be painfully obvious as to which method is more beneficial—but I'll be illustrating this to make the case, once again, for structured markup and using the right tool for the job.

What is the best way to mark up a numbered list of items?

Let's say you have a list of instructions to mark up, with each item preceded by a number. We'll take a look at two different ways we might approach that, and why one may be more appropriate than the other.

Method A: Unordered order

```
<ul>
  <li>1. Chop the onions.</li>
  <li>2. Saute the onions for 3 minutes.</li>
  <li>3. Add 3 cloves of garlic.</li>
  <li>4. Cook for another 3 minutes.</li>
  <li>5. Eat.</li>
</ul>
```

The preceding list could possibly be the worst recipe in culinary history, but it's there simply for the example's sake. It could use some salt or protein or... anyway, back to the important stuff.

For Method A we've chosen to mark the instructions up with an unordered list to take advantage of all the benefits that were outlined in Chapter 1. We've added structure and we know that most browsers, screen readers, and other devices can handle it properly. Later, we could style this list easily with CSS. Great! But...

The numbers game

Since this is a numbered list, we've added to the markup each number followed by a period to denote each separate step of the instructions. But what if we later needed to add a step in between steps 2 and 3? We'd need to renumber each step (by hand) that follows the one we've added. For this particular list, it's not such a big ordeal—but if you're dealing with a list of 100 items, you can start to see how tedious that could be.

Rendered bullets

Because we're using an unordered list to structure the example, we're going to see bullets in front of each numbered item (as in Figure 8-1). You may like the bullets, and if not you could, of course, turn these off with CSS, but an unstyled view of this list would always reveal them.

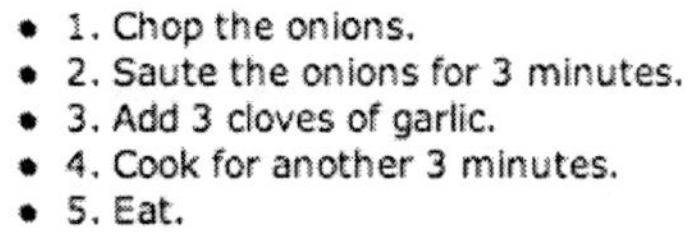

- 1. Chop the onions.
- 2. Saute the onions for 3 minutes.
- 3. Add 3 cloves of garlic.
- 4. Cook for another 3 minutes.
- 5. Eat.

Figure 8-1. Method A as viewed unstyled in a browser

There's an easier way—one that makes more semantic sense and is easier to maintain. Let's take a look at Method B.

8

Method B: An ordered list

```
<ol>
  <li>Chop the onions.</li>
  <li>Saute the onions for 3 minutes.</li>
  <li>Add 3 cloves of garlic.</li>
  <li>Cook for another 3 minutes.</li>
  <li>Eat.</li>
</ol>
```

I'm sure this is the obvious choice for many—but that doesn't mean we all haven't used Method A at some point for one reason or another. The <ol> stands for "ordered list," so semantically we're using the right element for the task at hand here. What else makes Method B so special?

Automatic numbering

You'll notice that we don't need to manually add a number to each list item. Numbers are generated automatically, in order, when using an <ol>. If our list of instructions was more like 100 steps, and we needed to later insert a new step right in the middle, we'd simply add another <li> item in the right position, and the renumbering would happen in the browser. Like magic.

With Method A, we'd need to manually change all those numbers we added to each item in the markup. I can certainly think of more enjoyable tasks to take care of.

Figure 8-2 shows how Method B would render in a typical browser, with the numbering preceding each instruction.

1. Chop the onions.
2. Saute the onions for 3 minutes.
3. Add 3 cloves of garlic.
4. Cook for another 3 minutes.
5. Eat.

Figure 8-2. Method B as viewed in a browser

Wrapper's delight II

Another advantage to using Method B is that when longer list items wrap to the next line, they are indented from the generated number, whereas with Method A, the lines would wrap underneath the marked-up number (see Figure 8-3 for a comparison).

Method A

- 1. Chop the onions.
- 2. Saute the onions for 3 minutes.
- 3. Add 3 cloves of garlic. Stir often to carmelize both the onions and the garlic.
- 4. Cook for another 3 minutes.
- 5. Eat.

Method B

1. Chop the onions.
2. Saute the onions for 3 minutes.
3. Add 3 cloves of garlic. Stir often to carmelize both the onions and the garlic.
4. Cook for another 3 minutes.
5. Eat.

Figure 8-3. Comparison of the wrapping of lines in Methods A and B

List types

While the default list style for ordered lists is most commonly Arabic numerals (1, 2, 3, 4, 5, etc.), using CSS, we can change this to a variety of styles using the list-style-type property. Here are some possible values:

- decimal: 1, 2, 3, 4, etc. (commonly the default)
- upper-alpha: A, B, C, D, etc.
- lower-alpha: a, b, c, d, etc.

- upper-roman: I, II, III, IV, etc.
- lower-roman: I, ii, iii, iv, etc.
- none: No numeral

So, for instance, if we wanted to have Method B generate uppercase Roman numerals instead of the default, we could write a CSS declaration like this:

```
ol li {
  list-style-type: upper-roman;
}
```

Figure 8-4 displays how this Method B, with the preceding CSS, would be viewed in a browser. Instead of the default Arabic numerals, our instruction list is numbered with Roman numerals. The markup, of course, stays exactly the same. Change your mind? One quick little CSS update using one of the values listed previously will change your list numbering to whatever you'd like.

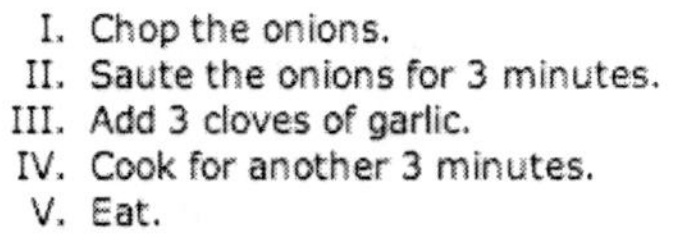

I. Chop the onions.
II. Saute the onions for 3 minutes.
III. Add 3 cloves of garlic.
IV. Cook for another 3 minutes.
V. Eat.

Figure 8-4. An ordered list with Roman numerals

Previously, you might have used the type attribute directly on the <ol> element to change the list type to Roman numerals, letters, and so forth. However, the type attribute has been deprecated in HTML 4.01 in favor of using the CSS rules outlined earlier. Therefore, you shouldn't use the type attribute but use CSS instead.

Later, in the "Extra credit" section, we'll take our ordered instruction list and style it with CSS. But first, let's take a look at another list type example.

What is the best way to mark up a set of terms and descriptions?

OK, the question is certainly leading, in that it almost answers itself. You'll see what I mean when we take a look at the following two methods. More important than the question, though, is that Method A is a common solution when marking up term and description pairs, and that Method B is a far underused type of list—but one that can be used in a variety of applications and provides a far more flexible structure.

First, let's quickly take a look at a potentially familiar way of dealing with term/definition pairs—specifically the definitions of a few standards defined by the W3C.

Method A

```
<ul>
  <li>CSS<br />
  A simple mechanism for adding style (e.g. fonts, colors, spacing) to ➡
Web documents.</li>
  <li>XHTML<br />
  A family of current and future document types and modules that ➡
reproduce, subset, and extend HTML, reformulated in XML.</li>
  <li>XML<br />
  A simple, very flexible text format derived from SGML.</li>
</ul>
```

This method seems to make sense, using an unordered list for structure and a <br /> element to separate the terms from their definitions.

However, what if we want to style each term (CSS, XHTML, or XML) differently from its definition? Our only option with Method A is to add some sort of style "hook" to the markup, such as an extra <span> or <strong> element. Maintenance-wise, though, that's not an ideal solution.

Figure 8-5 shows how Method A would appear in a typical browser, with each term and definition on its own line.

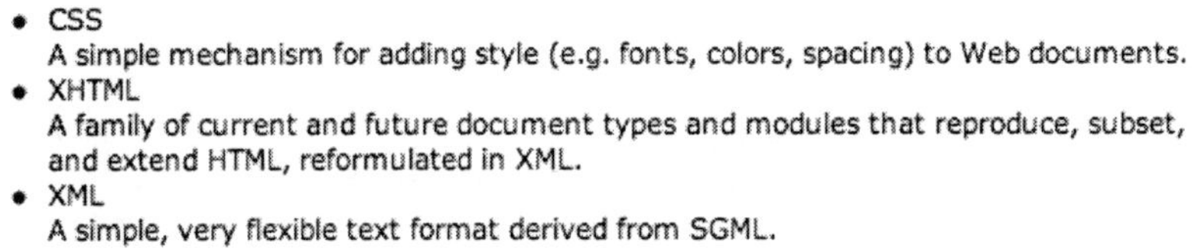

- CSS
  A simple mechanism for adding style (e.g. fonts, colors, spacing) to Web documents.
- XHTML
  A family of current and future document types and modules that reproduce, subset, and extend HTML, reformulated in XML.
- XML
  A simple, very flexible text format derived from SGML.

Figure 8-5. Method A as viewed in a typical browser

Aside from the inability to style each line uniquely, there isn't a whole lot wrong with Method A. But I bring this question up as an excuse to talk about the type of list found in Method B—the definition list.

Method B

```
<dl>
  <dt>CSS</dt>
  <dd>A simple mechanism for adding style (e.g. fonts, colors, spacing) ➡
to Web documents.</dd>
  <dt>XHTML</dt>
  <dd>A family of current and future document types and modules that ➡
reproduce, subset, and extend HTML, reformulated in XML.</dd>
  <dt>XML</dt>
  <dd>A simple, very flexible text format derived from SGML.</dd>
</dl>
```

A definition list (<dl>) consists of two additional elements, <dt> (term) and <dd> (description). For the purposes of our example, using a definition list makes perfectly good sense, as we're defining a series of term/description pairs.

By default, most visual browsers will render a definition list with the description (<dd>) on its own line and indented slightly (see Figure 8-6). We can, of course, change that indentation if we wish using CSS.

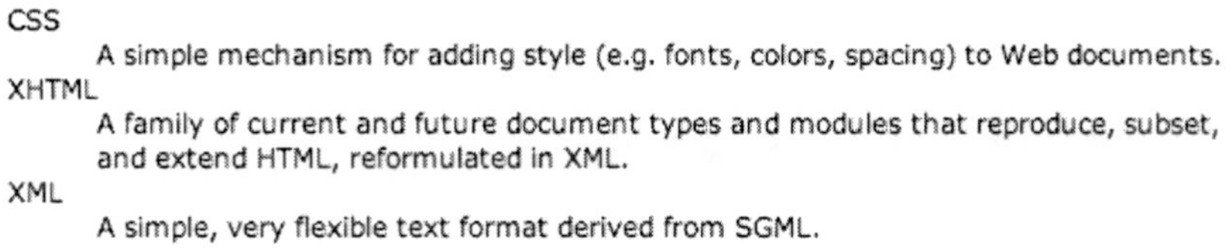

CSS
    A simple mechanism for adding style (e.g. fonts, colors, spacing) to Web documents.
XHTML
    A family of current and future document types and modules that reproduce, subset, and extend HTML, reformulated in XML.
XML
    A simple, very flexible text format derived from SGML.

Figure 8-6. Method B as viewed in a typical browser

Structure leads to style

Semantically, Method B is solid, giving us a separate element for each part of our list. This will enable us to style terms separately from their descriptions and vice versa.

For instance, something certifiably simple that we can do is to make bold the <dt>s with CSS. One declaration will do this for us, without adding anything additional to the markup:

```
dt {
  font-weight: bold;
  }
```

That's all there is to it, with no need to add <strong>, <b>, or even <span> elements to the list markup. Now, all <dt> elements will be bold, as you can see in Figure 8-7.

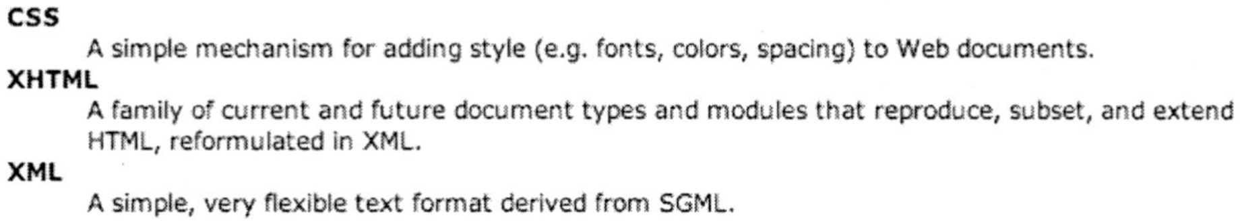

CSS
    A simple mechanism for adding style (e.g. fonts, colors, spacing) to Web documents.
XHTML
    A family of current and future document types and modules that reproduce, subset, and extend HTML, reformulated in XML.
XML
    A simple, very flexible text format derived from SGML.

Figure 8-7. Method B with font-weight: bold; applied to <dt> elements

Adding icons

You may have noticed that I like to add small images and icons to elements using CSS. The reason I like this is because by using the CSS background property, I can enrich pages, keeping decorative, nonessential graphics separated from the page content and structure.

Swapping out, adding, or removing these images becomes quick and easy when we don't have to touch the markup to make those updates.

For definition lists, it can be fun to add a small arrow icon pointing from the term down to the description. We can add this in easily with the following CSS rules:

```
dt {
  font-weight: bold;
  }

dd {
  margin-left: 15px;
  padding-left: 15px;
  color: #999;
  background: url(dd_arrow.gif) no-repeat 0 2px;
  }
```

What we've done here is close in the default indentation for <dd> elements a bit by saying margin-left: 15px;. Next, we've changed the color of the description to gray to further set it off from the <dt> element. A small orange arrow icon was added to sit to the left and 2 pixels down from the top of the description, as well as 15 pixels of padding on the left to let the icon show through. The results can be seen in Figure 8-8.

CSS
↳ A simple mechanism for adding style (e.g. fonts, colors, spacing) to Web documents.
XHTML
↳ A family of current and future document types and modules that reproduce, subset, and extend HTML, reformulated in XML.
XML
↳ A simple, very flexible text format derived from SGML.

Figure 8-8. A definition list with a background image denoting the relationships

As you can see, using the definition list structure, we can easily style each piece uniquely, creating a richer design—without touching the markup at all. We can also rest assured that viewed unstyled, the same list will display in a readable, organized fashion as well.

Other applications

It's important to point out that the uses for definition lists go further beyond just term/description pairs. Definition lists can be used for dialog, navigation, and even form layouts.

We can even quote the W3C on how they define definition lists in the HTML 4.01 Specification (www.w3.org/TR/html4/struct/lists.html):

"Definition lists, created using the <dl> element, generally consist of a series of term/definition pairs (although definition lists may have other applications)."

Don't be afraid to use definition lists for purposes other than common term/description pairings.

Summary

So far throughout this chapter, we've looked at two additional types of lists—ordered and definition. We've discovered that by using these structured lists, rather than an unordered list with additional markup, we gain more control over the style and we're also creating lists that are easier to maintain.

Next, let's take our ordered list of instructions from the beginning of the chapter, and customize it a bit using CSS.

Extra credit

Let's reacquaint ourselves with our ordered instruction list from earlier in the chapter:

```
<ol>
  <li>Chop the onions.</li>
  <li>Saute the onions for 3 minutes.</li>
  <li>Add 3 cloves of garlic.</li>
  <li> Cook for another 3 minutes.</li>
  <li>Eat.</li>
</ol>
```

Unstyled and in the absence of any CSS, this would appear in a browser as shown back in Figure 8-2. Just like any other structured markup example found in this book, an ordered list makes for an easily styled set of elements when CSS is added to the mix.

We know that, because we're using the proper structure here for this list, browsers that don't support CSS, or have it disabled, will display the list properly as well.

Let's get a little fancy and customize the numbers that appear before each instruction item.

Identify the parts

So that we can access each list item and replace its number with something a little more stylish, we'll need to add an id to each <li> element. We'll also add an id to the whole ordered list so that we can make specific style rules for *this* list and not *all* <ol>s:

```
<ol id="recipe">
  <li id="one">Chop the onions.</li>
  <li id="two">Saute the onions for 3 minutes.</li>
  <li id="three">Add 3 cloves of garlic.</li>
  <li id="four"> Cook for another 3 minutes.</li>
  <li id="five">Eat.</li>
</ol>
```

8

Now that we've identified everything, we'll have complete control, stylistically, over each element in the list. It's also worth mentioning that by adding a unique id to each list item here, we've lost the ability to rely on an ordered list's "automatic numbering" advantage. If we needed to add a new step in the middle of the others, we'd need to change the id values of the steps that follow. Just a disclaimer.

Custom numbers

Our first step for creating custom numbers for our list is to turn off the *default* generated numbers that will appear by using the list-style-type property on the #recipe element:

```
#recipe {
  list-style-type: none;
  }
```

Figure 8-9 shows our list with the numbers turned off by the preceding rule.

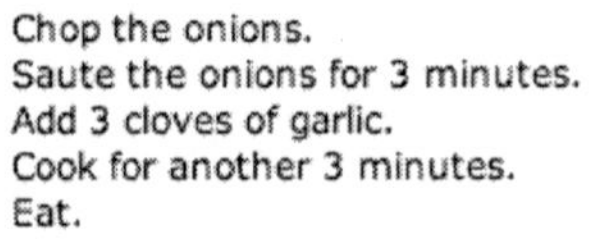

Chop the onions.
Saute the onions for 3 minutes.
Add 3 cloves of garlic.
Cook for another 3 minutes.
Eat.

Figure 8-9. Our ordered list with numbers turned off with CSS

Now that we've prevented the numbers from being generated, we can add our own graphic numbers instead. In Photoshop (or your favorite image editor), we can create five GIF images, one for each number. Figure 8-10 shows the five numbers I've created, using the Prensa typeface and red for the color.

1. 2. 3. 4. 5.

Figure 8-10. Five GIF images to be used for our ordered list

Adding the numbers to the CSS

Because of their larger size, we'll need to add some margins and padding around each list item in order to give enough room for the number image to show through as a background. We'll also add a light gray border to the bottom of each instruction.

We can use the descendent selector #recipe li to apply these rules to all <li> items within #recipe. This saves us from having to repeat these shared values on each number id.

```
#recipe {
  list-style-type: none;
  }

#recipe li {
  padding: 10px 50px;
  margin-bottom: 6px;
  border-bottom: 1px solid #ccc;
  }
```

With all the preceding values being applied to *all* <li> items within our list, we can now add each unique number image to its corresponding id:

```
#recipe {
  list-style-type: none;
  }

#recipe li {
  padding: 10px 50px;
  margin-bottom: 6px;
  border-bottom: 1px solid #ccc;
  }

#one {
  background: url(ol_1.gif) no-repeat 6px 50%;
  }

#two {
  background: url(ol_2.gif) no-repeat 2px 50%;
  }

#three {
  background: url(ol_3.gif) no-repeat 3px 50%;
  }

#four {
  background: url(ol_4.gif) no-repeat 0px 50%;
  }

#five {
  background: url(ol_5.gif) no-repeat 6px 50%;
  }
```

You'll notice that the position values differ slightly for each image, reflecting their horizontal placement. This is due to the fact that each of these images is variable in width because of the particular font I'm using. To compensate, we nudge each image to the right as necessary to get the dots of each number to line up just right.

Including "6px 50%" will place the image 6 pixels from the left and 50 percent from the top, essentially centering it vertically.

The results

Figure 8-11 shows the final results as viewed in a typical browser, with each image showing through on the left of each item. Gray lines are drawn at the bottom of each instruction to further provide separation.

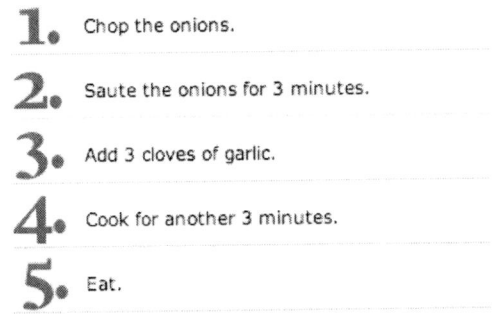

Figure 8-11. Our unordered list styled with custom number images

With a few images and CSS rules, we took a structured, ordered list and gave it some customized style—proving once again that we can keep nonessential images out of the markup for easy updates later on.

Wrapping up

Aside from the unordered variety, ordered and definition lists provide semantic structure as well as flexible styling options for those specific types. Let your imagination wander and experiment with different types of lists—using CSS to customize and spiff up the basic structure. To get you started, be sure to visit Listamatic, a site showcasing various CSS treatments on a single marked-up list: http://css.maxdesign.com.au/listamatic/.

In the end, you'll have a solid foundation that will display anywhere, but can then easily be modified with CSS for capable browsers.

CHAPTER 9

MINIMIZING MARKUP

Weblog
Articles
   How to Beat the Red Sox
   Pitching Past the 7th Inning
      ⊞ Part I
      ⊞ Part II
   Eighty-Five Years Isn't All That Long,
About
Photos
   Landscapes
   Objects
Services
   Design
      ⊞ Web
      ⊞ Print

Weblog
Articles
   How to Beat the Red Sox
   Pitching Past the 7th Inning
      ⊞ Part I
      ⊞ Part II
   Eighty-Five Years Isn't All That Long,
About
Photos
   Landscapes
   Objects
Services
   Design
      ⊞ Web
      ⊞ Print

Weblog
Articles
   How to Beat the Red Sox
   Pitching Past the 7th Inning
      ⊞ Part I
      ⊞ Part II
   Eighty-Five Years Isn't All That Long,
About
Photos
   Landscapes
   Objects
Services
   Design
      ⊞ Web
      ⊞ Print

We've been talking about how building pages with structure can help minimize your markup by separating that structure from the design details. Instead of using tables and images to create borders and customized layouts, we can turn to valid XHTML and CSS for the finishing touch.

One potentially bad habit that is easy to fall into when constructing sites with web standards (and especially those that rely heavily on CSS) is adding extraneous elements and class attributes—when they're not necessary at all.

By taking advantage of *descendant selectors* in our CSS, we can eliminate the need for unnecessary <div>s, <span>s, and classes. Minimizing your markup means faster, more easily maintained pages—and in this chapter, we'll discover a few simple ways to do it.

How can we minimize markup when building sites with web standards?

Minimizing markup is an important topic to talk about. A huge benefit to creating sites with valid XHTML markup and CSS for presentation is the markup reduction. Less code means faster downloads—absolutely key for users on slow, 56K modem connections as well as mobile users on Edge or other cellular-based networks. Less code also means less server space and bandwidth consumption—this makes the bosses and system administrators smile.

The problem is that just simply making sure your pages conform to the W3C's specifications does *not* mean there will automatically be less code used. It's possible to pepper your valid markup with all sorts of unnecessary elements. Sure, it's valid, yet it could be littered with extraneous code in order to make the application of CSS a little easier.

Fear not, there are some tips to writing compact markup that will be valid, but will also provide just the right amount of style control on the CSS end. Let's take a look at a few simple things we can do to minimize our markup.

Descendant selectors

Here we'll take a look at two methods for marking up a sidebar of a personal website that contains information, links, and other bits. We're stuffing all this good stuff inside of a <div> that we've given an id of sidebar in order to place it in a certain location of the browser window (more on CSS layouts in Part Two).

Method A: Class happy

```
<div id="sidebar">
  <h3 class="sideheading">About This Site</h3>
  <p>This is my site.</p>
  <h3 class="sideheading">My Links</h3>
  <ul class="sidelinks">
```

```
        <li class="link"><a href="archives.html">Archives</a></li>
        <li class="link"><a href="about.html">About Me</a></li>
    </ul>
</div>
```

I've seen markup similar to Method A on many sites. When designers first discover the power of CSS, it's easy to get carried away by assigning a class to any element that you'd like to style uniquely (often referred to as "classitis").

For the preceding example, we might have assigned the sideheading class to the two <h3> elements so that these headings will have a unique style from other headings on the page. We've also done the same for the <ul> and <li> elements.

Classified CSS

For style, let's say that we'd like the headings to be a serif font, orange, with a light gray bottom border. The sidelinks unordered list will have bullets turned off and the list items will be bold.

The CSS needed for the styling of Method A may look something like this:

```css
.sideheading {
  font-family: Georgia, serif;
  color: #c63;
  border-bottom: 1px solid #ccc;
  }

.sidelinks {
  list-style-type: none;
  }

.link {
  font-weight: bold;
  }
```

By referencing each class that was specified in the markup, we can apply unique styles to those components. You could even imagine other portions of the page that are organized in this fashion—the navigation, footer, and content areas, each of them littered with dozens of classes in order to have full control over any element.

Sure, it *works* just fine—but there's an easy way to reduce the markup that's needed for all of those classes, while at the same time making your CSS more readable and organized. Let's move on to Method B.

Method B: Natural selection

```html
<div id="sidebar">
  <h3>About This Site</h3>
  <p>This is my site.</p>
  <h3>My Links</h3>
```

9

```
        <ul>
          <li><a href="archives.html">Archives</a></li>
          <li><a href="about.html">About Me</a></li>
        </ul>
      </div>
```

Nice and compact! But wait, where did all the classes go? Well, you'll find that we don't really need them—primarily due to the fact that we've contained all of these elements within a <div> that has a unique ID, in this case sidebar.

Here's where the use of descendant selectors comes into play—by referencing elements that are contained within sidebar simply by their element names, we can eliminate all of those redundant classes.

Contextual CSS

Let's look at the same styles that were applied to Method A, but this time we'll use descendant selectors to access the elements within our sidebar:

```
#sidebar h3 {
  font-family: Georgia, serif;
  color: #c63;
  border-bottom: 1px solid #ccc;
  }

#sidebar ul {
  list-style-type: none;
  }

#sidebar li {
  font-weight: bold;
  }
```

By using the #sidebar ID as the reference, we can give unique styles to any of the elements contained within. For instance, only <h3> elements that are *within* the sidebar <div> will receive those specific rules.

This *contextual* way of assigning styles to elements becomes key for reducing markup. Oftentimes, we need not pepper our elements with class names when we've set up a semantic structure around them.

Not just for sidebars

While we've only illustrated one section of a page, the sidebar, the same can be applied to an entire page structure—by slicing your markup into logical sections (perhaps #nav, #content, #sidebar, #footer), and then applying unique styles to those sections with descendant selection.

For instance, let's say that you've used <h3> heading elements in both the #content and #sidebar areas of your page and would like each rendered in a serif font. However, you'd like the text contained in the <h3> element to appear purple in one section and orange in the other.

There's no need to alter the markup by adding a class to either heading. We can set a global style that contains shared rules for *all* <h3> elements, and then use descendant selectors to color the heading depending on where it lives.

```
h3 {
  font-family: Georgia, serif; /* All h3s to be serif */
}

#content h3 {
  color: purple;
}

#sidebar h3 {
  color: orange;
}
```

We've generically said that all <h3> elements should be in a serif font, while the color will be either purple or orange depending on its context. There is no need to repeat the shared rules (font-family in this case), which in turn minimizes the CSS and prevents repeating rules in multiple declarations.

Not only are we eliminating the need for extra markup in the form of class labels, but the CSS structure starts to make a lot more sense, making it more readable and easier to organize your declarations by page section. Going back to alter specific rules becomes all the easier—especially for large and complex layouts, where you may potentially have hundreds of CSS rules in one place.

For instance, in our example, if we had added the shared styles to each declaration and later wanted to change all <h3> elements to appear in sans serif, then we'd have to make that change three times instead of once.

Fewer classes mean easier maintenance

In addition to lessening the amount of code needed, using descendant selectors instead of assigning extraneous classes means future-friendly markup.

For instance, let's say that you would like the links in the sidebar to be red as opposed to the default blue that the rest of the page uses, so you went ahead and created a red class that you added to the anchor elements like this:

```
<div id="sidebar">
  <h3>About This Site</h3>
  <p>This is my site.</p>
  <h3>My Links</h3>
  <ul>
    <li><a href="archives.html" class="red">Archives</a></li>
    <li><a href="about.html" class="red">About Me</a></li>
  </ul>
</div>
```

9

137

And the CSS needed to turn those links red (provided that the default link color was something different) went something like the following:

```
a:link.red {
  color: red;
  }
```

This is all well and good and works perfectly fine. But, what if in the future you changed your mind and would like the same links to appear in green? Or more practically, your *boss* casually says, "Red is out this year. Make those sidebar links green." Sure, you could just make an alteration to the red class in the CSS and be done. But the markup is still saying red in the class attribute, which is of course semantically insignificant—as would be any *color* for the class name.

Although this makes a good case for using nonpresentational names for classes, it would take less effort (and code) and stay more semantically sound if we were to not assign a class at all; rather, we could just use descendant selectors to tap into those sidebar links to style them any way we wished.

The markup would be identical to Method B, and the CSS needed to turn the sidebar links would be as follows:

```
#sidebar li a:link {
  color: red;
  }
```

In essence, we're saying, "Only anchors using the href attribute that are found in <li> elements within the sidebar <div> should be colored red."

Now, our markup stays lean and mean, and our CSS is the only tool needed for future updating—whether we'd like the links to appear red, green, bold, italic, or whatever.

Next, let's look at an additional way we can minimize our markup—eliminating unnecessary <div> elements in favor of a preexisting block-level element.

The unnecessary <div>

In addition to reducing the number of class attributes needed for styling, there is another simple way we can reduce markup—by eliminating a <div> when a block-level element already exists as its child element. To demonstrate, let's look at two different methods.

Method A: <div> happy

```
<div id="nav">
  <ul>
    <li><a href="archives.html">Archives</a></li>
    <li><a href="about.html">About</a></li>
  </ul>
</div>
```

What we have here is an (extremely) small navigation menu that consists of nothing more than an unordered list. We've assigned the id of nav to the <div> that wraps around the whole list.

But why not assign the id directly to the <ul> element, which like the <div> is also block-level by nature? Let's look at Method B.

Method B: Lose the <div>

```
<ul id="nav">
  <li><a href="archives.html">Archives</a></li>
  <li><a href="about.html">About</a></li>
</ul>
```

Method B shows us that we can toss out the extra <div> in favor of identifying the <ul> directly. Any styling for positioning, margins, padding, and so forth can be applied to the <ul> just as easily as the <div>, so we in turn reduce our markup a bit by getting rid of the wrapper.

It's important to point out that this would only be appropriate if there are no other elements in addition to the <ul> contained within nav—for instance, a paragraph or <blockquote> or <form>. Since it's generally impractical for these elements to sit inside a <ul>, a <div> wrapper would make more sense. However, for instances such as I've outlined in Methods A and B, where the unordered list was the *only* element contained—then it makes sense to toss the <div> out. In fact, it's important to evaluate the existence of any containing element. Does it really need to be there? Is there already a block-level element that can be used? Compact markup awaits.

Other examples

Another example of where a <div> could be eliminated is when wrapping a <form>. For instance, instead of this:

```
<div id="myform">
  <form>
    ... form elements here ...
  </form>
</div>
```

we could more easily do this:

```
<form id="myform">
    ... form elements here ...
</form>
```

Likewise, for a footer of a website that contained a single paragraph, instead of

```
<div id="footer">
  <p>Copyright 1999-2004 Dan Cederholm</p>
</div>
```

9

139

we could also do this:

```
<p id="footer">Copyright 1999-2004 Dan Cederholm</p>
```

provided of course that the footer contained no more than *one* paragraph.

Summary

We've looked over two simple ways we can minimize our markup—by refraining from peppering elements with class attributes and instead using descendant selectors for styling, as well as assigning ids directly to preexisting block-level elements instead of wrapping them up in a <div>.

While using one of these methods may seem like an insignificant savings, when you start to add these up over an entire website, the compact, structured code becomes evident and the savings become real. You'll be further on your way to authoring code that is leaner, more semantically sound, and easier to maintain in the future.

For extra credit, let's take a look at how descendant selectors can be taken to the next level in styling nested lists that will make up a site map.

Extra credit

For this extra credit session, let's take a look at how we can use descendant selectors to uniquely style different levels of a set of nested lists. The example we'll work with is a portion of a small site map. We'll discover that we can keep the markup very basic, without needing to add extra class attributes in order to style the levels separately.

First, let's introduce ourselves to the markup.

The raw markup

At a very basic level, nested, unstyled lists deliver the perfect hierarchy for something like an outline or, for our example, a simple site map. By nesting the lists, we can guarantee the proper structure that all browsers and devices will read, while easily styling it with CSS later on.

The markup for a small site map might look something like this, with three top-level items and a few nested ones:

```
<ul>
  <li>Weblog</li>
  <li>Articles
    <ul>
      <li>How to Beat the Red Sox</li>
      <li>Pitching Past the 7th Inning
```

```
    <ul>
      <li>Part I</li>
      <li>Part II</li>
    </ul>
  </li>
  <li>Eighty-Five Years Isn't All That Long, Really</li>
</ul>
      </li>
      <li>About</li>
    </ul>
```

Figure 9-1 shows us how the preceding markup will render in most browsers. You can see that, by default, the structure that we're striving for is roughly in place. The hierarchy is evident, even in the absence of style. It's a little boring, though, so next let's start adding some CSS.

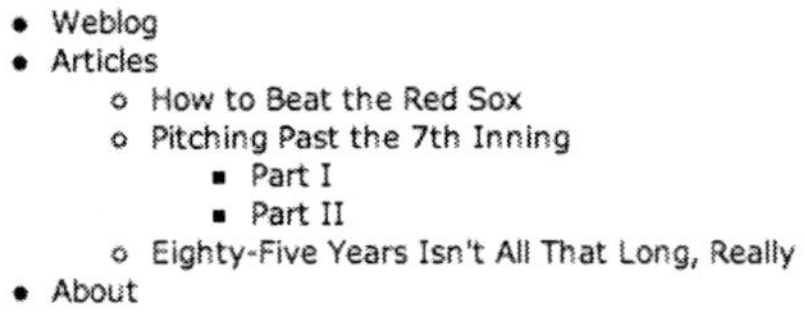

- Weblog
- Articles
  - How to Beat the Red Sox
  - Pitching Past the 7th Inning
    - Part I
    - Part II
  - Eighty-Five Years Isn't All That Long, Really
- About

Figure 9-1. Unstyled rendering of the nested list markup

Adding style

Let's say that we'd like to add some definition for certain levels of the site map. All we really need to add to the markup is a single id so that we may style this *particular* list differently from any other lists that may be on the same page, without any additional markup:

```
<ul id="sitemap">
  <li>Weblog</li>
  <li>Articles
    <ul>
      <li>How to Beat the Red Sox</li>
      <li>Pitching Past the 7th Inning
        <ul>
          <li>Part I</li>
          <li>Part II</li>
        </ul>
      </li>
      <li>Eighty-Five Years Isn't All That Long, Really</li>
    </ul>
  </li>
  <li>About</li>
</ul>
```

9

Again using descendant selectors, we can give a unique style to each separate level of the list. For instance, if we'd like the higher levels to be large, bold, and orange, with the inner levels progressively smaller, we'd first set the size, weight, and color for the entire list:

```
#sitemap {
  font-size: 140%;
  font-weight: bold;
  color: #f63;
  }
```

That will make the entire list big, bold, and orange. Next, we'll reduce the size and change the color for <li> elements that are nested at any level below:

```
#sitemap {
  font-size: 140%;
  font-weight: bold;
  color: #f63;
  }

#sitemap li ul {
  font-size: 90%;
  color: #000;
  }
```

The preceding CSS will ensure that all top-level items will be big, bold, and orange, while all lists that are nested within will be black in color with a font size of 90 percent (which in this case is 90 percent of 140 percent). See Figure 9-2 for the results.

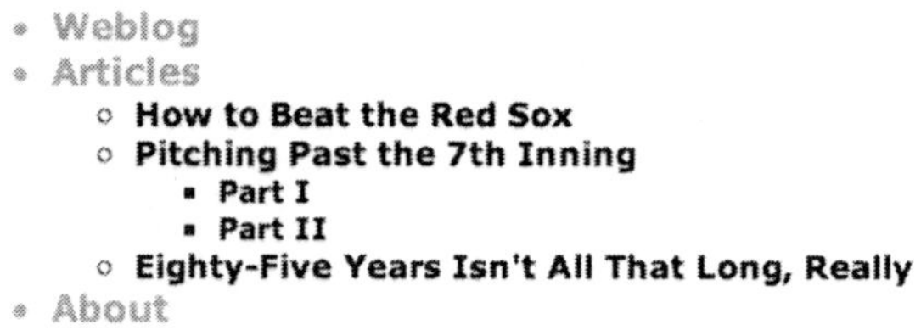

- Weblog
- Articles
  - **How to Beat the Red Sox**
  - **Pitching Past the 7th Inning**
    - **Part I**
    - **Part II**
  - **Eighty-Five Years Isn't All That Long, Really**
- About

Figure 9-2. Adding style to the top-level list items

We need not assign a smaller size for the third level, as it will automatically apply 90 percent of 90 percent (a little confusing, but it works!).

Now we have a descending font-size for each level of the list. Next, we'll add some bullets.

Custom bullets

Let's turn off default styling, and add a decorative bullet for only third-level items by using the background property. We'll first turn off list styling, in general, for all <li> elements, and then we'll specifically assign a background image for third-level items. For further separation, we'll also make third-level items font-weight: normal;—overriding the list's default of bold.

```css
#sitemap {
  font-size: 140%;
  font-weight: bold;
  color: #f63;
  }

#sitemap li {
  list-style: none; /* turns off bullets */
  }

#sitemap li ul {
  font-size: 90%;
  color: #000;
  }

/* for third-level */

#sitemap li ul li ul li {
  font-weight: normal;
  padding-left: 16px;
  background: url(bullet.gif) no-repeat 0 50%;
  }
```

Figure 9-3 shows the resulting site map with a custom bullet and normal font weight applied only to third-level <li> elements. We've added 16 pixels of padding on the left to account for the width of the decorative bullet image (plus a bit of whitespace). We're also telling the browser to align the image 0 pixels from the left and 50 percent from the top, which essentially aligns the bullet to the left and center of the text. While we could've used a pixel value here, using a percentage allows for similar bullet placement if text is resized.

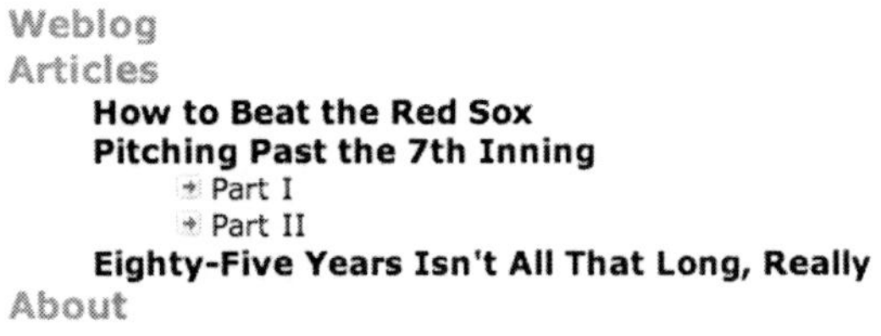

9

Weblog
Articles
How to Beat the Red Sox
Pitching Past the 7th Inning
  Part I
  Part II
Eighty-Five Years Isn't All That Long, Really
About

Figure 9-3. Custom bullets added to third-level items

Adding a border

To complete our site map, let's add a dotted border to the left side of the second-level list. This will further cue the user that the top-level item has suboptions that belong to it.

To achieve the border *only* on the second-level list, we'll add the following rules:

```
#sitemap {
  font-size: 140%;
  font-weight: bold;
  color: #f63;
  }

#sitemap li {
  list-style: none; /* turns off bullets */
  }

#sitemap li ul {
  margin: 6px 15px;
  padding: 0 15px;
  font-size: 90%;
  color: #000;
  border-left: 1px dotted #999;
  }

/* for third-level */

#sitemap li ul li ul {
  border: none;
  }

#sitemap li ul li ul li {
  font-weight: normal;
  padding-left: 16px;
  background: url(bullet.gif) no-repeat 0 50%;
  }
```

We've adjusted margins and padding a bit for the second level, as well as the addition of the dotted border. Following that rule, we'll turn *off* the border for third-level lists with the border: none; rule.

Figure 9-4 shows the resulting list with varying fonts, borders, and list images in place.

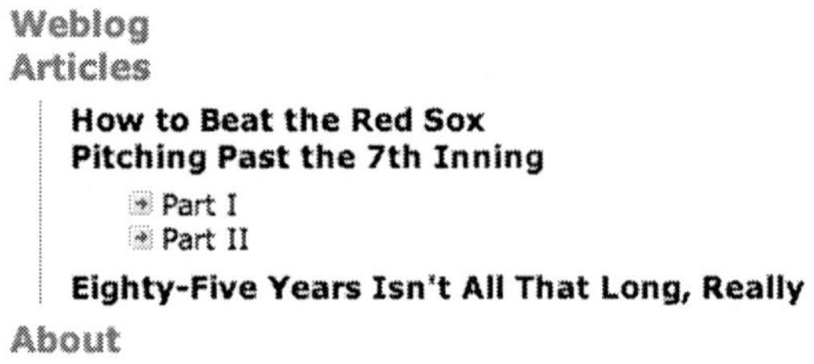

Weblog
Articles
    How to Beat the Red Sox
    Pitching Past the 7th Inning
        Part I
        Part II
    Eighty-Five Years Isn't All That Long, Really
About

Figure 9-4. Final styled site map, with dotted border applied to second-level lists

For building outline-like lists, nesting `ul`s makes for a structurally sound and easily styled solution. By assigning a single `id` to the top-level `ul`, we can let CSS do all the hard work of styling each level separately—without the need for extraneous presentational markup. And possibilities for creative styling go way beyond this simple example.

Figure 9-5 shows the same CSS applied to a slightly larger site map. Because the CSS assigns style depending on the level, the markup would be set up exactly the same. Depending on nesting level, the items would take on the appropriate style.

Weblog
Articles
> **How to Beat the Red Sox**
> **Pitching Past the 7th Inning**
>> Part I
>> Part II
> **Eighty-Five Years Isn't All That Long, Really**
About
Photos
> **Landscapes**
> **Objects**
Services
> **Design**
>> Web
>> Print

Figure 9-5. Expanded site map with nested lists and CSS

Conclusion

In this chapter, we explored two simple ways to minimize our markup using descendant selectors and tossing out unnecessary `<div>` elements.

Using descendant selectors eliminates the need for adding extraneous class attributes that will further muck up our markup. And eliminating `<div>` elements where a preexisting block-level element exists just below it can save us added bytes as well as reduce the code it takes to build complex layouts.

While it may seem trivial to save just a few characters by using these methods once over an entire website, these savings start to add up. Call it yet another tool for creating lean, structured markup.

With that lean markup, we also looked at how descendant selectors can be used to style a site map that is structured with nested unordered lists. Each level of the outline can be styled uniquely without the need for extra class attributes—again saving bytes and making it easier to update and restyle in the future. Yay for compact code!

PART TWO
SIMPLEBITS OF STYLE

CHAPTER 10
APPLYING CSS

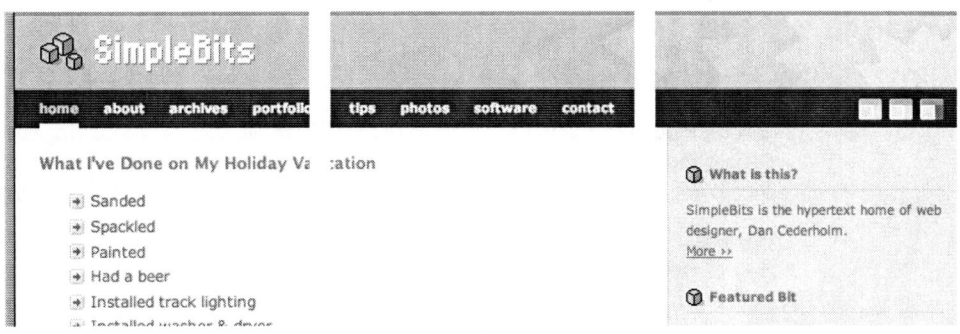

While the focus throughout Part One had been primarily markup examples, we also explored how CSS can be applied to that markup for design and style details. To begin Part Two, in this chapter we'll talk about the different methods used to apply CSS to a particular document, site, or even single element. In addition, we'll discuss how we can hide CSS from older browsers, enabling us to use advanced techniques without harming the markup structure that all browsers and devices can read.

Later, in the "Extra credit" section at the end of the chapter, we'll introduce alternate style sheets that can produce multiple themes, font sizes, and colors without the need for server-side scripting.

How do I apply CSS to a document?

We're going to look at four ways to apply CSS to a document, each with its own advantages and disadvantages. Depending on the situation, any one of these methods would be appropriate. Each method presented uses a valid and typical XHTML 1.0 Transitional framework for its document type, <html> element, and <head> setup.

Let's begin with Method A.

Method A: The <style> element

```
<!DOCTYPE html PUBLIC -//W3C//DTD XHTML 1.0 Transitional//EN"
  "http://www.w3.org/TR/xhtml1/DTD/xhtml1-transitional.dtd ">
<html xmlns="http://www.w3.org/1999/xhtml" xml:lang="en" lang="en">
<head>
  <meta http-equiv="content-type" content="text/html; charset=utf-8" />
  <title>Applying CSS</title>
  <style type="text/css">
    <![CDATA[
    ... CSS declarations here ...
    ]]>
  </style>
</head>
```

This method, also known as an embedded style sheet, allows you to write all of your CSS declarations right in the actual XHTML document. The <style> element sits inside the <head> section of a page and can contain any number of CSS rules you desire.

The type attribute with the text/css value ensures that the browser understands what type of style language we're presenting and is required. We're also using CDATA comment syntax that is recommended by the W3C to hide the style rules from older browsers that can't understand them (www.w3.org/TR/xhtml1/#h-4.8).

Partial understanding

One important downside to using Method A is that some older browsers will do their best to render CSS that is contained in <style> elements. This can be a bit of a problem if you have any advanced CSS rules that only modern browsers will understand for layout and positioning. If complicated CSS is kept within <style> elements, it's possible that users of older browsers may receive a jumbled, unusable mess.

Uncached

Another downside to embedded style sheets is that since they are on the page, they are required to be downloaded each time that page is loaded. Conversely, the method that follows requires the styles to be downloaded once, and then cached by the browser.

Multiple changes

Along with the fact that embedded style sheets appear on the XHTML page, including an embedded style sheet also means duplicating these styles if you want them to be applied to multiple pages within a site. If you need to change these styles, you must make the changes on each page that includes the style sheet. Lots of changes. Lots of work.

Good for development

On the upside, I find that when I'm initially building and testing CSS, it's very convenient to write all of the rules on the page I'm testing using Method A. It allows me to work on a single document for both markup and style when making frequent changes. After testing is complete, I'll apply CSS to the public version using a different method. Let's take a look at a few more.

Method B: External style sheets

```
<!DOCTYPE html PUBLIC "-//W3C//DTD XHTML 1.0 Transitional//EN"
  "http://www.w3.org/TR/xhtml1/DTD/xhtml1-transitional.dtd ">
<html xmlns="http://www.w3.org/1999/xhtml" xml:lang="en" lang="en">
<head>
  <meta http-equiv="content-type" content="text/html; charset=utf-8" />
  <title>Applying CSS</title>
  <link rel="stylesheet" type="text/css" href="styles.css" />
</head>
```

10

Method B demonstrates how we can link to external style sheets—where all of the CSS declarations are kept in a separate file, and then referenced in the head section of the XHTML of the document with the <link> element.

The href attribute points to the location of the file. The value can be a relative path (as in the case of Method B), or an absolute path, using the full http:// location of the document. Also note that <link> is a single element, or empty element, and is required to have the self-closing / at the end.

Separate file = easy maintenance

Having all your CSS rules in a file separate from your markup has an obvious advantage—any style changes for an entire site can be made on that *one* file, rather than repeating CSS declarations on *every* page, as you would need to do if using Method A.

This, of course, is especially critical for large-scale sites where hundreds or thousands of pages can all share the same style instructions from a single document.

Download once

An additional advantage to linking styles in an external style sheet is that the file is often only downloaded once and cached by the browser, saving download time for repeat visits—or for other pages that reference the same style sheet.

Still not completely hidden

Like Method A, Method B also has the possibility of being interpreted by older browsers that have limited support for CSS. Any styles that are targeted for modern browsers may wreak havoc in an unsupported browser.

Hmm, that's the second time I've mentioned that problem. The next method *has* to solve it, right?

Method C: @import

```
<!DOCTYPE html PUBLIC "-//W3C//DTD XHTML 1.0 Transitional//EN"
  "http://www.w3.org/TR/xhtml1/DTD/xhtml1-transitional.dtd ">
<html xmlns="http://www.w3.org/1999/xhtml" xml:lang="en" lang="en">
<head>
  <meta http-equiv="content-type" content="text/html; charset=utf-8" />
  <title>Applying CSS</title>
  <style type="text/css">
    <![CDATA[
      @import "styles.css";
    ]]>
  </style>
</head>
```

Similar to Method B, using the @import rule allows us to import CSS from an external document, either by a relative path (as in Method C) or an absolute path.

Method C shares the same benefits when using the <link> element. Because the styles are held in an external document, making changes and updates to a single file can affect an entire site—and can be done so quickly and easily. External style sheets are cached by the browser, saving download times for pages that import the same file.

Hide and seek

The major historical advantage for using Method C is that Netscape versions 4.x and below don't support the @import rule, essentially "hiding" the CSS that is being referenced. This is certainly a handy "hack," in that we can target advanced CSS for tasks such as layout and other design details to modern browsers that can handle them, while older browsers will ignore them.

The problem with Netscape 4.x is that it thinks it supports CSS as well as browsers that actually do. Therefore, with the exception of Netscape 4.x, we can send along any CSS that we wish, letting the browser decide if it can display it or not.

This is an important point for building sites with web standards—that we can separate our structured markup from the presentation as much as possible, and then hold design details and styles for browsers that support them. Older browsers will receive the structure that they can easily read, but the advanced CSS will be hidden from them.

What this does do is allow designers and developers to move forward now, rather than continue to use methods that cater to prehistoric browser versions that may choke on advanced CSS rules.

Styles on, styles off

As a comparison, take a look at Figures 10-1 and 10-2, which show my personal site with full CSS, and then without, as an older browser may render it. The structure without CSS is still evident and is readable and usable to all. If I hadn't hidden the CSS that's required to present the design, users of older browsers may have received quite an unreadable mess.

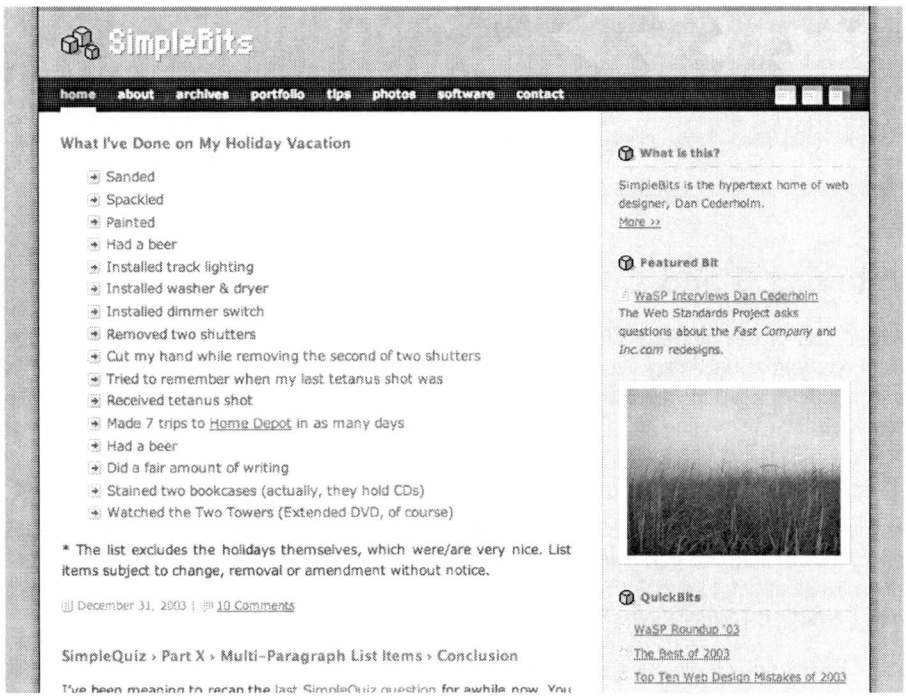

Figure 10-1. My personal site with CSS

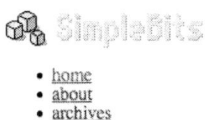

- home
- about
- archives
- portfolio
- tips
- photos
- software
- contact

What I've Done on My Holiday Vacation

- Sanded
- Spackled
- Painted
- Had a beer
- Installed track lighting
- Installed washer & dryer
- Installed dimmer switch
- Removed two shutters
- Cut my hand while removing the second of two shutters
- Tried to remember when my last tetanus shot was
- Received tetanus shot
- Made 7 trips to Home Depot in as many days
- Had a beer
- Did a fair amount of writing
- Stained two bookcases (actually, they hold CDs)
- Watched the Two Towers (Extended DVD, of course)

* The list excludes the holidays themselves, which were/are very nice. List items subject to change, removal or amendment

Figure 10-2. The same page, without CSS, as an older browser may render it

Combining B and C for multiple style sheets

Sometimes, it can be beneficial to import more than one style sheet to a document. For instance, you could keep your entire layout in one style sheet and typography rules in another. For large, complex designs, this can make maintaining the high number of rules much easier.

The chameleon effect

In the case of *Fast Company* magazine's website, I wished to make the colors of the website change each month to correspond to the magazine's monthly cover image. To make the routine change easier, I kept all CSS rules related to color in one file, while the rest of CSS that *didn't* change each month was held in another.

Each month I could make quick, easy updates to the colors file without hunting through the hundreds of rules that were needed to make up the rest of the design. Instantly the entire site's colors would change with the modification of that single file.

How it's done

To combine Methods B and C for importing multiple style sheets, we would use the <link> element in the <head> of the document to reference a master CSS file—just like Method B illustrates, by linking to a styles.css file.

The contents of styles.css would simply contain @import rules to import any number of CSS files that we wish.

For instance, if we'd like to import three style sheets, one for layout, one for fonts, and one for colors, styles.css would contain the following:

```
/* hidden from old-school browsers */

@import url("layout.css");
@import url("fonts.css");
@import url("colors.css");
```

Now, our <link> element can stay the same throughout an entire site, referencing only the styles.css file. That one file can import multiple style sheets with the @import rule. New style sheets could be added to this one file that would in turn affect the entire site.

This makes updates and CSS file shuffling very easy. For instance, if down the road you would like to further separate your CSS into *four* files, you can easily change the import URLs in this single file, rather than being bothered with modifying the XHTML markup.

Lo-fi and hi-fi styles

Another trick when using Method C's @import rule to hide CSS from old browsers is to use the cascade effect in CSS to serve lo-fi styles that *old* and modern browsers should be able to recognize, using either Method A or Method B, and then use @import to serve advanced styles to browsers that support them.

Older browsers get only what they can support, while more modern browsers receive *all* the styles intended.

Let's take a look at how this would appear in code:

```
<!DOCTYPE html PUBLIC "-//W3C//DTD XHTML 1.0 Transitional//EN"
  "http://www.w3.org/TR/xhtml1/DTD/xhtml1-transitional.dtd ">
<html xmlns="http://www.w3.org/1999/xhtml" xml:lang="en" lang="en">
<head>
  <meta http-equiv="content-type" content="text/html; charset=utf-8" />
  <title>Applying CSS</title>
  <link rel="stylesheet" type="text/css" href="lofi.css" />
  <style type="text/css">
    @import "hifi.css";
  </style>
</head>
```

10

where `lofi.css` would contain basic CSS rules like link colors and font sizes, and `hifi.css` may contain advanced rules like layout, positioning, and backgrounds.

We can achieve sending lo-fi and hi-fi versions of the design—without the need for scripting or server-side browser identification of any kind.

Order is important

The order in which we've placed the `<link>` and `<style>` elements in the markup is important. The "cascade" of CSS refers to the priority that is placed on rules—depending on what order they appear.

For instance, since modern browsers support both methods, they will receive both style sheets and apply all the styles from each. Style rules in `hifi.css` will override styles that refer to the *same* elements in `lofi.css`. The reason? Because `hifi.css` comes *after* `lofi.css` in the markup.

Older browsers will ignore `hifi.css` because of the @import rule used; therefore, they will only apply rules found in `lofi.css`.

Embrace the cascade

You can use the cascade property of CSS to your advantage in a variety of ways. One example is a scenario where you have an entire site sharing one external CSS file for all of its layout, positioning, fonts, colors, and so forth. You can use Method C on each page of the site to import the file, hiding it from older browsers.

Let's say there is *one* page on the site that shares the layout and positioning, but needs custom colors or fonts. For this one page (which is different from the rest of the site), we can still import the main CSS file, but also just after that in the `<style>` element, import a second CSS file containing customized styles for that particular page. Any styles in the second CSS file will take priority and override styles that reference the same elements found in the first CSS file.

Let's look at an example to illustrate this. `master.css` contains CSS that the entire site uses for structure, fonts, and so forth, while `custom.css` is imported only on a particular page with the overriding of a few elements.

```
<!DOCTYPE html PUBLIC "-//W3C//DTD XHTML 1.0 Transitional//EN"
  "http://www.w3.org/TR/xhtml1/DTD/xhtml1-transitional.dtd ">
<html xmlns="http://www.w3.org/1999/xhtml" xml:lang="en" lang="en">
<head>
  <meta http-equiv="content-type" content="text/html; charset=utf-8" />
  <title>Applying CSS</title>
  <style type="text/css">
    @import "master.css";
    @import "custom.css";
  </style>
</head>
```

Because custom.css comes *second* in the markup order, its declarations of the same elements will override those found in master.css.

For instance, let's say that in main.css we had all <h1> elements appear serif and red, while all <h2> appear serif and blue:

```
h1 {
   font-family: Georgia, serif;
   color: red;
   }

h2 {
   font-family: Georgia, serif;
   color: blue;
   }
```

On our customized page, we'd like to change only the styles for <h1> elements, while <h2> should stay the same. In custom.css, we need only declare the new styles for <h1>:

```
h1 {
   font-family: Verdana, sans-serif;
   color: orange;
   }
```

This declaration will override the one found in master.css (because custom.css is imported last). Pages that import custom.css after master.css will have <h1> elements that appear in Verdana and orange, while <h2> elements will still show in a serif font and blue—the declaration found in master.css wasn't overridden in custom.css.

Using the cascade property in CSS can be a handy way to share common styles while overriding only those that need to be customized whenever desired.

Method D: Inline styles

```
<h1 style="font-family: Georgia, serif; color: orange;">This is a ➥
Title</h1>
```

There is a fourth method of applying CSS that we need to talk about as well: inline styles. The style attribute can be added to almost any element, allowing CSS rules to be applied directly at the element level, as shown in Method D.

Since inline styles are at the lowest level possible in the cascade, they will override any styles that are declared in external style sheets, or rules held in the <style> element in the <head> of the document.

This can be a simple way of adding style here and there to documents, but it comes at a price.

10

157

Style tied to markup

If we rely on Method D too much for adding style to documents, we're not really separating our content from our presentation. Going back to make changes means going directly to the markup, when keeping CSS in a separate file makes for easier maintenance.

Abusing Method D is almost like littering your markup with <font> elements and other presentational gobbledygook. These design details always belong in a separate place.

Use with caution

There are certainly real-world uses for inline styles—and they can be a savior in a pinch, where adding style to a document is necessary, but accessing an external file or the <head> of the document is impossible; or additionally, if they are merely temporary styles, not meant to be shared with other elements on the page.

For instance, if there is one page that will be announcing a bake sale on your website that will eventually be taken down afterward, and you'd like this particular page to have unique styles, you may opt to embed these unique rules rather than adding them to a permanent style sheet.

Just proceed with caution. Know that these styles can't be modified easily, across an entire page or site.

Summary

We've looked over four different methods for applying CSS to markup, showing that each has its merits depending on the situation. Let's recap the methods and the advantages and disadvantages that they each may have.

Method A:

- This method requires styles to be in the <head> section of each document. Styles can't be shared with multiple documents and are required to be downloaded each time the page loads.
- Styles contained in the <style> element won't be completely hidden from all older browsers.
- This method is good for testing and development stages. Markup and style can each be modified in the same file.

Method B:

- This method enables one set of styles to be shared among multiple documents or an entire site.
- External style sheets are downloaded once and often cached by the browser, saving download time for repeat visits.
- Keeping shared styles in one file means easy maintenance for design updates.
- Styles referenced with the <link> element won't be hidden from older browsers.

Method C:

- This method enables one set of styles to be shared among multiple documents or an entire site.
- External style sheets are downloaded once and often cached by the browser, saving download time for repeat visits.
- Keeping shared styles in one file means easy maintenance for design updates.
- Using @import hides styles from Netscape 4.x browsers.

Method D:

- Styles are coded inline, keeping the design too closely tied to the markup.
- Styles can't be shared among other elements, entire documents, or sites.
- Maintenance can be tedious and inefficient.
- This method is good for temporary solutions or when accessing an external file within the <head> of the document is impossible.

Now that we've recapped the various ways that we can link up our styles to our markup, let's go a step further in the "Extra credit" section to take a look at *alternate style sheets*.

Extra credit

For extra credit, let's dive a little deeper into the style sheet world to look closely at alternate style sheets (multiple styles for the same markup) and how we can give users more control over what styles they select.

Alternate styles

Previously in this chapter, we talked about four ways to apply CSS to a document, while showing the advantages of linking or importing our styles in an external style sheet. We can take this a step further and reference alternate style sheets where the user can potentially choose larger text sizes, various color themes, or even alternate layouts.

We can do this by referencing multiple style sheets with the <link> element (much like Method B from earlier), but adding the value "alternate stylesheet" for the rel attribute.

For instance, if we want to give users the choice between two additional text sizes, we link the main style sheet normally, and then the alternate style sheets follow:

```
<head>
  <meta http-equiv="content-type" content="text/html; charset=utf-8" />
  <title>Applying CSS</title>
  <link rel="stylesheet" type="text/css" href="default.css" ➥
title="default"/>
  <link rel="alternate stylesheet" type="text/css" ➥
href="largetext.css" title="large" />
```

```
<link rel="alternate stylesheet" type="text/css" ➦
href="largertext.css" title="larger"/>
</head>
```

You'll notice that, along with the "alternate stylesheet" value for the rel attribute on the last two <link> elements, we've added a title attribute to each, naming each style sheet so that they may be selected later.

The "default" style sheet will always be on and activated by the browser. large.css and larger.css will be downloaded, but not used unless activated by other means (which we'll talk about later). The presence of the "alternate stylesheet" value in the rel attribute is what prevents that style sheet from being "on" by default when the page loads.

> If we wish to hide the alternate styles from older browsers, such as Netscape 4.x, we need not use the @import method. Netscape 4.x doesn't support the "alternate stylesheet" value for the rel attribute, and therefore those styles will never be applied.

Three font sizes

Let's talk a little more about what would be contained in those alternate style sheets. If, for instance, we'd like to give the user the option of enlarging the font size on the page, we could specify a larger size in each of the alternate style sheets that, when activated, would override the rules found in default.css.

This would be especially handy if we chose to specify our font sizes in pixels—where some browsers don't allow the user to increase the font size. If we chose to set the base font size at a pixel amount that was hard to read for low-vision users, we can use alternate style sheets to give them larger options.

So, in default.css, we may have set a base font size for the site:

```
body {
   font-size: 12px;
   }
```

And in large.css, we'd override that rule with a slightly larger font size:

```
body {
   font-size: 16px;
   }
```

And similarly in larger.css, we'll boost it up another notch:

```
body {
   font-size: 20px;
   }
```

When activated (and I promise we'll get to that in a minute), the large.css and larger.css style sheets will override the default rule, increasing the font size for the page.

Still cascading

It's important to note that the cascade effect of CSS still applies, and alternate style sheets work just like any other style sheet, in that *only common rules* are overridden when the alternate styles are active. So if we had layout, positioning, and other site-wide rules in default.css that weren't repeated in the alternate style sheets, those default rules would still work.

Getting alternate styles to work

Great. So we have these alternate style sheets sitting there, waiting to be used. How does the user activate them? Unfortunately, only a few browsers have a built-in mechanism for choosing alternate style sheets: Firefox, Safari, and Opera, for example.

If alternate style sheets are present in Firefox, for example, users can choose to activate an alternate style from the View ~TMA Page Style menu (see Figure 10-3).

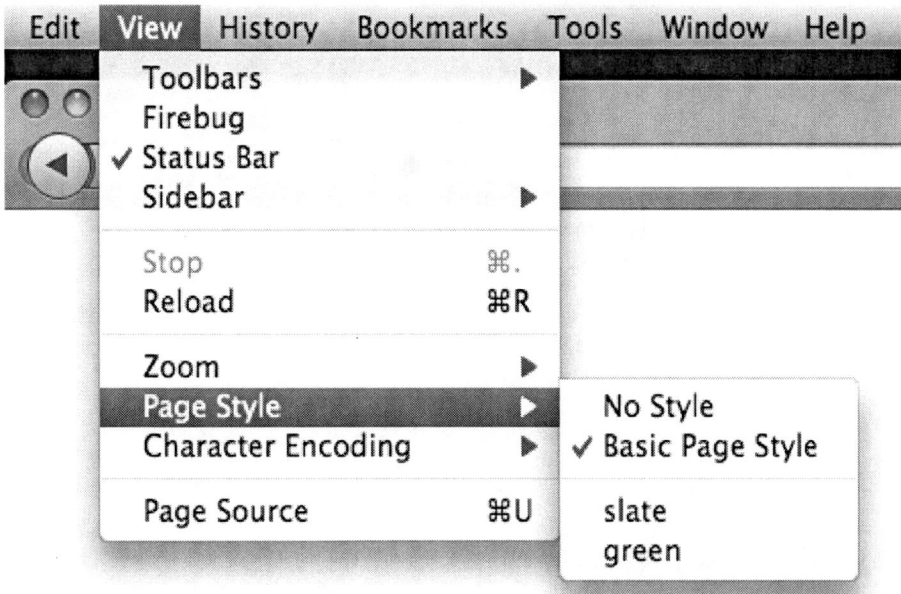

Figure 10-3. Firefox's alternate style sheet selection menu

Hopefully more browser makers will implement similar mechanisms as time goes on, but until then, there is another way to toggle alternate style sheets on or off—even saving the user's choice, through the magic of cookies.

161

Paul Sowden has written an indispensable tutorial at *A List Apart*, titled "Alternative Style: Working with Alternate Style Sheets" (www.alistapart.com/articles/alternate/). In it, he explains a set of JavaScript functions that can be used to activate and deactivate alternate style sheets in modern browsers.

The toggling is handled by a hyperlink on the page, effectively switching between any one of the style sheets by its title attribute. The JavaScript remembers the user's last selection by storing a cookie so that the next time the user visits the page, the correct alternate styles will be activated in addition to any default style sheets.

As an example, a few years ago I offered three color schemes on my personal website. Each scheme was activated by clicking the appropriate icon, which in turn referred to Paul Sowden's script. The first icon was the default, while the second and third activated two additional alternate style sheets for different color schemes. See Figure 10-4 for an illustration.

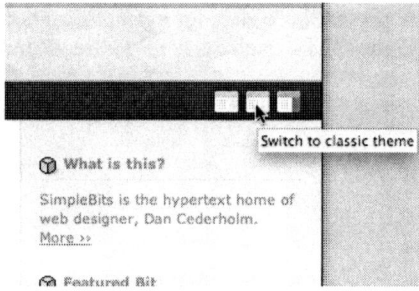

Figure 10-4. Alternate style sheet being activated by the clicking of an icon

Because the JavaScript used was client-side based, the switching happened instantly, without the need for refreshing the entire page. It was very fast.

> *The complete JavaScript code is available for download in Paul Sowden's article at* A List Apart (www.alistapart.com/articles/alternate/).

More than just font sizing

In addition to the popular "text sizer," as it's sometimes referred to, there are endless style switching possibilities. Some sites allow the user to choose from a rainbow variety of color themes, while others offer the choice between fonts, font sizes, or even different layouts of the page.

By experimenting with the cascade—overriding certain default rules and placing them in alternate style sheets—some really interesting and interactive things can start happening on your websites. All with a simple script and a few CSS rules. Low bandwidth, high impact.

Courtesy of DOM

We can thank another W3C standard for the ability to use scripting to access alternate style sheets. The DOM, or *Document Object Model* is, well... let's hear what the W3C has to say about it:

"The Document Object Model is a platform- and language-neutral interface that will allow programs and scripts to dynamically access and update the content, structure, and style of documents. The document can be further processed and the results of that processing can be incorporated back into the presented page. This is an overview of DOM-related materials here at W3C and around the web."

Sounds familiar, doesn't it? That is exactly what we're doing with the style sheet switcher script—dynamically accessing and updating the style of documents. We can do this if we follow W3C standards, allowing developers to author scripts that can access predictable elements in our markup. If we strive toward standards-based markup, we can ensure that more DOM-based scripts can be written in the future, enhancing the user's experience of the pages we build.

The style switcher only scratches the surface of the possibilities for DOM-based scripting. But it's yet another example of the benefits gained when building a site with standards.

Reset styles

While we've talked about the various ways in which we can apply CSS to documents, it's a good time to also mention the concept of using a *reset style sheet*. Eric Meyer has led the way with a fair amount of research and writing on the subject, and explains on his blog:

"The goal of a reset stylesheet is to reduce browser inconsistencies in things like default line heights, margins and font sizes of headings, and so on" (http://meyerweb.com/eric/tools/css/reset/).

In other words, all browsers have default styles—CSS that is applied at the browser level to render HTML elements a certain way. For example, an <h1> is usually large and bold with margins and/or padding above and below it before you apply any of your own CSS. Ordered and unordered list items are often indented. The problem, as Meyer points out, is that these default styles can vary, depending on the browser and/or operating system. To get everyone down to a common baseline, a reset.css file is applied first in order to "zero out" any values the browser might apply.

In addition to achieving consistency, a reset style sheet can save a considerable amount of code as well. In a large style sheet, we often find ourselves setting margin: 0; padding: 0; on elements that have default margins and padding. This is repeated throughout the style sheet for every declaration where it's needed. A reset style sheet will do this once, clearing up your main style sheet of duplicated rules.

10

An example reset.css

Here is Eric Meyer's version of a *reset.css*, which as you can see, applies various global rules to remove the default styling the browsers might apply to each element:

```css
/* v1.0 | 20080212 */

html, body, div, span, applet, object, iframe,
h1, h2, h3, h4, h5, h6, p, blockquote, pre,
a, abbr, acronym, address, big, cite, code,
del, dfn, em, font, img, ins, kbd, q, s, samp,
small, strike, strong, sub, sup, tt, var,
b, u, i, center,
dl, dt, dd, ol, ul, li,
fieldset, form, label, legend,
table, caption, tbody, tfoot, thead, tr, th, td {
  margin: 0;
  padding: 0;
  border: 0;
  outline: 0;
  font-size: 100%;
  vertical-align: baseline;
  background: transparent;
  }
body {
  line-height: 1;
  }
ol, ul {
  list-style: none;
  }
blockquote, q {
  quotes: none;
  }
blockquote:before, blockquote:after,
q:before, q:after {
  content: '';
  content: none;
  }

/* remember to define focus styles! */
:focus {
  outline: 0;
  }

/* remember to highlight inserts somehow! */
ins {
  text-decoration: none;
  }
```

```
del {
  text-decoration: line-through;
  }

/* tables still need 'cellspacing="0"' in the markup */
table {
  border-collapse: collapse;
  border-spacing: 0;
  }
```

It's important to mention that your reset.css doesn't have to include everything shown here. Feel free to customize your own version, zeroing out what you think is helpful in your own projects.

The idea here is to include this style sheet *first*, before applying your own styles, to have that baseline in place. Using the method described earlier in the chapter, we would import the reset style sheet before all others in the styles.css file that was linked in the markup, like so:

```
/* hidden from old-school browsers */

@import url("reset.css");
@import url("layout.css");
@import url("fonts.css");
@import url("colors.css");
```

With the browser defaults for various common elements zeroed out, the baseline is then set for your own styles to build upon.

I highly recommend exploring the use of reset style sheets in your own work, as it can save time and code. I now start every new project with a reset.css file included from the get-go, and it consistently saves me from duplicating countless CSS rules in order to start from a fresh base.

10

Conclusion

In this chapter, we've discovered the various ways in which we can apply CSS to elements, documents, and entire sites. We've also learned how to hide CSS from older browsers and how to import multiple style sheets. We then talked about serving lo-fi and hi-fi CSS to browsers that support either—without the need for scripts or server-side browser sniffing.

Lastly, we learned about alternate style sheets—how through a bit of DOM-based JavaScript they can offer the user a dynamically switchable experience, whether allowing font size, color, or layout choices. We also discussed using a reset style sheet to help override those default styles that most browsers apply, giving us a clean slate to work from.

I hope these techniques get you off on the right foot in applying style to structure.

CHAPTER 11
PRINT STYLES

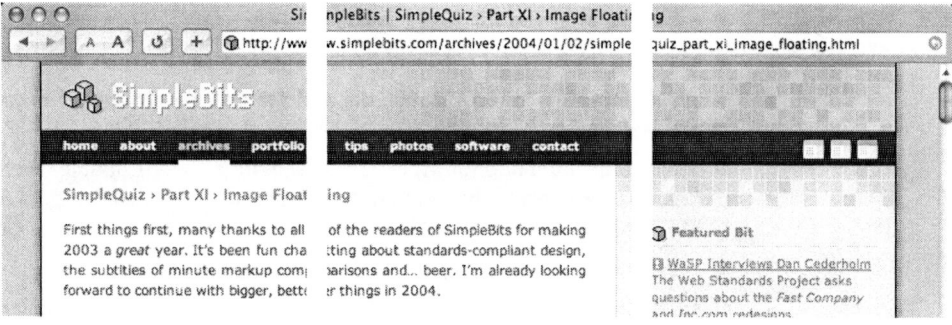

Previously, in Chapter 10, we learned of the various methods available to apply CSS to your documents. In this chapter, we'll explore print styles—assigning CSS that is used specifically when printing a web page. With a few CSS rules, we can ensure that our structured markup looks as good on paper as it does onscreen.

To begin, we'll talk about media types and how they relate to serving device-specific CSS.

How can we specify styles for print?

Before we answer that question, we need to familiarize ourselves with the idea that we can assign media types to our CSS. Declaring a media type enables us to target our styles to a specific medium.

For instance, if we'd like a certain linked style sheet to be intended only for computer screens, we could add the media attribute to the <link> element as follows:

```
<link rel=stylesheet" type="text/css" media="screen" ➥
href="screenstyles.css" />
```

The preceding code ensures that the styles linked in this statement are intended *only* for computer screens. You may be asking, "What else would we be targeting?" The answer is... quite a few possibilities.

Media types

In addition to the screen value used in the preceding code, there are a handful of other possible values. Here's a full list of the recognized media types, defined by the W3C in their CSS 2.1 specification (found at www.w3.org/TR/CSS21/media.html):

- all: Suitable for all devices.
- braille: Intended for Braille tactile feedback devices.
- embossed: Intended for paged Braille printers.
- handheld: Intended for handheld devices (typically small screen, limited bandwidth).
- print: Intended for paged material and for documents viewed onscreen in print preview mode.
- projection: Intended for projected presentations—for example, overhead projectors. Please consult the section on paged media (www.w3.org/TR/CSS21/page.html) for information about formatting issues that are specific to paged media.
- screen: Intended primarily for color computer screens.
- speech: Intended for speech synthesizers. Note: CSS2 had a similar media type called aural for this purpose. See the appendix on aural style sheets (www.w3.org/TR/CSS21/aural.html) for details.

- tty: Intended for media using a fixed-pitch character grid (such as teletypes, terminals, or portable devices with limited display capabilities). Authors shouldn't use pixel units with the tty media type.
- tv: Intended for television-type devices (low resolution, color, limited scrollability screens, sound available).

We'll be most concerned with the all, print, and screen media types for this chapter.

Two ways to target

The W3C tells us that there are two ways that we can assign media types to CSS. We illustrated one of the methods at the beginning of the chapter using the <link> element and media attribute. Let's take a look at both side by side.

Method A: The media attribute

```
<link rel="stylesheet" type="text/css" media="screen" ➡
href="screenstyles.css" />
```

Just as we demonstrated earlier, in Method A we're specifying the screenstyles.css file to apply only to computer screens. That should exclude the rules that are contained in screenstyles.css from being applied when printing the page or when the page is being viewed on a projector, handheld device, or screen reader.

Partial support

It's important to note that concrete support for all media types is somewhat wishy-washy. In an ideal world, all devices and browsers would adhere to whatever media type is specified. For instance, if we had said

```
<link rel="stylesheet" type="text/css" media="handheld" ➡
href="handheldcss." />
```

one would hope that *only* handheld devices such as PDAs, phones, etc., would recognize those styles. Unfortunately, standards haven't exactly reached that far beyond the browser at the time of this writing, and not every device will support their respective media type.

For this reason, we're focusing on types that have real-world uses—such as print styles.

Method B: @media or @import

```
<style type="text/css">
  @import url("screenstyles.css") screen;
  @media print {
    /* style sheet rules for print go here */
  }
</style>
```

11

The second method for assigning media types happens in conjunction with an @import or @media directive. For instance, when we're using the @import method for referencing external style sheets, a media type can be added along with it.

Also, the @media rule allows us to section off rules that are specific to a certain media type. As in Method A, we're using the @media rule to assign styles specifically for print.

In the head or externally

We've put Method A in <style> elements as an example, where it would live in the <head> section of a document. But we could also put the @import and @media rules in an external style sheet that we're referencing with the <link> element (see the section "Combining B and C for Multiple Style Sheets" in Chapter 10).

> *While the default value when specifying a media type is screen, typically all is recognized when no media type is assigned. This means that, by default, CSS is meant for all devices—screen, handhelds, projectors, screen readers, and so forth.*

Multiple values allowed

When using either method, it's allowable to assign multiple media types at one time. For instance, if we'd like to assign a style sheet to both print *and* screen using Method A, it would look something like this:

```
<link rel="stylesheet" type="text/css" media="screen, print" ➥
 href="screenstyles.css" />
```

Multiple values are separated by commas within the media attribute. Similarly, if we'd like to use Method B to assign multiple media types, we'd use code like this:

```
<style type="text/css">
  @import url("screenandprint.css") screen, print;
  @media print {
    /* style sheet rules for print go here */
  }
</style>
```

In the preceding example, screenandprint.css is assigned to both screen and print by specifying multiple media type values; after that we're using the @media rule to section off styles for print only.

Now that we've outlined the two methods for specifying media types, let's look at how we'd use them to serve screen and print styles.

Separating screen and print styles

Let's imagine that we'd like to serve two CSS files for the same document—one for screens and one used when printing the page. We'll use my personal site as an example.

I use the <link> element to reference master styles (styles.css) for the entire site. The contents of the styles.css file is simply an @import rule that applies an external style sheet, while at the same time hiding it from older browsers like Netscape 4.x.

So, in the <head> of the page, I link the master styles.css file:

```
<link rel="stylesheet" type="text/css" href="/css/style.css" />
```

I also have created a separate style sheet specifically for printing (print.css). Inside the print.css file, I write rules that pertain only to the page when it's printed:

```
<link rel="stylesheet" type="text/css" href="/css/style.css" />
<link rel="stylesheet" type="text/css" href="/css/print.css" />
```

So, how can we ensure that each of these CSS files is used only for the intended medium? We just add the media attribute to the <link> element (as illustrated in Method A, from earlier in this chapter):

```
<link rel="stylesheet" type="text/css" media="screen" href="/css/ ➥
styles.css" />
<link rel="stylesheet" type="text/css" media="print" href="/css/ ➥
print.css" />
```

By specifying screen for the styles.css file, we can ensure that the styles contained in styles.css are only applied for computer screens. Similarly, by specifying the print value for the media attribute, we ensure that the styles contained within print.css will only be applied when the user prints the page.

Now that we've separated screen and print styles, let's talk a little about what styles would be appropriate in our print style sheet.

Building a print style sheet

While our styles.css file may contain CSS for the layout, fonts, position, backgrounds, etc., we have a blank slate with the print.css file to customize styles for the printed page.

The key thing to remember when building a print style sheet is the targeted medium. Since we're dealing with a page, rather than a browser window, pixel dimensions and sizing aren't the best choice.

11

Make a point

It makes perfectly good sense to use point values for font sizes in a print style sheet. So the first rule of our print style sheet might define a base font size for the body element—in points.

```
body {
    font-family: "Times New Roman", serif;
    font-size: 12pt;
    }
```

Simple enough, and we have a better idea of how 12-point text would look on a printed page, rather than a pixel value. We also made the text serif, which tends to print out nicely and is more easily readable on a printed page.

Save ink by hiding unnecessary elements

There may be plenty of page elements on the screen version of a site that aren't necessary on the printed page. Elements like navigation links, sidebars, forms, and advertising can often be wasted ink when printed—and we can choose not to display them by using the display property in the print style sheet. Often, it's the *content* that the user desires to print.

For instance, if a typical site had #nav, #sidebar, #advertising, and #search elements that contained the site navigation, sidebar items, and search form, respectively, we could turn these off in our print style sheet with the following declaration:

```
body {
    font-family: "Times New Roman", serif;
    font-size: 12pt;
    }

#nav, #sidebar, #advertising, #search {
    display: none;
    }
```

By setting the display: none in our print style sheet, we'll be hiding those elements on the *printed* page.

By experimenting with turning off desired portions of your pages, you can quickly and easily create a customized "printer-friendly" version of your site from the same markup. No need to use server-side solutions to pump out an entirely parallel version of a site with a stripped-down template—just an extra CSS file, assigned with the print media type, does the trick.

This also reinforces the fact that organizing your structure into logical page "sections" can make styling easier after the fact. If your page has an advertising banner, assign an id to it that makes sense, so that you can have complete control over the banner with CSS—in this case, you can turn it off for printing.

Turning off backgrounds and colors would be another way to save ink and produce a more easily readable print version.

For instance, if we had previously assigned a background image or color to the <body> element, we could turn it off like this:

```
body {
  background: none;
  }
```

We could, of course, do the same for any element that we've assigned a background for in the screen version using the preceding method.

Expose links

Another neat trick that unfortunately only modern browsers that fully support the CSS2 specification can take advantage of is exposing hyperlink URLs so they appear in print after the hyperlinked text.

Using the :after pseudo-class, we can write a CSS rule that will print the URL of a hyperlink after its text in the browsers that support it (try Mozilla, Firefox, or Safari to see it in action). At the same time, it's painless for users of browsers that don't support the :after pseudo-class—only the hyperlinked text will show (see Eric Meyer, "CSS: Design: Going to Print," www.alistapart.com/articles/goingtoprint/).

Let's add a rule that will expose hyperlink URLs (in our content area *only*) to our print style sheet:

```
body {
  font-family: "Times New Roman", serif;
  font-size: 12pt;
  }

#nav, #sidebar, #search {
  display: none;
  }

#content a:link:after, #content a:visited:after {
  content: " (" attr(href) ") ";
  }
```

11

We've essentially told the print version of the page to reveal the hyperlink URLs after the hyperlinked text, putting the URL in between a set of parentheses with a single space before and after. This will only be done to hyperlinks within the #content section of the site. While we could've written a generic rule to expand all hyperlinks, we've chosen to only expand in the content area of the page—excluding links in headers, footers, and other areas.

Again, although this only works in a few browsers at the time of this writing, it's harmless to browsers that don't support the :after pseudo-class—they will simply ignore it.

Link text

While we've gone ahead and done something fancy for link URLs, let's not forget to call out linked text in a unique way so that it's easy to differentiate linked words from the normal flow of text:

```
body {
  font-family: "Times New Roman", serif;
  font-size: 12pt;
  }

#nav, #sidebar, #search {
  display: none;
  }

a:link, a:visited {
  color: blue;
  text-decoration: underline;
  }

#content a:link:after, #content a:visited:after {
  content: " (" attr(href) ") ";
  }
```

We could, of course, choose any color we wished here. I opted for default blue and under-lined, as it's easily recognizable as a link. For black-and-white printing, experiment to get a shade that shows enough of a contrast between a link and normal text.

Save ink with print preview

Another tip for saving ink is to use the browser's print preview function to test print versions of our pages without actually printing an entire page on paper.

In most browsers, the File ➤ Print dialog box contains a Preview option to view how the printed page will appear. You can get a good look at how your print style sheet is operating here.

How it looks

The print style sheet that I've used on my personal site looks much like the preceding example that we've been building. By comparing Figures 11-1 and 11-2, you can see how I've customized the print styles to turn off things like navigation and sidebars and have expanded links and changed fonts and sizes for optimal readability.

You can easily see that with just a tiny CSS file, we can serve an entirely customized version of any number of pages specifically for printing. It's an easy feature to add to any project, yet it will enhance users' experience when they go ahead and print your pages.

The next time your boss says, "We need to build a new template for a printer-friendly version of the site and have a completely parallel directory structure," you can pull this little trick out your back pocket (or wherever you can fit this book).

> *For more on print styles, be sure to read CSS guru Eric Meyer's helpful articles,* "CSS Design: Going to Print" (www.alistapart.com/articles/goingtoprint) *and* "Print Different" (www.meyerweb.com/eric/articles/webrev/200001.html).

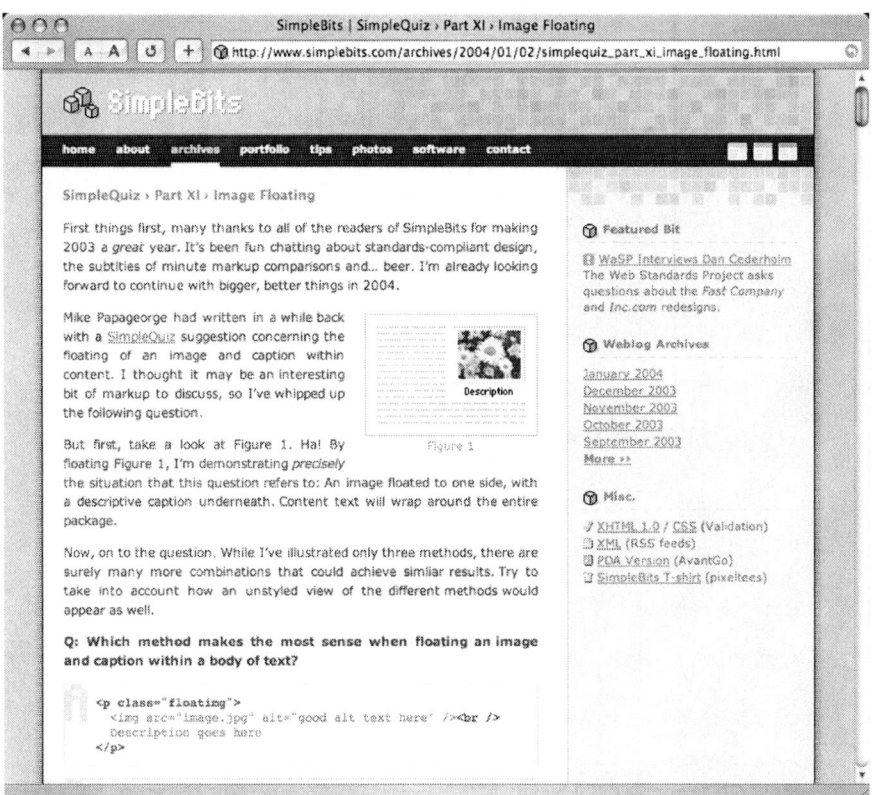

Figure 11-1. SimpleBits as viewed in a browser with screen styles enabled

11

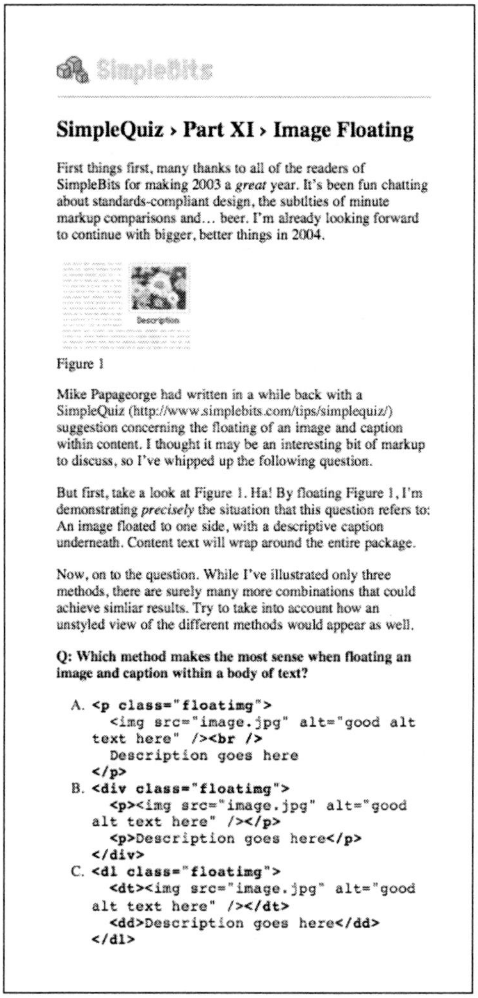

SimpleQuiz › Part XI › Image Floating

First things first, many thanks to all of the readers of SimpleBits for making 2003 a *great* year. It's been fun chatting about standards-compliant design, the subtlties of minute markup comparisons and… beer. I'm already looking forward to continue with bigger, better things in 2004.

Figure 1

Mike Papageorge had written in a while back with a SimpleQuiz (http://www.simplebits.com/tips/simplequiz/) suggestion concerning the floating of an image and caption within content. I thought it may be an interesting bit of markup to discuss, so I've whipped up the following question.

But first, take a look at Figure 1. Ha! By floating Figure 1, I'm demonstrating *precisely* the situation that this question refers to: An image floated to one side, with a descriptive caption underneath. Content text will wrap around the entire package.

Now, on to the question. While I've illustrated only three methods, there are surely many more combinations that could achieve similiar results. Try to take into account how an unstyled view of the different methods would appear as well.

Q: Which method makes the most sense when floating an image and caption within a body of text?

```
A. <p class="floatimg">
      <img src="image.jpg" alt="good alt
   text here" /><br />
      Description goes here
   </p>
B. <div class="floatimg">
      <p><img src="image.jpg" alt="good
   alt text here" /></p>
      <p>Description goes here</p>
   </div>
C. <dl class="floatimg">
      <dt><img src="image.jpg" alt="good
   alt text here" /></dt>
      <dd>Description goes here</dd>
   </dl>
```

Figure 11-2. SimpleBits, print version

Summary

We've just scratched the surface of what can be included in print style sheets. Because we can separate print and screen styles by assigning media types, customizing each medium becomes simple and easily maintained and organized. Building an entire site of printer-friendly pages becomes unnecessary when we can utilize the same structured markup with a different CSS file associated with it.

In the future, I hope that more media types are widely supported in other devices. When designers can start to rely on styling device-specific CSS for devices such as PDAs, phones, and all screen readers while using the same structured XHTML, it will make our lives all the easier.

11

CHAPTER 12
CSS LAYOUTS

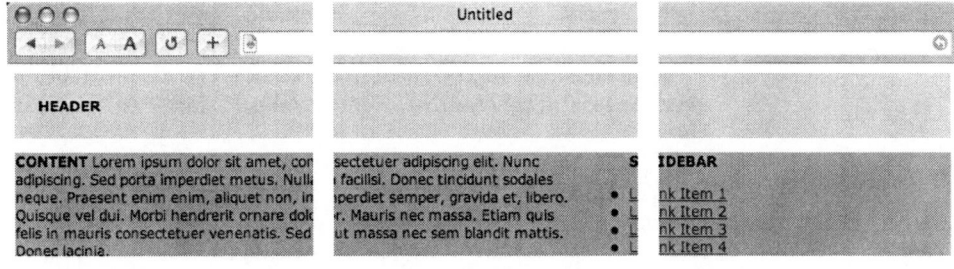

Throughout the book, we've been talking primarily about the *insides* of web page elements—the guts. But what about the framework? For years, designers have relied on tables for structuring columnar layouts, often nesting multiple tables inside each other to achieve just the right amount of spacing or visual effect. These bloated layouts can be slow to download and slow to work with in terms of code maintenance—not to mention often unreadable in text browsers, screen readers, and small-screened devices.

In this chapter, we'll combine CSS and structured markup to create a two-column layout using four popular methods. In turn, we'll show that it's possible to create columnar designs without nested tables and spacer GIFs.

Later, in the "Extra credit" section, we'll discuss the box model problems found in Internet Explorer 5 for Windows and how to get around it. We'll also share a simple secret for getting equal-length columns with CSS.

How can I use CSS to build a two-column layout?

The answer is several ways. To get you started, and to help you understand the fundamental difference between two of the most popular methods (floating and positioning), I've decided to focus on four options—all of which result in a two-column layout with a header on top and a footer at the bottom.

My hope is that by using this chapter as a guide, you can begin to build the framework for sites that contain many of the rest of this book's examples.

Each of the four methods that we'll focus on take place between the <body> and </body> elements of the document, and I've introduced the markup structure that we'll be using at the beginning of each method.

To give you an idea of the entire page structure that surrounds the methods, let's outline what else would be included:

```
<!DOCTYPE html PUBLIC "-//W3C//DTD XHTML 1.0 Transitional//EN"
  "http://www.w3.org/TR/xhtml1/DTD/xhtml1-transitional.dtd">
<html xmlns="http://www.w3.org/1999/xhtml" lang="en" xml:lang="en">
<head>
<title>CSS Layouts</title>
<meta http-equiv="Content-Type" content="text/html; charset=utf-8" />
</head>

<body>

...method examples...

</body>
</html>
```

And to give you a general idea of the layout we're aiming for throughout each method, take a look at Figure 12-1 for a visual overview of the columnar layout we'd like to achieve.

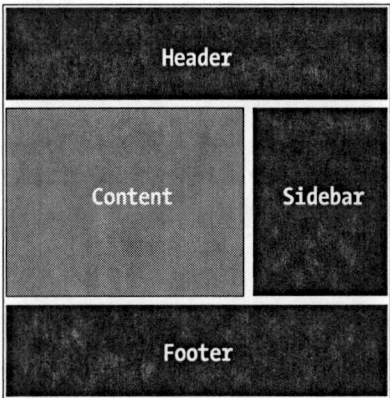

Figure 12-1. Wireframe of the intended two-column layout

Let's get started by introducing the first method that utilizes the float property.

Method A: Floating the sidebar

```
<div id="header">
   ...header content here...
</div>

<div id="sidebar">
   ...sidebar content here...
</div>

<div id="content">
   ...main content here...
</div>

<div id="footer">
   ...footer content here...
</div>
```

The preceding example is the markup we'll be using to create a columnar layout with CSS using the float property. We've divided our page elements into logical segments using <div> elements—each of which have a unique id attached to them:

- #header: Contains a logo, navigation, or other top-level items
- #sidebar: Contains extra contextual links and information

12

- #content: Contains the main body of text and focus of the page
- #footer: Contains copyright information, credits, ancillary links, etc.

Sectioning off these elements of the page enables us to take full control of the layout. By applying a few CSS rules, we'll have a two-column layout working in no time.

Styling the header and footer

The first step we'll take in making our structure a columned layout is to add some background color and padding to the header and footer. This will make it a bit easier to visualize.

```
#header {
  padding: 20px;
  background: #ccc;
  }

#footer {
  padding: 20px;
  background: #eee;
  }
```

Adding the preceding CSS to Method A's structure will give us what's shown in Figure 12-2. I've added a bit of faux content to fill out the sections.

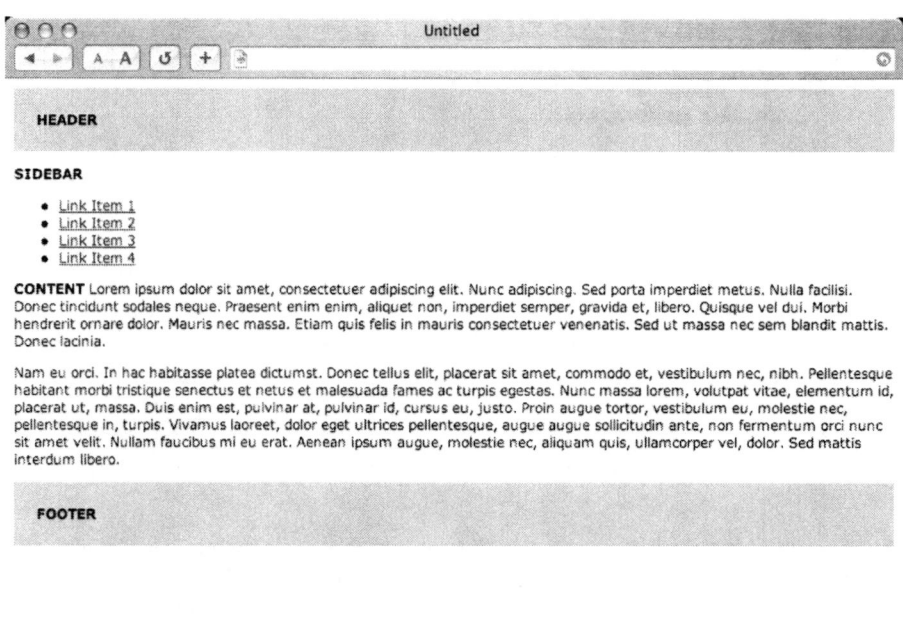

Figure 12-2. Adding style to the header and footer

Within these declarations for #header and #footer you could, of course, continue to add styles that are unique to those sections, such as font-family, color, and link colors. Now let's create two columns.

Floating the sidebar

The essence of Method A is that it uses the float property to place the #sidebar to either side of the content <div>. For this example, we'll be placing it to the right of the content, but the reverse would work as well.

The key to floating the #sidebar is that it must appear *before* the content <div> in the markup. This way, the sidebar's top will line up with the content area's top.

We'll add the float property to the #sidebar as well as give it a width of 30 percent and a background color:

```
#header {
  padding: 20px;
  background: #ccc;
  }

#sidebar {
  float: right;
  width: 30%;
  background: #999;
  }

#footer {
  padding: 20px;
  background: #eee;
  }
```

Figure 12-3 shows us the results of adding the preceding CSS. You can see that the sidebar sits on the right, with the content area flowing around it.

True columns

We could stop right there, but as Figure 12-3 shows, we don't exactly have a two-column layout just yet. To finish the effect, we'll give the #content <div> a right margin of the same width as the right column, effectively creating a right column space for the #sidebar to fit in.

12

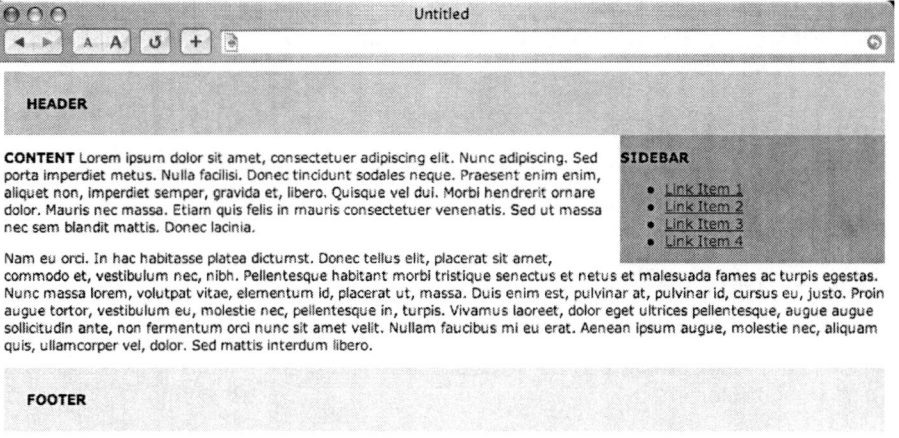

Figure 12-3. Floating the #sidebar to the right of the content

The CSS added would be as simple as

```
#header {
  padding: 20px;
  background: #ccc;
  }

#sidebar {
  float: right;
  width: 30%;
  background: #999;
  }

#content {
  margin-right: 34%;
  }

#footer {
  clear: right;
  padding: 20px;
  background: #eee;
  }
```

Notice that we've given the right margin 4 percent more than the width of the #sidebar. This will give us some extra space between the two columns. Figure 12-4 shows us the results as viewed in a browser, where you can see that by adding a right margin to the content <div>, it creates the illusion of a second column.

Also note that we've added a clear: right; rule to the #footer declaration. This is important, and will ensure the footer will always appear below the sidebar and content areas—regardless of the height of either column. The footer will *clear* any floats that come before it.

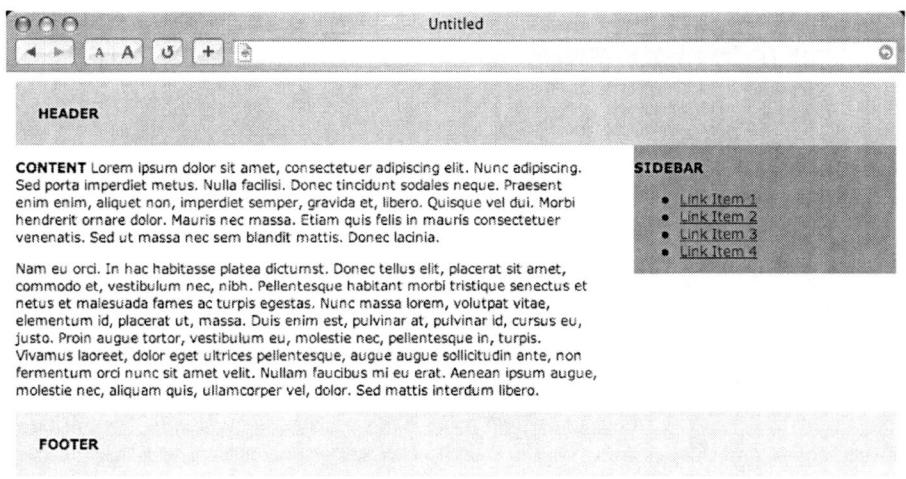

Figure 12-4. A two-column layout

We now have a working two-column layout, and can easily add more padding, backgrounds, borders, and other elements to the existing CSS declarations to make it look more appealing.

We've been using percentage widths for the columns thus far, essentially creating a flexible-width layout (the columns will expand and contract depending on the user's window width). We could easily use pixel amounts for the columns for a fixed-width layout as well, but you need to be aware of IE5/Windows' misinterpretation of the CSS box model when adding margins and padding to either column (if support for that ancient browser is required). More on the box model and successful workarounds can be found in "The box model problem" in the "Extra credit" section for this chapter.

Method B: The double float

```
<div id="header">
  ...header content here...
</div>

<div id="content">
  ...main content here...
</div>

<div id="sidebar">
  ...sidebar content here...
</div>

<div id="footer">
  ...footer content here...
</div>
```

One downside to using Method A is that in order to float the sidebar, we're having to place it in *before* the content <div> in the markup. Text browsers, screen readers, and other devices that don't support CSS will show (or read) the sidebar's content before the main page content. Not exactly ideal.

We can still use the float method and get around this problem by swapping the positions of the content and sidebar <div>s in the markup (as can be seen earlier), and then floating each to opposite sides with CSS:

```
#header {
  padding: 20px;
  background: #ccc;
  }

#content {
  float: left;
  width: 66%;
  }

#sidebar {
  float: right;
  width: 30%;
  background: #999;
  }

#footer {
  clear: both;
  padding: 20px;
  background: #eee;
  }
```

By floating the two <div>s apart from each other, we can order the source in the optimal fashion—content before sidebar content in the markup—yet still achieve the same results shown in Figure 12-4.

Clear both

It's also important to set your clear property in the #footer declaration to both, so that regardless of the length of either column, the footer will always appear below the columns.

The results should appear identical to Figure 12-4, yet the order of the markup has been improved.

Method C: Floating the content

```
<div id="header">
  ...header content here...
</div>

<div id="content">
  ...main content here...
</div>

<div id="sidebar">
  ...sidebar content here...
</div>

<div id="footer">
  ...footer content here...
</div>
```

There is one more method worth mentioning that uses a single float property and still places the content <div> *before* the sidebar in the markup.

This time, we'll be floating the *content* <div> to the left and giving it a width that's less than 100 percent. This will open up enough space for the sidebar to fit nicely on the right.

The CSS

The CSS that's needed for Method C is as basic as it gets—with a single float property, a desired width for the content area, and a small margin between the two columns.

```
#header {
  padding: 20px;
  background: #ccc;
  }

#content {
  float: left;
  width: 66%;
  }
```

12

```
#sidebar {
  background: #999;
  }

#footer {
  clear: left;
  padding: 20px;
  background: #eee;
  }
```

Notice that we need not define a width for the sidebar, as it will just fill in the remaining width that the content <div> doesn't use (in this case 34 percent).

Background woes

Figure 12-5 shows us the results. Oops. In some popular browsers, the background color of the sidebar will show through underneath the content area. Because the sidebar isn't assigned a specific width, it wants to expand as wide as the browser window.

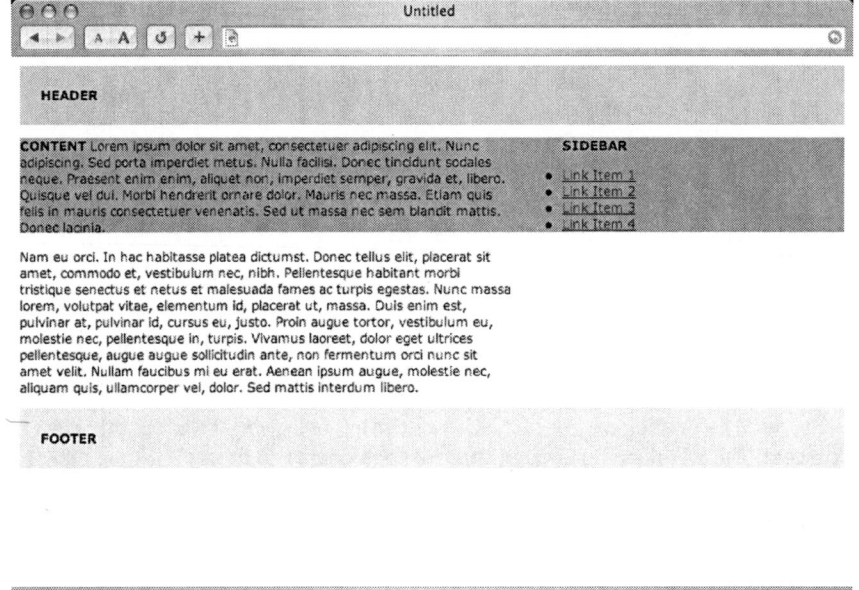

Figure 12-5. Floating the content, with the sidebar's background color showing through

We can avoid this by adding a left margin to the sidebar that equals the width of the content area. We'll actually make the margin a bit larger than the content's width so as to add some white space between columns.

```
#header {
  padding: 20px;
  background: #ccc;
  }
```

```
#content {
  float: left;
  width: 66%;
  }

#sidebar {
  margin-left: 70%;
  background: #999;
  }

#footer {
  clear: left;
  padding: 20px;
  background: #eee;
  }
```

Plain and simple

Alternatively, if no background color is required by the design, then the left margin isn't necessary. Figure 12-6 shows the layout results with the entire #sidebar declaration removed and a small right margin added to the content <div>. Both columns share whatever default background color is specified for the page.

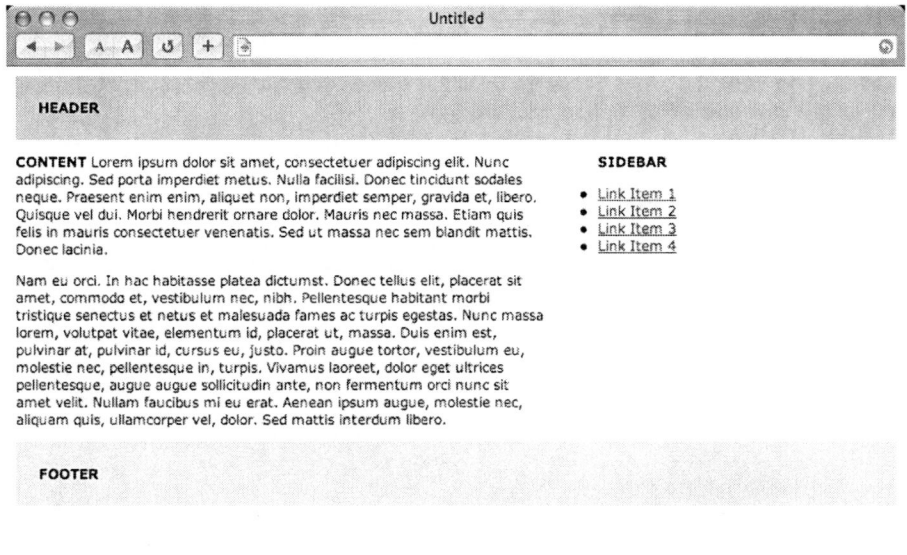

Figure 12-6. Floated content with background color omitted

12

The CSS would be reduced to

```
#header {
  padding: 20px;
  background: #ccc;
  }

#content {
  float: left;
  width: 66%;
  margin-right: 6%;
  }

#footer {
  clear: left;
  padding: 20px;
  background: #eee;
  }
```

> *Along with adding a left margin (or omitting a background color), there exists an alternative way of achieving colored columns using a background image instead—and I'll reveal this little secret in the "Extra credit" section at the end of this chapter*

In addition to using the `float` property, we can create a columnar layout using positioning. Let's take a look at the final option, Method D.

Method D: Positioning

```
<div id="header">
  ...header content here...
</div>

<div id="content">
  ...main content here...
</div>

<div id="sidebar">
  ...sidebar content here...
</div>

<div id="footer">
  ...footer content here...
</div>
```

For Method D, we'll use the same markup structure, and right off the bat we'll order the <div>s the most efficient way—with the content coming before the sidebar. Nonstyled viewers or readers will receive the content first, the sidebar second. When we use positioning, the order of the markup becomes independent from the location where the elements appear on the page.

Predictable height

The CSS will look somewhat similar to that used in the first three methods. The first difference will be assigning a pixel value height to the header. We'll need a predictable height in order to position the sidebar later.

I'm using an arbitrary value here—and this would change depending on the contents that you needed to contain in the header, such as a logo and/or navigation, search form, and so forth.

```
#header {
    height: 40px;
    background: #ccc;
    }

#footer {
    padding: 20px;
    background: #eee;
    }
```

Space for the column

Next, let's give the #content <div> a right margin, much as we did in the previous methods. This will leave the space for the right column, which we'll drop in by using absolute positioning, rather than floating.

```
#header {
    height: 40px;
    background: #ccc;
    }

#content {
    margin-right: 34%;
    }

#footer {
    padding: 20px;
    background: #eee;
    }
```

12

Drop in the sidebar

Finally, we'll place the #sidebar <div> in the margin of the #content area using absolute positioning. We'll also zero out any default margins and/or padding that the browser may place on the entire page perimeter. This will give our positioning coordinates equal value across all browsers.

```css
body {
  margin: 0;
  padding: 0;
  }

#header {
  height: 40px;
  background: #ccc;
  }

#content {
  margin-right: 34%;
  }

#sidebar {
  position: absolute;
  top: 40px;
  right: 0;
  width: 30%;
  background: #999;
  }

#footer {
  padding: 20px;
  background: #eee;
  }
```

By specifying position: absolute, we can use the top and right coordinates to drop the #sidebar right where we want it (see Figure 12-7).

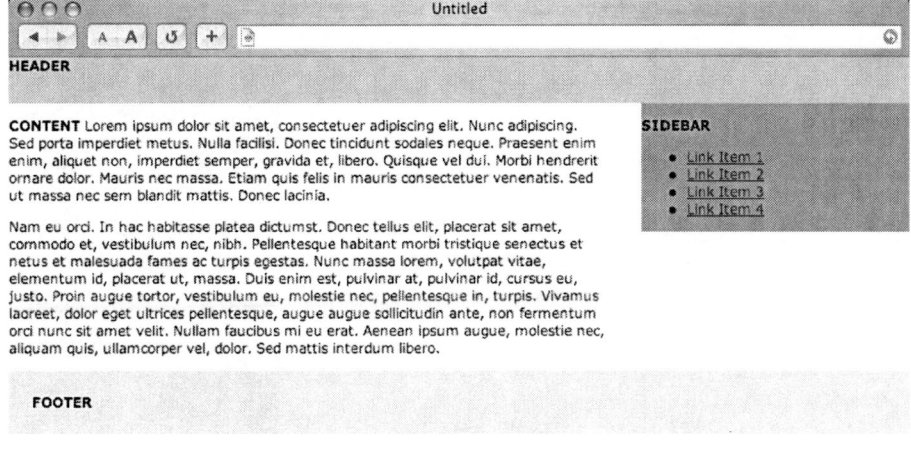

Figure 12-7. Two-column layout using positioning

We're saying, "Put the #sidebar <div> 40 pixels from the top of the browser window and 0 pixels from the right side of the browser window." Alternative properties we could have used for coordinates are bottom and left.

The footer issue

When floating columns as in the previous methods, we could use the clear property to ensure that the footer extends the entire width of the browser window, regardless of how tall the content or sidebar columns are.

With positioning, the sidebar is taken out of the normal flow of the document, so that in the event that the sidebar was ever longer in length than the content area, it would overlap the footer (see Figure 12-8).

12

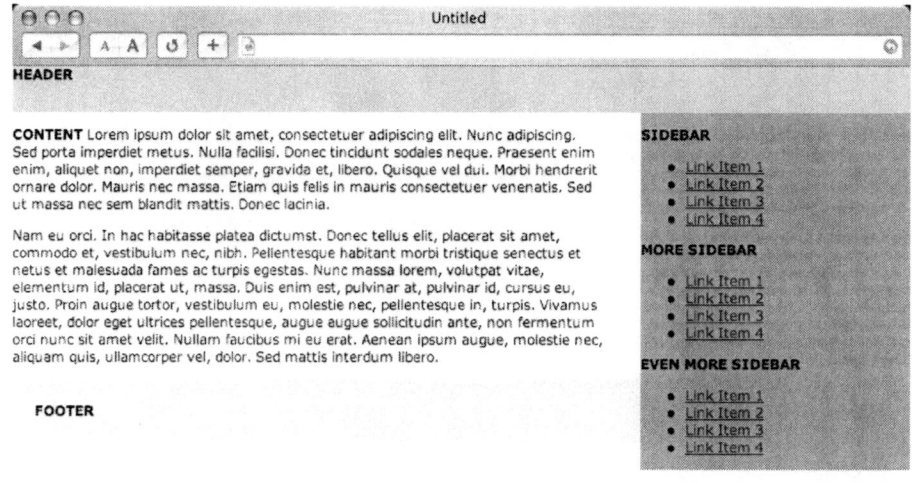

Figure 12-8. Overlapping sidebar and footer

One solution to this problem that I've often used is to give the footer the same right margin that the content area has, effectively extending the right column past the footer as well as the content.

The CSS would be adjusted like so:

```
body {
  margin: 0;
  padding: 0;
  }

#header {
  height: 40px;
  background: #ccc;
  }

#content {
  margin-right: 34%;
  }
```

```
#sidebar {
  position: absolute;
  top: 40px;
  right: 0;
  width: 30%;
  background: #999;
  }

#footer {
  margin-right: 34%;
  padding: 20px;
  background: #eee;
  }
```

This solution can look odd on pages with short content and long sidebars—but hey, it works. The results can be seen in Figure 12-9, where the overlapping of the sidebar and footer is avoided.

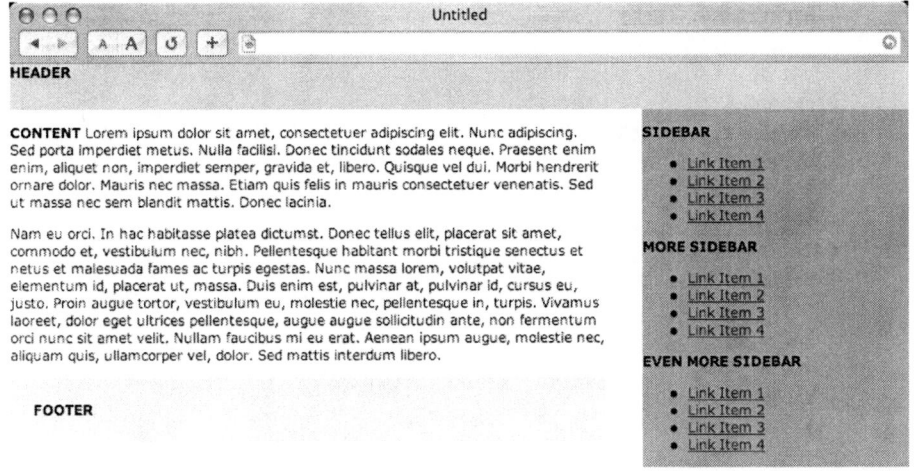

Figure 12-9. Footer with margin-right matching the content area

Three's company

But what if we'd like a three-column layout? No problem, and it's very easy to add when using positioning. What we'll need to do is add a left margin for the content and footer areas for whatever width that we'd like the third column to be.

The additional sidebar can sit anywhere we'd like in the markup, since we'll use positioning once again to place it.

Let's say that we've added a second sidebar, called #sidecolumn. We'll add the following CSS rules to make room for it, and then position it on the left.

```css
body {
  margin: 0;
  padding: 0;
}

#header {
  height: 40px;
  background: #ccc;
}

#content {
  margin-right: 24%;
  margin-left: 24%;
}

#sidecolumn {
  position: absolute;
  top: 40px;
  left: 0;
  width: 20%;
  background: #999;
}

#sidebar {
  position: absolute;
  top: 40px;
  right: 0;
  width: 20%;
  background: #999;
}

#footer {
  margin-right: 24%;
  margin-left: 24%;
  padding: 20px;
  background: #eee;
}
```

What we've done here is opened up a left margin on the content and footer areas (to avoid overlap), just as we've done previously for the right sidebar. Then we've dropped in a new #sidecolumn using absolute positioning—placing it 40 pixels from the top and 0 pixels from the left.

You'll notice that we've changed the widths a bit to allow for that third column. Because we're using percentages, these layouts will expand and contract proportionately depending on the browser's width. Alternatively, you could assign pixel widths to any or all of these columns to achieve a fixed-width layout.

Figure 12-10 shows the results as viewed in a browser—a flexible, three-column layout created with CSS and absolute positioning.

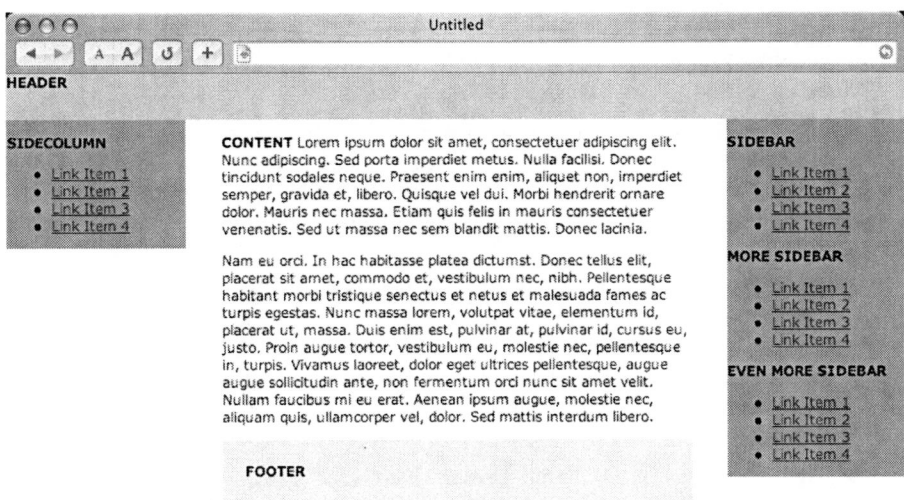

Figure 12-10. A flexible three-column layout using positioning

Summary

What we've accomplished in this chapter is essentially scratching the surface of what is possible when creating CSS-based layouts. The intention here is to give you a foundation on which to grow, by showing the two main methods: floating and positioning.

I hope that you'll dig deeper into what is possible with CSS layout techniques, ridding your pages of nested tables in favor of lean, structured markup that is accessible to more browsers and devices.

For more information on CSS-based layouts, be sure to check out the following resources:

- "The Layout Reservoir" (www.bluerobot.com/web/layouts/): Great examples of multicolumn layouts created with absolute positioning.

- "From Table Hacks to CSS Layout: A Web Designer's Journey" (www.alistapart.com/articles/journey/): A great tutorial by Jeffrey Zeldman that chronicles the steps needed to create a two-column layout.

- "CSS Layout Techniques: For Fun and Profit" (www.glish.com/css/): Eric Costello's large resource of various CSS layouts.

- "Little Boxes" (www.thenoodleincident.com/tutorials/box_lesson/boxes.html): A beautiful and simple interface to many CSS layout demonstrations by Owen Briggs.

- "Layouts.IronMyers.com" (http://layouts.ironmyers.com/): Jacob C. Myers' collection of 224 grid and CSS layouts. Various configurations are available for preview and download.

- "CSS Zen Garden" (www.csszengarden.com/): "A demonstration of what can be accomplished visually through CSS-based design." Cultivated by Dave Shea, the "garden" showcases cutting-edge CSS designs (including layouts, of course) submitted by readers, using a single XHTML file. A fantastic resource to view CSS layouts at their best.

- "Elastic Design" (http://www.alistapart.com/articles/elastic/): We didn't talk about em-based (or "elastic") layouts, but I encourage you to take a look at this alternative way of creating CSS layouts with relative units, based on the current base font size. Author Patrick Griffiths discusses how adjusting the text also adjusts the calculated widths of the layout columns, therefore providing a flexible, scalable design.

- "The Incredible Em & Elastic Layouts with CSS" (http://jontangerine.com/log/2007/09/the-incredible-em-and-elastic-layouts-with-css): Designer Jon Tan walks you through the construction of an em-based layout, with detailed explanation. A great tutorial for those interested in experimenting with em-based layouts.

Extra credit

Now that we've gone over the basics of creating basic CSS layouts, it's important we talk about Internet Explorer 5 and 5.5 for Windows and their unfortunate misinterpretation of the CSS box model. These browsers are certainly long in the tooth, and support for them may not be required for you, but it's good to understand the problem nonetheless. Later, we'll also share a secret for achieving equal-height columns by the use of a tiled background image.

The box model problem

Earlier in this chapter we talked about building multicolumn CSS layouts, using only the width property to define each column's space. Things get a little more complicated when you start to add padding and/or borders directly to those columns. Why?

Unfortunately, version 5 of Internet Explorer for Windows incorrectly calculates the width of a container when padding and/or borders are added to the mix.

For instance, in any CSS1-compliant browser but IE5/Windows, a container's total width is a culmination of its specified width, padding, and border. This is the way the W3C intends all browsers to handle the CSS box model.

But IE5/Windows calculates the border and padding as part of the specified width. Confused? Not to worry; taking a visual look at the problem will help.

Seeing is believing

Let's compare Figures 12-11 and 12-12. Figure 12-11 shows a 200-pixel-wide box with 10 pixels of padding on either side, as well as a 5-pixel border. Add up all of these values horizontally, and you'll come up with a grand total of 230 actual pixels.

This is the box model as it was intended—the width property always defines the content area of a box and padding and borders are added to that value.

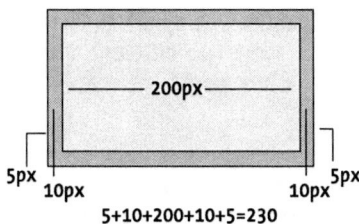

Figure 12-11. Correct calculation of the box model

So, if we gave a sidebar a width of 200 pixels and added padding and borders, the CSS declaration would go something like this:

```
#sidebar {
  width: 200px;
  padding: 10px;
  border: 5px solid black;
  }
```

We've specified a width of 200 pixels, but the physical space that the sidebar will require is 230 pixels—except in IE5/Windows, where the column will be a *total* of 200 pixels wide, including the padding and borders being placed *inside*.

12

Figure 12-12 shows that when we specify 200 pixels with the width property, our padding and border widths take away from the content area rather than add to it.

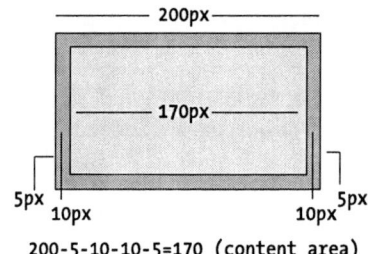

200-5-10-10-5=170 (content area)

Figure 12-12. IE5/Windows' incorrect calculation of width, padding, and borders

Wavering widths

What we're up against when using padding and borders for boxes is varying widths, depending on which browser the user is using. Yuck. This can throw off designs only for the scant handful of folks who still might be using the ancient IE/5.x on Windows. While it's not crucial nowadays to worry about box model problems because of dwindling statistics for IE5, it's good to know *why* this was a problem, historically, and why you might see these fixes in legacy code.

So what did we do? Well, fortunately, there's a hack to fix these width discrepancies in IE5/Windows. The hack enables us to serve two different widths—one for IE5/Windows and one for everyone else that gets the box model correct.

The Box Model Hack

Lovingly crafted by Tantek Çelik, the Box Model Hack (www.tantek.com/CSS/Examples/boxmodelhack.html) allows us to serve two widths—one that is adjusted and will only be recognized by Internet Explorer 5 for Windows, and another for every other browser.

By taking advantage of a CSS parsing bug that manifests itself only in IE5 and IE5.5/Windows, we can specify a width that is wider (to accommodate for the padding and borders), and then override that value with the actual width that other browsers will understand correctly.

Code by example

For instance, if we wished our sidebar's content area to be 200 pixels wide with 10 pixels of padding and a 5-pixel border, again our CSS declaration would look like this:

```
#sidebar {
  width: 200px;
  padding: 10px;
  border: 5px solid black;
  }
```

For IE5/Windows, we'll want to specify a width of *230* pixels (the grand total with padding and border on both sides), and then override with the 200 pixels that are originally intended for compliant browsers:

```
#sidebar {
  padding: 10px;
  border: 5px solid black;
  width: 230px; /* for IE5/Win */
  voice-family: "\"}\"";
  voice-family: inherit;
  width: 200px; /* actual value */
  }
```

Notice that IE5/Windows' value comes first, followed by a few rules that make IE5/Windows believe that the declaration has ended. Here, we use the voice-family property, which was chosen simply because it won't affect the visual display for browsers that understand it. Lastly, the actual width value is specified, thereby overriding the first width rule. The second width rule is ignored by IE5/Windows.

The results would be identical for both IE5/Windows and all other CSS2-compliant browsers. Without the hack, IE5/Windows users would get a skinnier column than desired.

Be nice to Opera

For CSS2-compliant browsers that also fall prey to the parsing bug that IE5/Windows does, we'll want to add an additional declaration following any instances of the Box Model Hack. Dubbed the "Be nice to Opera" rule, it will make sure all capable browsers don't get "hung up" on the parsing bug and thus deliver the intended width.

```
#sidebar {
  padding: 10px;
  border: 5px solid black;
  width: 230px; /* for IE5/Win */
  voice-family: "\"}\"";
  voice-family: inherit;
  width: 200px; /* actual value */
  }

html>body #sidebar {
  width: 200px;
  }
```

With that, we've completed the workaround for IE5/Windows' misinterpretation of the CSS box model, and everyone should be happy.

Not just for widths

While we've used the Box Model Hack for getting equal widths in this example, the hack can also be used anytime we need to deliver different CSS to IE5/Windows. Any hack should be used with caution and with the understanding that it should be used only when

12

necessary. It's a good idea to keep track of where you've used the Box Model Hack so that in the future you may easily remove it.

This particular hack is indispensable while millions of web users are still using IE5/Windows at the time of this writing.

> *The following section, "Faux columns," originally appeared at* A List Apart *magazine in January 2004 (www.alistapart.com/articles/fauxcolumns/).*

Faux columns

One of the questions I get asked the most often regarding my personal site's design is the following:

"How do you get the right column's background color to extend all the way down the page?"

It's a simple concept, really—and one that can be applied to any of the layout methods that I described earlier in the chapter.

Vertical stretch

One of the somewhat frustrating properties of CSS is the fact that elements only stretch vertically as far as they need to. That means if a 200-pixel tall image is contained within a <div> element, the <div> element will only expand down the page 200 pixels.

This becomes an interesting dilemma when you use <div>s to section your markup, and then apply CSS to create a columnar layout like we did earlier in this chapter. One column may be longer than the other (see Figure 12-13). Depending on the amount of content contained, it becomes difficult to create a layout with two equally tall columns when a unique background color is desired for each column.

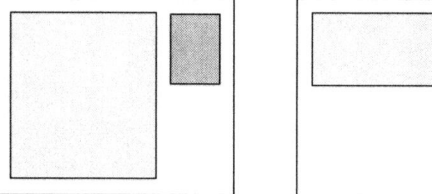

Figure 12-13. Columns of unequal length

There are a few ways to make the columns appear equal in length, regardless of the content that they contain. I'm sharing my particular solution (for use with an absolutely positioned layout), which happens to be pretty darned simple.

The cheat

The embarrassingly simple secret is to use a vertically tiled background image to create the illusion of colored columns. For a previous incarnation of SimpleBits (www.simplebits. com), my background image looked something like Figure 12-14 (proportions changed for demonstration), with a decorative stripy thing on the left, a wide white section for the content column, a 1-pixel border, and a light brown section for the right column's background followed by the reverse of the left side's decorative border.

Figure 12-14. `tile.gif`: A 2-pixel-tall background image, with widths allotted for columns

The whole image was no more than a few pixels tall, but when vertically tiled, it created the colored columns that will flow all the way down to the bottom of the page—regardless of the length of content in the columns.

The CSS

This elementary CSS rule was added to the `<body>` element:

```
background: #ccc url(tile.gif) repeat-y 50% 0;
```

Essentially, we're making the entire page's background color gray and tiling it vertically only (repeat-y). The 50% 0 bit refers to the positioning of the background image—in this case, 50 percent from the left side of the browser window (resulting in a centered image) and 0 pixels from the top.

Positioned columns

With the background image in place, my positioned layout sat on top, with padding and margins set for the left and right columns, ensuring that they lined up in the right place—within the faux columns created by the background image (see Figure 12-15).

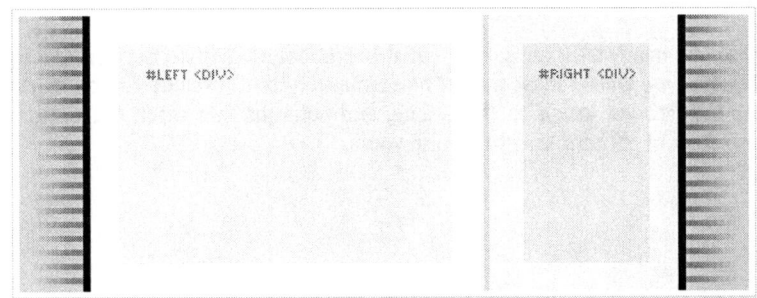

Figure 12-15. The tiled background image creates the colored columns.

12

203

It's important to note that if borders, padding, and margins are desired on either column, then we must still make up for IE/Windows' botching of the box model with Tantek Çelik's Box Model Hack (see "The box model problem" earlier in this chapter).

Alternatively, if borders or padding can be avoided altogether by just using margins instead (or if supporting the ancient IE5/Win browser isn't a requirement, and I'd be surprised if it was in this day and age), then the Box Model Hack won't be necessary. And if the column's content is simply sitting (transparently) on top of the tiled background, then it should be easy to avoid the hack.

Whatever floats your boat

While I used absolute positioning to create a two-column layout on my own site, equally fine results could be achieved via any of the layout methods described earlier in the chapter.

The same idea applies: tile the background image, and then float a column in position to overlay the faux-column backdrop behind.

It's a simple concept, but one that may alleviate one of the frustrations that designers frequently encounter when building CSS-based layouts.

Wrapping up

I hope this chapter gets you off on the right foot when delving into the exciting world of CSS layouts. To begin the chapter, we looked at four different methods for building layouts—three of them using the float property and one using absolute positioning. Be sure to visit the additional resources I listed for more layout techniques and demonstrations.

We also talked about the importance of the Box Model Hack when creating column widths with padding and borders, making sure these look consistent in IE5/Windows as well as other browsers. You might not need to get things looking consistent in IE5/Windows, with statistics for the browser becoming next to nothing at the time of this revision. If ignoring the ancient browser is OK with your client or boss, then consider yourself lucky, and you've at least learned something about CSS's storied past.

Lastly, I shared a handy trick for getting equal-height columns when building CSS layouts—something that you would think should be elementary but in reality can be frustrating. A little tiling background image to the rescue, and columns that reach the bottom of the page (regardless of content length) can be yours.

CHAPTER 13
STYLING TEXT

A Painting Tip

I f you're painting with latex paints, and the job is going to take more than a day (or you just need a longish break), putting used brushes and rollers in the refrigerator prevents them from drying out and more importantly, prevents you from having to clean the brushes until you're done with the job for good.

I hate cleaning brushes, so this tip is a life saver. Just put the brushes in a plastic bag (I prefer the recyclable grocery bag variety) and pop it in the veggie drawer or wherever. I find allotting certain sections of the refrigerator for different paint types helpful. And you may as well.

When you need them again, they'll be ready to go. Who would've thought you'd get such great home improvement advice here? Then again, maybe you haven't.

A Painting Tip

I f you're painting with latex paints, and the job is going to take more than a day (or you just need a longish break), putting used brushes and rollers in the refrigerator prevents them from drying out and more importantly, prevents you from having to clean the brushes until you're done with the job for good.

I hate cleaning brushes, so this tip is a life saver. Just put the brushes in a plastic bag (I prefer the recyclable grocery bag variety) and pop it in the veggie drawer or wherever. I find allotting certain sections of the refrigerator for different paint types helpful. And you may as well.

When you need them again, they'll be ready to go. Who would've thought you'd get such great home improvement advice here? Then again, maybe you haven't.

A Painting Tip

I f you're painting with latex paints, and the job is going to take more than a day (or you just need a longish break), putting used brushes and rollers in the refrigerator prevents them from drying out and more importantly, prevents you from having to clean the brushes until you're done with the job for good.

I hate cleaning brushes, so this tip is a life saver. Just put the brushes in a plastic bag (I prefer the recyclable grocery bag variety) and pop it in the veggie drawer or wherever. I find allotting certain sections of the refrigerator for different paint types helpful. And you may as well.

When you need them again, they'll be ready to go. Who would've thought you'd get such great home improvement advice here? Then again, maybe you haven't.

I think it'd be a good idea to bring it back down to basics for a chapter to talk about using CSS to style text. Manipulating type is probably the area where CSS gets most of its use—even for sites that aren't fully embracing web standards throughout. Stripping repeated `<font>` elements from site markup was (and is) attractive for designers, and it's not hard to see a major advantage of controlling typography via CSS—further separating the presentation from the content.

We now know, from many of the examples throughout this book, that CSS is capable of so much more—yet styling text can be one of the simplest ways to add design to even the most elementary of web pages. And by relying on CSS to style text, we can avoid adding unnecessary images to our pages.

Throughout this chapter, we'll go over some examples of how CSS can be used creatively to take a block of boring, normal hypertext to new heights (as well as new colors, sizes, and typefaces).

How can I make hypertext look cool?

Styling text is something that CSS can do well—often even in older browsers where more advanced CSS was never supported fully. In the past, designers and developers alike may have leaned on images for any instances where styling text beyond sizing or making it bold was required. Some sites began to take this too far, resulting in an accessibility nightmare that is simply not tolerable by today's standards. (Ever try to read a site whose text is mostly handled by images—in a text browser?)

In order to give you some alternatives to creating images and to answer the question posed previously, we'll take a nonstyled block of hypertext and progressively add various CSS rules to transform it into something attractive.

Times they are a-changin'

To begin, let's look at the block of text we'll be manipulating when viewed with the default font of the browser—in my case, Times at 16 pixels. I'm using the Safari browser on Mac OS X, and because of it, we're seeing text being rendered as antialiased. Similar results will occur with ClearType enabled on Windows.

Times (or the variant Times New Roman) is the default font of many browsers—however, this could easily be changed by users to whatever they fancy, and of course shouldn't be relied upon.

Figure 13-1 shows us the nonstyled text that we'll be using throughout the chapter: a simple title marked up with an <h1> element, followed by three paragraphs of riveting home improvement advice.

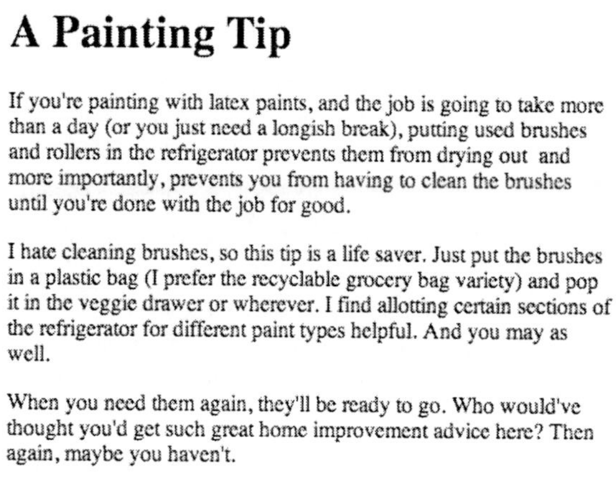

A Painting Tip

If you're painting with latex paints, and the job is going to take more than a day (or you just need a longish break), putting used brushes and rollers in the refrigerator prevents them from drying out and more importantly, prevents you from having to clean the brushes until you're done with the job for good.

I hate cleaning brushes, so this tip is a life saver. Just put the brushes in a plastic bag (I prefer the recyclable grocery bag variety) and pop it in the veggie drawer or wherever. I find allotting certain sections of the refrigerator for different paint types helpful. And you may as well.

When you need them again, they'll be ready to go. Who would've thought you'd get such great home improvement advice here? Then again, maybe you haven't.

Figure 13-1. Heading and text as viewed by default in the browser

Adjusting leading (a.k.a. line-height)

One of the simplest and most effective ways we can style text is by applying the line-height property. Providing some extra space between lines can make paragraphs more readable and attractive. It'll do wonders for your pages.

Adding the following CSS rule to the <body> element does the trick nicely. We could also add the following rule to any element we'd like—for instance, if we'd like only <p> elements to receive the increased line height:

```
body {
    line-height: 1.5em;
}
```

We're essentially saying that above that text on the page should be a line height of *one and a half* times the height of the character. I like using em units for line-height, as they will increase or decrease relative to the font size.

13

209

Figure 13-2 shows the results of the line-height property being applied to our example.

It's looking better already. It's amazing what a little line-height will do.

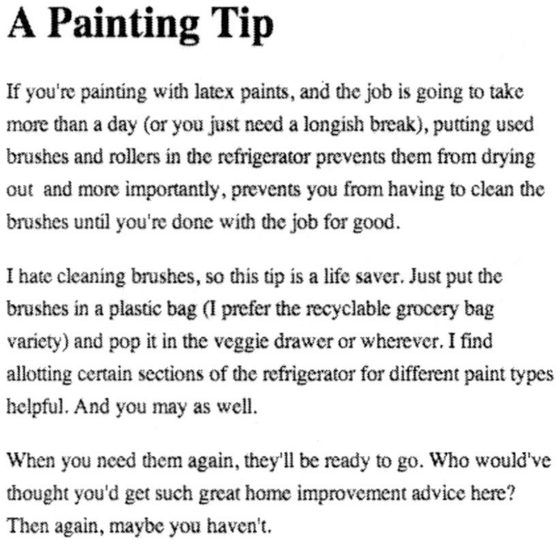

A Painting Tip

If you're painting with latex paints, and the job is going to take more than a day (or you just need a longish break), putting used brushes and rollers in the refrigerator prevents them from drying out and more importantly, prevents you from having to clean the brushes until you're done with the job for good.

I hate cleaning brushes, so this tip is a life saver. Just put the brushes in a plastic bag (I prefer the recyclable grocery bag variety) and pop it in the veggie drawer or wherever. I find allotting certain sections of the refrigerator for different paint types helpful. And you may as well.

When you need them again, they'll be ready to go. Who would've thought you'd get such great home improvement advice here? Then again, maybe you haven't.

Figure 13-2. Default text with increased line height

All in the family

We can, of course, change the typeface as well, keeping in mind that we're limited to whatever fonts may be installed on the user's system.

Let's assign a set of preferred fonts for our example using the font-family property. The idea here is to specify a list of fonts separated by commas—in the order of preference. If the user doesn't have the first font on the list installed, the browser will choose the next in the list, and so on.

```
body {
  font-family: Georgia, Times, serif;
  line-height: 1.5em;
  }
```

In the preceding example, we're saying, "Render all text using the Georgia typeface. If the user doesn't have Georgia installed, use Times. If the user doesn't have Times installed, use the default *serif* font."

Figure 13-3 shows the example text with the font-family property added.

A Painting Tip

If you're painting with latex paints, and the job is going to take more than a day (or you just need a longish break), putting used brushes and rollers in the refrigerator prevents them from drying out and more importantly, prevents you from having to clean the brushes until you're done with the job for good.

I hate cleaning brushes, so this tip is a life saver. Just put the brushes in a plastic bag (I prefer the recyclable grocery bag variety) and pop it in the veggie drawer or wherever. I find allotting certain sections of the refrigerator for different paint types helpful. And you may as well.

When you need them again, they'll be ready to go. Who would've thought you'd get such great home improvement advice here? Then again, maybe you haven't.

Figure 13-3. Our example rendered with the Georgia typeface

Font names with spaces

For specifying font names that include spaces (e.g., Lucida Grande), we'll need to enclose those names with quotation marks.

In the example that follows, we're specifying Lucida Grande (a popular Macintosh font) as the preferred font, with Trebuchet MS (a popular Windows font) as the second alternative. Lastly, we'll add a catch-all sans-serif choice for the users' default sans-serif font, in case they don't have the previous two fonts installed.

```
body {
    font-family: "Lucida Grande", "Trebuchet MS", sans-serif;
    line-height: 1.5em;
    }
```

Kerning (a.k.a. letter-spacing)

Kerning is a word used to describe the spacing between characters in the typography world. The equivalent CSS property is letter-spacing. Next, let's use the letter-spacing property on the <h1> element to spice up the title in our example.

13

By applying letter-spacing to <h1> elements, we can start to achieve stylish titles—without having to open an image-editing application to create graphic text.

First, let's apply *negative* letter-spacing to tighten the letters in the title:

```
h1 {
    letter-spacing: -2px;
    }
```

This results in the example shown in Figure 13-4.

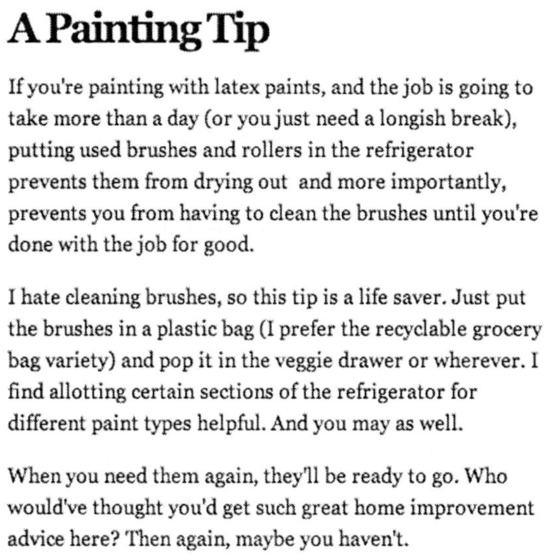

A Painting Tip

If you're painting with latex paints, and the job is going to take more than a day (or you just need a longish break), putting used brushes and rollers in the refrigerator prevents them from drying out and more importantly, prevents you from having to clean the brushes until you're done with the job for good.

I hate cleaning brushes, so this tip is a life saver. Just put the brushes in a plastic bag (I prefer the recyclable grocery bag variety) and pop it in the veggie drawer or wherever. I find allotting certain sections of the refrigerator for different paint types helpful. And you may as well.

When you need them again, they'll be ready to go. Who would've thought you'd get such great home improvement advice here? Then again, maybe you haven't.

Figure 13-4. Negative letter-spacing applied to our <h1>

Alternatively, let's try adding a *positive* letter-spacing amount and also use the font-style property to make the title appear in italics.

```
h1 {
    letter-spacing: 4px;
    font-style: italic;
    }
```

Figure 13-5 shows the results. Pretty stylish for just hypertext, isn't it? It's wise not to apply too much letter spacing in either direction, as it can easily begin to make the text more difficult to read. And who cares if text is stylish when it's unreadable, right?

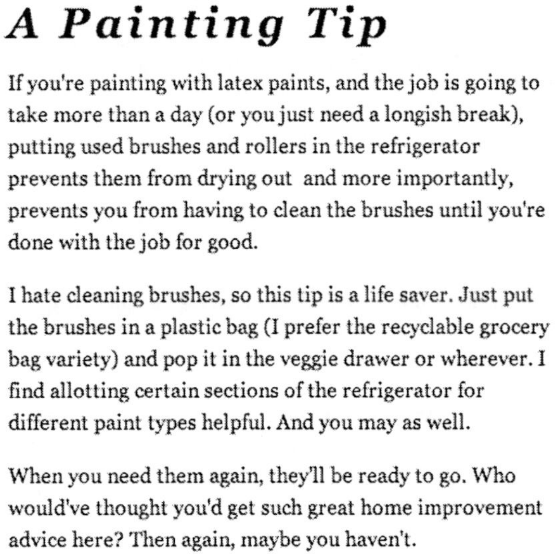

A Painting Tip

If you're painting with latex paints, and the job is going to take more than a day (or you just need a longish break), putting used brushes and rollers in the refrigerator prevents them from drying out and more importantly, prevents you from having to clean the brushes until you're done with the job for good.

I hate cleaning brushes, so this tip is a life saver. Just put the brushes in a plastic bag (I prefer the recyclable grocery bag variety) and pop it in the veggie drawer or wherever. I find allotting certain sections of the refrigerator for different paint types helpful. And you may as well.

When you need them again, they'll be ready to go. Who would've thought you'd get such great home improvement advice here? Then again, maybe you haven't.

Figure 13-5. Positive letter-spacing and italics applied

Drop caps

Commonplace in print, drop caps add a certain panache and elegance to paragraphs of type—and yes, it's possible to achieve them without images, using only CSS.

First, we'll need to add a "style hook" to the markup so that we'll be able to call out the first letter of the first paragraph uniquely. We'll wrap the "I" with a <span> element and give it a drop class so that we may reuse it throughout a page or site.

```
<p><span class="drop">I</span>f you're painting with latex paints, ➥
and the job ...
```

It's possible in some modern browsers that get the CSS2 specification completely right to use the :first-letter pseudo-class to access the first letter of the paragraph—without adding the extraneous <span> element. While it's semantically superior, the effect would unfortunately not appear in Internet Explorer versions 5, 6, and 7, and support in Firefox 2 and Opera would be inconsistent. Safari however, has had good support of :first-letter since version 1.

13

213

Now that we have complete control over the "I" in the first paragraph, let's add the CSS declaration that will enable us to enlarge the letter and float it to the left (so that other text will flow around it). We'll also add a decorative background and border:

```
.drop {
  float: left;
  font-size: 400%;
  line-height: 1em;
  margin: 4px 10px 10px 0;
  padding: 4px 10px;
  border: 2px solid #ccc;
  background: #eee;
}
```

Coupled with the styles we've been adding to the example so far, Figure 13-6 demonstrates how the resulting drop caps would appear in the browser—all without the need for images, and using simply CSS and markup.

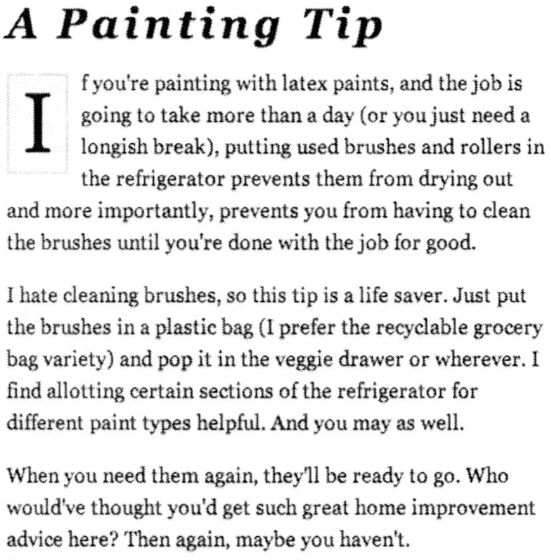

A Painting Tip

I f you're painting with latex paints, and the job is going to take more than a day (or you just need a longish break), putting used brushes and rollers in the refrigerator prevents them from drying out and more importantly, prevents you from having to clean the brushes until you're done with the job for good.

I hate cleaning brushes, so this tip is a life saver. Just put the brushes in a plastic bag (I prefer the recyclable grocery bag variety) and pop it in the veggie drawer or wherever. I find allotting certain sections of the refrigerator for different paint types helpful. And you may as well.

When you need them again, they'll be ready to go. Who would've thought you'd get such great home improvement advice here? Then again, maybe you haven't.

Figure 13-6. Drop caps example created with CSS

Text alignment

Again looking to the print world for inspiration, we could apply justification to our text using the text-align property. Justified text spaces words out so that each line is of equal length, making a tight, defined column.

The CSS for turning justification on for all text in our example would be as simple as

```
body {
    font-family: Georgia, Times, serif;
    line-height: 1.5em;
    text-align: justify;
    }
```

Figure 13-7 shows the example block of text, now justified!

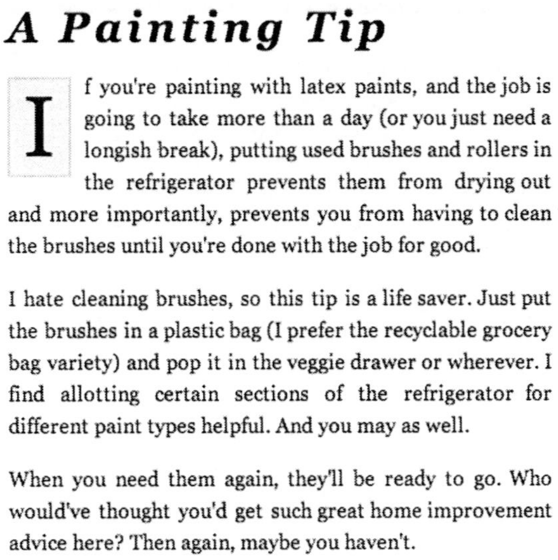

A Painting Tip

I f you're painting with latex paints, and the job is going to take more than a day (or you just need a longish break), putting used brushes and rollers in the refrigerator prevents them from drying out and more importantly, prevents you from having to clean the brushes until you're done with the job for good.

I hate cleaning brushes, so this tip is a life saver. Just put the brushes in a plastic bag (I prefer the recyclable grocery bag variety) and pop it in the veggie drawer or wherever. I find allotting certain sections of the refrigerator for different paint types helpful. And you may as well.

When you need them again, they'll be ready to go. Who would've thought you'd get such great home improvement advice here? Then again, maybe you haven't.

Figure 13-7. An example of justified text, using the text-align property

Notice that the text lines up evenly on both the left *and* right sides of the paragraphs. Other possible values for the text-align property are left, right, and center.

For instance, we could also apply the text-align property to the <h1> element to center the title of our example by adding the following rule:

```
h1 {
    letter-spacing: 4px;
    font-style: italic;
    text-align: center;
    }
```

Figure 13-8 shows the results of the centered title.

13

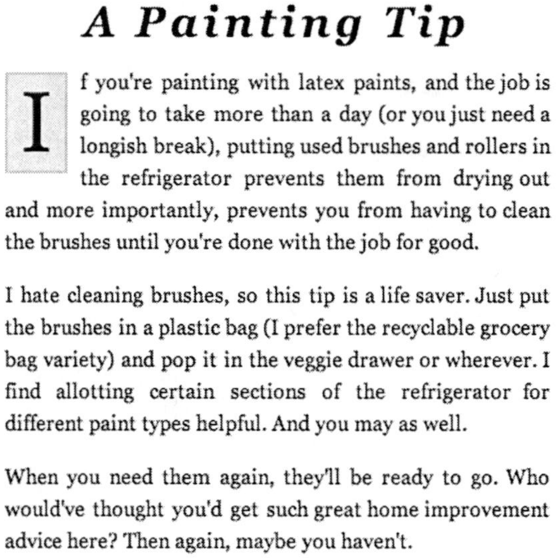

A Painting Tip

I f you're painting with latex paints, and the job is going to take more than a day (or you just need a longish break), putting used brushes and rollers in the refrigerator prevents them from drying out and more importantly, prevents you from having to clean the brushes until you're done with the job for good.

I hate cleaning brushes, so this tip is a life saver. Just put the brushes in a plastic bag (I prefer the recyclable grocery bag variety) and pop it in the veggie drawer or wherever. I find allotting certain sections of the refrigerator for different paint types helpful. And you may as well.

When you need them again, they'll be ready to go. Who would've thought you'd get such great home improvement advice here? Then again, maybe you haven't.

Figure 13-8. Centered <h1> using the `text-align` property

Transforming text

The `text-transform` property can modify the capitalization of text—regardless of how capitalization appears in the markup. For instance, in our example, our title is marked up with the following:

```
<h1>A Painting Tip</h1>
```

Using the `text-transform` property in our CSS, we could capitalize (or place in lowercase if we wished) the entire title—without changing the markup. In addition to the previous styles we've added to <h1> elements, the CSS to capitalize our title would be simply the following:

```
h1 {
    letter-spacing: 4px;
    font-style: italic;
    text-align: center;
    text-transform: uppercase;
}
```

resulting in what we see in Figure 13-9. Without having to mess about with the markup, we can change capitalization of certain elements on the page or even entire sites at will, modifying only the CSS.

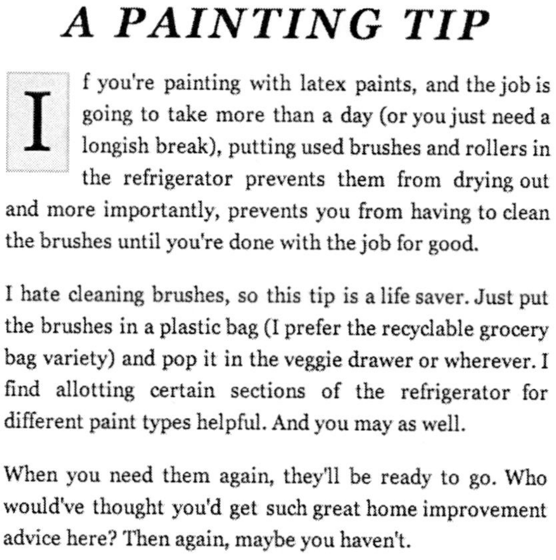

A PAINTING TIP

I f you're painting with latex paints, and the job is going to take more than a day (or you just need a longish break), putting used brushes and rollers in the refrigerator prevents them from drying out and more importantly, prevents you from having to clean the brushes until you're done with the job for good.

I hate cleaning brushes, so this tip is a life saver. Just put the brushes in a plastic bag (I prefer the recyclable grocery bag variety) and pop it in the veggie drawer or wherever. I find allotting certain sections of the refrigerator for different paint types helpful. And you may as well.

When you need them again, they'll be ready to go. Who would've thought you'd get such great home improvement advice here? Then again, maybe you haven't.

Figure 13-9. Capitalization of the heading using CSS

Small caps

Most browsers will recognize the font-variant property, allowing us to render type in small caps (where the text is capitalized with varying character sizes).

Let's apply the font-variant property to the heading of our example:

```
h1 {
    letter-spacing: 4px;
    text-align: center;
    font-variant: small-caps;
}
```

Figure 13-10 shows us the results of our heading in small caps—yet another way to mimic the print world using only markup and CSS.

13

217

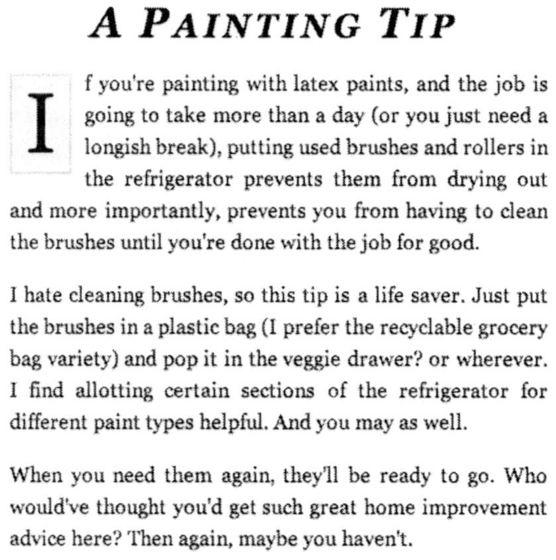

A PAINTING TIP

I f you're painting with latex paints, and the job is going to take more than a day (or you just need a longish break), putting used brushes and rollers in the refrigerator prevents them from drying out and more importantly, prevents you from having to clean the brushes until you're done with the job for good.

I hate cleaning brushes, so this tip is a life saver. Just put the brushes in a plastic bag (I prefer the recyclable grocery bag variety) and pop it in the veggie drawer? or wherever. I find allotting certain sections of the refrigerator for different paint types helpful. And you may as well.

When you need them again, they'll be ready to go. Who would've thought you'd get such great home improvement advice here? Then again, maybe you haven't.

Figure 13-10. Our heading rendered in small caps

Paragraph indentation

Looking again to the print world (gee, are you seeing a trend here?), we can indent the first line of paragraphs by using the text-indent property. Adding a positive value will indent the text by that amount.

Therefore, let's indent each paragraph in our example 3em—or about the maximum width of three characters. I'm going to go ahead and remove the drop caps from the results, so as not to interfere with the indentation of the first line of the first paragraph.

The CSS for indenting the first line of all <p> elements would look like this:

```
p {
  text-indent: 3em;
  }
```

Figure 13-11 shows the results, where you can see that only the first line of each paragraph is indented the amount we've specified. I chose to use em units, as the indentation's width will remain relative to the font size—especially helpful if users decide to increase (or reduce) the size of fonts themselves.

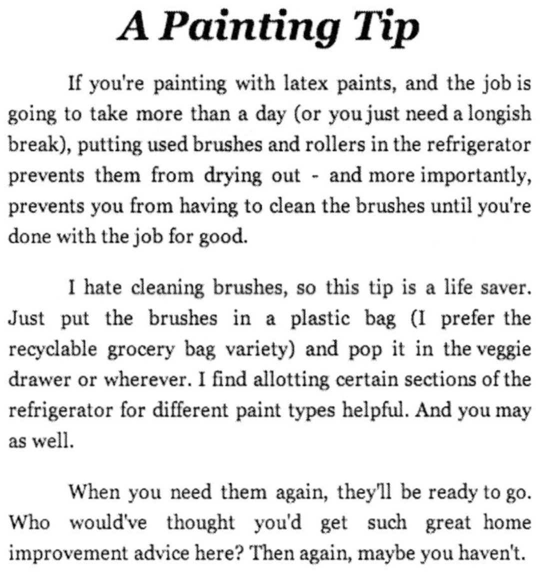

A Painting Tip

If you're painting with latex paints, and the job is going to take more than a day (or you just need a longish break), putting used brushes and rollers in the refrigerator prevents them from drying out - and more importantly, prevents you from having to clean the brushes until you're done with the job for good.

I hate cleaning brushes, so this tip is a life saver. Just put the brushes in a plastic bag (I prefer the recyclable grocery bag variety) and pop it in the veggie drawer or wherever. I find allotting certain sections of the refrigerator for different paint types helpful. And you may as well.

When you need them again, they'll be ready to go. Who would've thought you'd get such great home improvement advice here? Then again, maybe you haven't.

Figure 13-11. Indented paragraphs as a result of the `text-indent` property

Contrast

Another important thing to keep in mind when it comes to typography on the Web is *contrast*. By default, most browsers render pure black text (#000) on a white (#fff) background. Much pleasantness can be gained from knocking that black down a notch or two. For example, if your design called for black text on a white background, you could set the default on the body element to a black that is slightly less, well... *black*:

```
body {
  color: #333;
  background: #fff;
  }
```

It's subtle, but the text will appear less harsh and easier on the eyes.

Conversely, if your design called for white text on a black background, you could improve readability by knocking down that pure white a tad, to say a very light gray:

```
body {
  color: #ddd;
  background: #000;
  }
```

Again, it's extremely subtle, but tiny details like these can make all the difference in a hypertext-heavy design.

13

219

Summary

By sharing a few CSS properties that relate to the styling of text, my hope is that you've come to realize that there are times when you don't have to rely on an image creation tool to handle styled text. Often a bit of style applied to markup does the job just fine—and in some cases, very well.

There are certainly instances where we may have to create text as a graphic—be it a company's logo, or where a particular font is necessary to the design of certain page elements. The key with anything is balance. Try using CSS styling first, and your markup will be cleaner and more accessible.

CSS gives us the control to shape and style text with surprisingly good results, adding a tool to your design arsenal that will allow your markup to remain lean and mean.

CHAPTER 14
IMAGE REPLACEMENT

- home
- about
- archives
- bits
- photos
- software
- portfolio
- contact

In years past, as more designers and developers were turned on to the advantages of using web standards in the early days of their adoption, and specifically CSS, new techniques were discovered every day and the envelope was continually pushed. New, better ways of accomplishing goals evolved regularly.

A prime example of this evolution can be found in the art of "image replacement"—a technique for using CSS to replace plain hypertext with stylized images.

How can I use CSS to replace text with images?

It would be ideal to hold all presentational (nonessential or decorative) graphics within CSS, allowing you to easily swap out updated images, while keeping the markup exactly the same. Also, we can ensure all browsers and devices get the meaning of the markup first, whether or not they fully support the advanced CSS required to swap text for images. I've been preaching advantages like this throughout the entire book.

No perfect solution

However, finding the "perfect" method to swap text for images that are referenced only by CSS is much like the search for the Holy Grail. It doesn't yet exist. There are methods that work in all browsers, but fail in assistive software, such as a screen reader. There are other methods that work fine, unless users have specified that their browser show no images yet still enable CSS.

While no one method at the time of this writing satisfies everyone, or every user, the techniques *are* used today on a variety of sites. You should use caution when applying any image replacement method and understand the drawbacks that come attached.

Use, but with caution

This is the purpose of this chapter—to explain the flexibility that comes with image replacement, but to also show where it falls short. As time passes, more CSS aficionados may discover better ways to accomplish the same results. And until then, we'll have to work with what we have, weighing the pros and cons.

To get you familiar with the idea of image replacement, let's take a look at several popular methods out there, beginning with the Fahrner Image Replacement (FIR) technique that started it all.

Method A: Fahrner Image Replacement (FIR)

Named for Todd Fahrner, who developed the technique, FIR is the original method used to replace text with an image using the background (or background-image) property in CSS.

Douglas Bowman popularized the method with his fantastic tutorial, "Using background-image to Replace Text" (http://stopdesign.com/archive/2003/03/07/replace-text.html). To demonstrate, let's run through a simple example using FIR to swap a heading element of text with a stylized graphic.

The markup

The markup we'll use for the replacement will be the following:

```
<h1 id="fir">Fahrner Image Replacement</h1>
```

Just a simple heading element, with the text we wish to replace later with a graphic. You'll notice we've assigned a unique id to the <h1> element, so that we'll have full control over this particular heading with CSS.

Figure 14-1 shows the results of the markup in a typical browser—the heading is rendered in the browser's default font (in this case the Verdana typeface). Predictable and boring so far.

Fahrner Image Replacement

Figure 14-1. Default rendering of our heading

The extra element

FIR requires an extra element (in addition to the heading element) to surround the text in the markup. While we could use any element we wished, the generic quality of the <span> element makes it the perfect tool for the job. Looking at the nonstyled markup, the <span> will have no effect on the appearance.

Our modified markup now looks like this:

```
<h1 id="fir"><span>Fahrner Image Replacement</span></h1>
```

Now that we have the extra <span> element in place, we're ready for the CSS.

The CSS

The essence of Method A is to use the two elements that we have to accomplish two separate tasks. We'll use the <span> element to "hide" the text, and then we'll assign a background image of styled type to the <h1> element. It's because of these two steps that we need two elements to work with.

Hide the text

First, let's hide the text by using the display property on the <span> element:

```
#fir span {
  display: none;
  }
```

14

This will completely hide the text that is within <span> elements in this particular heading. Browsers will show nothing. That's the first step—get rid of the text completely. No need to show you a screen shot of the results—as you can imagine, it would be blank.

Assign a background

Figure 14-2. `fir.gif`, the image we'll be using to replace the text

I've created what I think is a stylish graphic version of the text in Photoshop (see Figure 14-2). You could do the same in your favorite image editor as well. Take note of the pixel dimensions, as we'll need those in just a moment.

The pixel dimensions of the graphic shown in Figure 14-2 are 287 pixels wide by 29 pixels high. We'll take both the image and dimensions and plug them in as a background image assigned to the <h1> element:

```
#fir {
  width: 287px;
  height: 29px;
  background: url(fir.gif) no-repeat;
  }

#fir span {
  display: none;
  }
```

While previously we hid the text using the display property on the <span> element, here we specify the height and width of the image we're using for replacement, as well as the image itself, using the background property.

We've opened a "window" on the <h1> element that shares the exact dimensions as the image (287 × 29 pixels), while the image will shine through behind the text that we're hiding with the display property.

Figure 14-3 shows us the results of the heading as seen in the browser. All we see is the stylized image. Perfecto!

Figure 14-3. The results of using the Fahrner Image Replacement method

Advantages

By using CSS to serve the image, rather than the markup, we can ensure browsers and devices that don't support CSS will simply display the raw text. Swapping out graphics is as easy as updating a single CSS file—rather than updating the markup.

But with these benefits come a few drawbacks that are very important to mention.

Drawbacks

Accessibility expert Joe Clark has done extensive research on how the Fahrner Image Replacement method breaks down for those using screen readers or other assistive software to read web pages.

The results of his testing can be read in full in his article "Facts and Opinion About Fahrner Image Replacement" (www.alistapart.com/articles/fir/). In it, he finds (among other things) that most screen readers (perhaps wrongly) obey this CSS declaration:

```
#fir span {
  display: none;
  }
```

The text is not only hidden visually, but also completely omitted by those browsing with screen readers because of the rule. Some will argue that the display property by its very nature should be recognized only by *screened* devices, and that perhaps a new CSS media type should be created specifically for screen readers to give designers better control over how systems may present future image replacement techniques—or that screen-reading software should adhere to one of the existing media types such as aural.

In addition to text display issues for screen readers, there are two other drawbacks to the FIR method:

- The semantically insignificant <span> element that is necessary for this particular method to work.
- In the rare event that users have disabled images in their browser (often for bandwidth-saving reasons), but have kept CSS enabled, neither the text nor the background image will appear.

Weigh the pros and cons

The fact remains that by using FIR, designers run the risk of serving incomplete content to those with disabilities, and run the (remote) risk of doing the same for those with the "images off/CSS on" combination. The trick here is to weigh the pros and cons—understand the drawbacks and use caution.

There are a few instances when FIR would still make sense—and I'll share two of them in the "Extra credit" section, later in this chapter.

14

Because of these accessibility findings that have come to surface, other designers and developers have been continually tweaking the concept of image replacement—finding new ways to "hide" normal text, while assigning an image as a background. Let's look at a few more methods.

Method B: Leahy/Langridge Image Replacement (LIR)

Simultaneously developed by Seamus Leahy (www.moronicbajebus.com/playground/css-play/image-replacement/) and Stuart Langridge (www.kryogenix.org/code/browser/lir/), the LIR method set out to handle image replacement—without the meaningless but necessary <span> element that FIR required.

Instead of using the display property to hide the text, LIR moves it out of the way by setting the height of the containing element (in our example, the <h1>) to 0 and setting padding-top to equal the height of the replacement image.

The markup and CSS

Since we don't need the extra <span> element for this method, our markup would be reduced simply to

```
<h1 id="lir">Leahy/Langridge Image Replacement</h1>
```

And the CSS that's necessary to replace the text with the image shown in Figure 14-4 is the following single declaration:

```
#lir {
  padding: 90px 0 0 0;
  overflow: hidden;
  background: url(lir.gif) no-repeat;
  height: 0px !important; /* for most browsers */
  height /**/:90px; /* for IE5/Win */
  }
```

Figure 14-4. lir.gif, created in an image editor

The image chosen to replace the text with is 90 pixels in height, hence the padding on top of the same value. For most browsers, we're setting the height to 0, which effectively gets rid of the text (or anything else that's contained within the <h1> element). We've used the !important rule to make certain that the preceding value is recognized over the one that follows (for IE5/Windows only). Competent browsers (including IE6+) will ignore the second height rule, while IE5/Windows will recognize it.

Box model woes

The final rule is put in place to make up for IE5/Windows' misinterpretation of the CSS box model (see "The box model problem" in Chapter 12). Since padding is added *in addition* to height and width values in IE5/Windows, we'll need to serve an adjusted value specifically for those browsers.

In this case, the height will always equal that of the height of the image we're using for replacement.

Again, you may not need to support such an ancient browser (IE5/Windows), whose numbers are dwindling down to next to nothing these days. If that's the case, disregard this hack.

Drawbacks

While Method B makes it possible to lose the extraneous <span> element (trimming code is always a good thing), it shares a drawback with Method A in that users with images disabled but CSS enabled will see nothing at all.

We could also argue that another drawback of the LIR method is the fact that it requires a Box Model Hack in order for IE5/Windows to behave properly.

Since Method B doesn't use the display property to hide the text, one could assume that this method is a better choice to allow users of screen-reading software. But like Method A, the Leahy/Langridge method should also be used with caution—taking into consideration the accessibility concern of an "images off/CSS on" scenario.

Let's take a look at one more variation on image replacement, developed by Mike Rundle.

Method C: The Phark Method

One of the great things about the Web is that people are constantly improving techniques, looking for alternative ways to accomplish the same goals. In August 2003, developer Mike Rundle came up with his own variation on image replacement (http://phark.typepad.com/phark/2003/08/accessible_imag.html), using the unique idea of assigning a large, negative text-indent value to the text he intended to hide. The text is still there on screen—but just so far out of range that it'll never be seen even on the largest of monitors. Rather ingenious.

14

The markup and CSS

Like Method B, the Phark Method (named for the moniker of Mike's site) also sidesteps the need for extra markup in order to work properly. Our heading markup would be the following:

```
<h1 id="phark">The Phark Method</h1>
```

The extra <span> element that was necessary for FIR isn't needed for this method. Let's take a look at the simplistic CSS that's used to hide the text and replace it with the image shown in Figure 14-5.

Figure 14-5. phark.gif, the 26-pixel-tall image we'll use for replacement

```
#phark {
  height: 26px;
  text-indent: -5000px;
  background: url(phark.gif) no-repeat;
  }
```

As you can see, Method C is by far the simplest and doesn't need the Box Model Hack or extraneous markup. By indenting the text an absurd amount of negative pixels, the text is pushed out of the way and unseen by the user.

Like with Method B, users of screen-reading software should be able to still read the text just fine using this method, which is certainly an improvement.

Still not perfect

While the Phark Method is the easiest to implement, it still fails in the "images off/CSS on" scenario. As rare an occurrence as that sounds, it still means that at the time of this writing, there is no perfect solution just yet.

Method D: sIFR

sIFR, short for *Scalable Inman Flash Replacement*, is an ingenious set of scripts that allows HTML text to be replaced by a Flash movie, thereby giving the designer the ability to use any typeface they wish. Since the fonts are embedded in Flash, and hidden to the user, it enables rich typography to be inserted into any web page that supports JavaScript and Flash.

Figure 14-6 shows a test page created by early sIFR pioneer, Mike Davidson, where the text shown is hypertext replaced with fancy fonts that not every user would likely have. sIFR makes it possible with JavaScript and Flash.

Figure 14-6. A test page for sIFR created by Mike Davidson

sIFR is arguably the most accessible technique of those mentioned previously, since it uses no additional markup and plays nice with screen readers. If JavaScript and/or Flash is turned off or unsupported, the text will still be readable (and backup CSS styles could be applied).

While sIFR offers unlimited font choice and controls, it can be tricky to implement. Fortunately, there are many examples and good documentation to help you along the way. Getting the necessary CSS, JavaScript, and Flash files set up and in the right place can be confusing for the beginner. However, once set up, sIFR delivers what no other method can: any font you'd like, without using images.

For more info on sIFR, be sure to visit http://wiki.novemberborn.net/sifr3 and http://www.mikeindustries.com/blog/sifr/.

Let's now recap each of the four methods presented, noting their differences.

14

Summary

We've looked closely at four popular image replacement methods, starting with the original Fahrner Image Replacement and three of its successors. While none of the four are perfect solutions, techniques such as Mike Rundle's are pretty darn close, and may have applications in the real world, as long as the pitfalls and drawbacks aren't taken lightly.

Let's break down the main differences between the four methods presented:

Method A:

- This method requires a meaningless extra <span> element.
- Screen-reader software in common use at the time of this writing will speak nothing due to acknowledging the display property (based on Joe Clark's findings).
- Nothing will appear in an "images off/CSS on" scenario.

Method B:

- This method doesn't require additional markup.
- Screen-reader software should read the text normally.
- The Box Model Hack is necessary for IE5/Windows.
- Nothing will appear in an "images off/CSS on" scenario.

Method C:

- This method doesn't require additional markup.
- Screen-reader software should read the text normally.
- Nothing will appear in an "images off/CSS on" scenario.

Method D:

- This method doesn't require additional markup.
- This method plays nice with screen-reader software.
- This method allows any typeface to be embedded by the designer.
- This method requires JavaScript and Flash in order to render custom fonts.
- This method can be confusing and tricky to implement.

Except for Method D (sIFR), all of the current popular methods share that last drawback. It's been several years since a new image replacement technique has been discovered, so there's a good chance we're stuck with the options presented in this chapter.

There *is* hope in the way of the Web Fonts module in CSS3 (http://www.w3.org/TR/css3-webfonts/), which introduces the @font-face property, enabling the CSS author to link to an actual font file via a URL, much like they would an image, video, or other downloadable file. The promise is wonderful: being able to embed any typeface you wish, while styling it with CSS. But it also opens up a host of legal issues and concerns for type designers and foundries. Here's hoping this gets sorted out before the next millennium. Until then, there are a couple of practical applications for the general idea of image replacement, and we'll take a look at two of them in the "Extra credit" section of this chapter.

> It's important to mention that standards-compliant designer Dave Shea has been extensively monitoring the state of image replacement, and has been keeping a nicely organized page that covers all of the methods presented in this chapter and more. Be sure to keep an eye on Dave's "Revised Image Replacement" (www.mezzoblue.com/tests/revised-image-replacement/).

Extra credit

For extra credit, let's look at two instances in which image replacement just might have a legitimate place in the real world. First up, we'll take on the useful act of logo swapping, first explained to me by Douglas Bowman, who popularized the original Fahrner Image Replacement technique of Method A. Second, I'll share how the navigation system tabs on *Fast Company*'s site was designed using JavaScript-free image replacement.

Logo swapping

Earlier in this chapter, we looked at how CSS can be used to replace text with an image. Certain drawbacks are attached to each of those methods—but these drawbacks will fall by the wayside when using one of the methods to replace an image... *with another image.*

But why would you want to do that?

Hi-fi and lo-fi

One reason for swapping an image with another image would be to serve varying site logos—one for browsers that handle CSS properly (referenced with the background property) and one that's served to old browsers, handheld devices, screen readers, and so forth.

This is especially handy when your fancy, CSS-friendly logo has transparency or colors that are specific to the CSS design of the site. You may want to have the nonstyled version display a lo-fi version of the logo that still looks good when CSS isn't supported or enabled.

The example

To skirt around copyright lawyers, I'll use my own personal site yet again as an example, which not only swaps logos, but also takes into account that on any page other than the home page the CSS-enabled version of the logo is still clickable as a hyperlink back to the index page.

14

Let's look at the markup that I used for the logo on a previous design of my home page, as well as the markup used on subsequent pages.

For the home page:

```
<div id="logo">
  <span><img src="/images/logo_lofi.gif" width="173" height="31"➥
alt="SimpleBits" /></span>
</div>
```

All other pages had a clickable logo to direct users back to the home page.

```
<div id="logo">
  <span><a href="/"><img src="/images/logo_lofi.gif" width="173"➥
height="31" alt="SimpleBits" /></a></span>
</div>
```

A pair of logos

Figures 14-7 and 14-8 show the two logos I used—the former one that's marked up inline on the page for the nonstyled version (lo-fi), and the latter one that was referenced by the CSS for the modern browser version (hi-fi).

Figure 14-7. `logo_lofi.gif` that nonstyled viewers will see (lo-fi)

Figure 14-8. `logo_corn.gif` that
CSS-enabled viewers will see (hi-fi)

The text of the hi-fi logo was white with a transparent background that was meant to sit on a corn backdrop, and therefore would look odd for viewers of the nonstyled version of the site. This is the reason I'd chosen to use CSS to swap logos—to allow me to serve one or the other, depending on the browser's capabilities.

The CSS

So let's pull this all together with the CSS that makes everything possible.

First, we'll hide the inline image by setting its width to 0—remember that by not using the display property to hide the lo-fi logo, we have a better chance of screen-reading software reading the image that's being hidden (by way of the alt text provided):

```
#logo img  {
   display: block;
   width: 0;
   }
```

Next, let's assign the hi-fi logo by way of the background property on the <span> element that I snuck in there. Yes, it's meaningless and semantically meaningless—let's make an exception in this case.

```
#logo span {
   width: 173px;
   height: 31px;
   background: url(../images/logo_corn.gif) no-repeat;
   }
```

You'll notice that all we must do is assign height and width that is equal to the logo that we're using for replacement and set the background image to the hi-fi version.

Regain the hyperlink

Finally, for pages other than the home page, we still want people to be able to click the logo to get back to the index. But how can we do this, if we've set the image's width to 0? There would be literally no clickable area.

We can add a declaration for the logo's <a> element that will "stretch" its clickable area over the background image. The width will equal that of the replaced image.

```
#logo a  {
   border-style: none;
   display: block;
   width: 173px;
   }
```

By setting the width of the <a> in CSS, we could conceivably serve two logos that were of different dimensions as well. In this example, they are the same size.

We've also added the top rule to get rid of the default border that most browsers place around hyperlinked images (see Figure 14-9).

14

SimpleBits
home
about
archives
portfolio
tips
photos

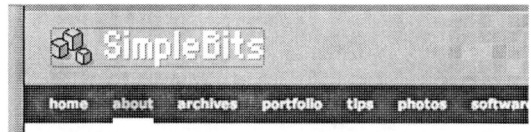

Figure 14-9. Hyperlinked logo, with clickable area shown

The results

By taking a look at Figures 14-10 and 14-11, you can see that with the markup and style just demonstrated, two logos could be served for both nonstyled and CSS-enabled users. For times when the logo is hyperlinked, we could still specify the clickable area using a simple CSS rule.

I believe this example shows how image replacement can be used without guilt in the real world—specifically for replacing an existing inline image with another image that's referenced in CSS.

SimpleBits
home
about
archives
bits
photos
software
portfolio

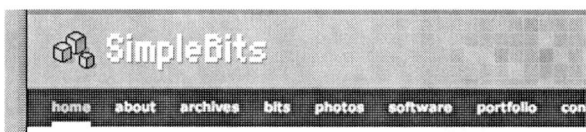

Figure 14-10. Hi-fi logo for CSS-enabled browsers

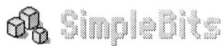

SimpleBits
home
about
archives
bits
photos
software
portfolio
contact

Figure 14-11. Lo-fi logo for nonstyled viewers

Next, let's take a look at another real-world case study, a navigation system I designed for the *Fast Company* website back in 2003 that combines an unordered list with image replacement... and a twist.

Accessible image-tab rollovers

To call this particular solution "accessible" could be a bit false. The image-tab navigation I devised for *Fast Company*'s website shares a drawback with the image replacement techniques described earlier in this chapter—that users with "images off/CSS on" will most likely see nothing.

However, for scenarios in which you *must* use images for navigation, whether it be space constraints or typography requirements, this method is valuable to understand.

The accessible part comes from the fact that, while in the end we're using images for navigational tabs, the markup is still a lean, mean unordered list—accessible by all browsers, phones, handheld devices, and so forth.

Let's take a look at how everything comes together.

The problem

While I was a member of the *Fast Company* web team, we needed to fit more items into FC's top navigation. But we ran out of room. Previously, navigation markup was handled by a simple, styled, unordered list. But at a window resolution of 800 × 600, there wasn't enough additional horizontal space to add even one more item using the current design.

The solution

I chose to combine and modify the approach in Czech author Petr Stanicek's (a.k.a. Pixy) "Fast Rollovers, No Preload Needed" (http://wellstyled.com/css-nopreload-rollovers.html) and the Leahy/Langridge Image Replacement method described earlier in this chapter to create accessible, JavaScript-free, image-tab rollovers (see Figure 14-12).

Figure 14-12. FastCompany.com's tabbed navigation, circa February 2004

How does it work?

The markup: One list to rule them all

I wanted to continue to use a simple unordered list for the navigation in the markup. Much has already been said in this book about using lists for navigation: they're compact, lightweight, and accessible to text browsers, screen readers, handheld devices, and phones.

Here's what the list looked like originally (I've deleted some of the items to make it more convenient to demonstrate):

14

```
<ul id="nav">
  <li><a href="/" class="selected">Home</a></li>
  <li><a href="/guides/">Guides</a></li>
  <li><a href="/magazine/">Magazine</a></li>
  <li><a href="/articles/">Archives</a></li>
</ul>
```

Nice and simple. Now let's add a unique id to each <li> element so that we can do some fancy stuff with it (namely, replace the boring text with stylized graphics for each tab):

```
<ul id="nav">
  <li id="thome"><a href="/" class="selected">Home</a></li>
  <li id="tguides"><a href="/guides/">Guides</a></li>
  <li id="tmag"><a href="/magazine/">Magazine</a></li>
  <li id="tarchives"><a href="/articles/">Archives</a></li>
</ul>
```

Now we're ready to create some tab images using Photoshop, or your favorite image editor.

One image, three states

The essence of Pixy's brilliant fast rollovers approach involves creating *one* image for each navigation item that includes normal, hover, and active states stacked on top of each other. Later, we'll use CSS to change the background-position that reveals each state at the appropriate time.

This method eliminates the need to use what was historically JavaScript to swap images and preload multiple sets of images. What a production time-saver—not to mention a means of providing faster downloading.

Figure 14-13 shows an example image that I've created and used for the *Fast Company* site's navigation. Each state is 20 pixels tall with a total image height of 60 pixels. The top 20 pixels are the normal state, the next 20 pixels show the hover state, and the final 20 pixels show the active state (which is also used for the "you are here" effect). There are similar images for each tab we'd like to use.

Figure 14-13.
A single image
containing the
three states

Using one image for each state allows us to toss out ugly JavaScript that is traditionally used for such effects and instead make use of simple CSS rules for hover effects. This is good. It also eliminates the "flicker" effect that other CSS methods suffer from, where separate on/off images are necessary. This is good. We also don't have to preload any additional images. Again... this is good.

The CSS: This is where the magic happens

First we'll set up the rules that all navigation items will need. This will save us from writing duplicate rules for each tab. Then we'll add a separate rule for each list item id, giving the <li> its own background-image and width—the only two variables that will be different for each tab.

The CSS goes something like this:

```
#nav {
  margin: 0;
  padding: 0;
  height: 20px;
  list-style: none;
  display: inline;
  overflow: hidden;
  }

#nav li {
  margin: 0;
  padding: 0;
  list-style: none;
  display: inline;
  }

#nav a {
  float: left;
  padding: 20px 0 0 0;
  overflow: hidden;
  height: 0px !important;
  height /**/:20px; /* for IE5/Win only */
  }

#nav a:hover {
  background-position: 0 -20px;
  }

#nav a:active, #nav a.selected {
  background-position: 0 -40px;
  }
```

The preceding code essentially turns off padding and list styles, makes the list horizontal, and hides the text that's between each hyperlink in the list. Notice the :hover and :active rules. These are generic for every <a> element within #nav so that we don't have to repeat those particular rules for each item.

14

I've also assigned a "selected" class to a tab that I wish to highlight permanently, signifying which section of the site you're currently on. This is shared with the :active state.

You may also notice that list-style: none; and display: inline; are repeated in both the #nav and #nav li selectors. This was to keep IE5/Windows happy. In a perfect world, declaring this once for #nav would be perfectly sufficient, and with IE5 usage across the Web now at next to nil, it'd likely be fine.

Next, we'll add the rule for each id and assign its background-image and width. Here's one example:

```
#thome a  {
  width: 40px;
  background: url(home.gif) top left no-repeat;
  }
```

There is, of course, a similar declaration for each tab needed.

The results

Figure 14-14 shows the resulting tabs in normal, hover, and selected states. To see it all working in action, check out the working example with source code on SimpleBits (www. simplebits.com/bits/tab_rollovers.html).

Figure 14-14. Resulting tabbed navigation with each of the three states demonstrated

Why use it?

- **It's lightweight**: Just an unordered list in the markup.
- **It's accessible**: Using Stuart's method, we can ensure screen readers will read the text links.
- **No JavaScript**: We don't need to preload or create multiple images for each state. We also don't need extra JavaScript to control hover effects. Thanks, Pixy.
- **It's stylized**: Fitting hypertext into defined areas can be tricky; this allows for using stylized images.

But wait, the text doesn't scale!

Following a great suggestion from Douglas Bowman, and in response to legibility issues and the inability to resize image text, I went a step further and created a second set of tab images with larger text labels. I could then override rules on the existing "medium" and "large" alternative style sheets. The alternative styles are activated using Paul Sowden's style sheet switcher, which I talked about back in the "Extra credit" section of Chapter 10.

An example of the overridden rule looks almost identical to the original, with a new width and image path:

```
#thome a  {
  width: 46px;
  background: url(guides_lg.gif) top left no-repeat;
  }
```

Figure 14-15 shows the larger tabs as they appeared on the *Fast Company* site, where you'll notice that the horizontal spacing is tighter, while the vertical size remains the same as the original. But, by adding the ability to increase the size of hypertext as well as the tab images, we've helped out low-vision users, while still working with our particular design constraints.

Figure 14-15. Tab navigation with larger image set activated from an alternative style sheet

Compatibility

This method has been tested and should work in all modern browsers past version 5.0.

Wrapping up

Now that you're up to speed on the wonders of image replacement, I hope that you're armed with the knowledge that, while no perfect solution exists yet, the concept is an important one to understand and experiment with.

Additionally, by showing you two real-world examples of how image replacement can be utilized, my hope is that the wheels will start turning, and you... yes, you... could be the one who discovers the next best method. Fame and fortune await.

14

CHAPTER 15
STYLING <BODY>

One of the benefits of separating content from presentation is flexibility. By using CSS to control a site's layout (as we saw in Chapter 12), we can control an entire site's design. Change a few rules, and instantly and dramatically update thousands of pages.

Just one example of the flexibility gained from choosing to use CSS to control a site's layout comes from styling the <body> element. By adding a class or id to the <body> element, you can take advantage of customized control over any element on the page, eliminating the need for duplicating shared rules.

In this chapter, you'll discover how adding class to the <body> element enables you to toggle between two separate layouts while sticking with the same markup structure.

Two and sometimes three columns

When we redesigned the website for *Fast Company* using a CSS-based layout, one of the challenges was that while sections like navigation and footer information were shared on every page, we needed to create two different page layouts.

One layout would be used for "index pages" (see Figure 15-1)—pages that have navigational purposes, allowing the user to drill further down into the directory structure of the site. We decided these pages should have a three-column layout.

The second type of page layout was an "article page" (see Figure 15-2). Any page that was considered a destination had this type of layout. For increased readability, we chose to omit the left column, leaving two—one large column for content, and one for advertising.

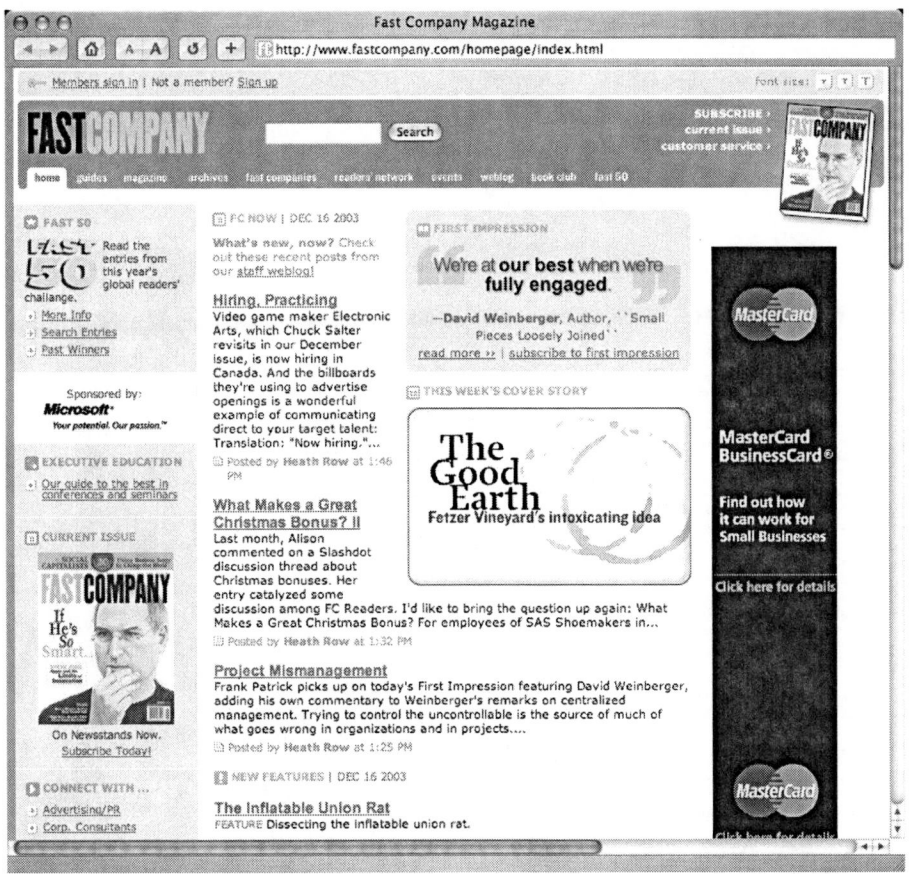

Figure 15-1. Example of a *Fast Company* "index page" with three columns

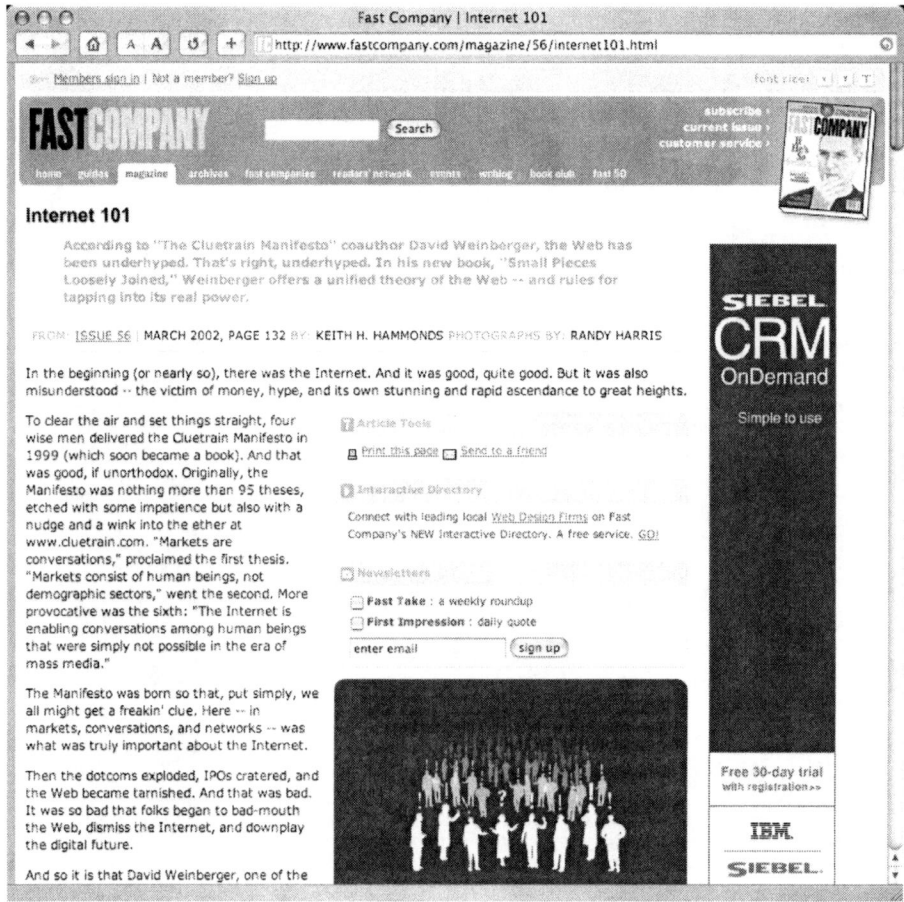

Figure 15-2. Example of a *Fast Company* "article page" with two columns

The reason I explained all of that wasn't to prove that we had cracked some brilliant layout puzzle—but rather to show how applying a class to the <body> element allowed us to adjust the column widths and drop or omit a third column depending on the page type. All of this was done without duplicating any rules or without importing additional style sheets.

Markup and style structure

This will start to make more sense when I describe a distilled version of the markup structure that was used for both types of pages. To achieve the columnar layout, I used the absolute positioning method, as described in Chapter 12.

Article page

For article pages, a simplified look at the markup structure went something like this:

```
<div id="header">
  ...header info here...
</div>

<div id="content">
  ...content here...
</div>

<div id="right">
  ...right column info...
</div>

<div id="footer">
  ...footer info...
</div>
```

CSS rules were put in place to give the #content and #footer a right margin wide enough for the #right column to be placed using absolute positioning; in this case, 190 pixels was just enough.

```
#content, #footer {
  margin: 10px 190px 10px 10px;
  }
```

Index page

For index pages, the markup structure was kept exactly the same, saving the need for duplicating shared CSS rules—yet an additional <div> is added for a third column (#left) to the left of the #content.

```
<div id="header">
  ...header info here...
</div>

<div id="content">
  ...content here...
</div>

<div id="left">
  ...left column info...
</div>

<div id="right">
  ...right column info...
</div>

<div id="footer">
  ...footer info...
</div>
```

15

For this three-column structure, we'll need not only a right margin on #content and #footer to accommodate the right column, but also a *left* margin to accommodate the new left column.

But we've previously specified the left margin to be only 10 pixels for the default article-style layout that only contains two columns. We're stuck.

This <body> has class

Here is where the <body> element comes into play. By assigning a class to the <body>, signifying that this is an index-style page, we can write rules that are specific only to that class.

For example, to override the default left margin of 10 pixels, we add the following class to the <body> element on index-style pages only:

```
<body class="index">
```

Following the original rule that sets the margin for the #content and #footer, we can add the following to the CSS:

```
#content, #footer {
  margin: 10px 190px 10px 10px;
  }
body.index #content, body.index #footer {
  margin-left: 190px;
  }
```

For pages with the index class attached to the <body> element exclusively, an increased left margin of 190 pixels (matching the right column) is applied to accommodate a left column. If the index class isn't present, the left margin will be 10 pixels as designated in the default declaration.

Now we can toggle between two- and three-column layouts, simply by assigning the class to the <body> element and dropping in the additional <div> to the markup when desired. Additional classes could be set up as well, with no limit to how many page types can be included.

Markup sections and names can remain the same, while being slightly customized depending on page type.

Not just for columns

While I've used the toggling of columns for the *Fast Company* website as an example, this same idea can be applied to customize *any* element on the page.

For instance, if on index-style pages you would also like all page titles marked up with an <h1> element to be orange instead of their default color, you could add an additional CSS declaration following the default.

For all pages, you'd use the following:

```
h1 {
  font-family: Arial, Verdana, sans-serif;
  font-size: 140%;
  color: purple;
  }
```

And this would apply to index-style pages only:

```
body.index h1 {
  color: orange;
  }
```

You'll notice that in the index-specific declaration we need only put rules that we want to differ from the default values. In this case, on pages where <body class="index"> is specified, <h1> elements will be styled in Arial at 140 percent and orange—without the need to add a class to the <h1> elements or any other additional markup.

I'm using pretty simple examples here—but you can start to imagine the possibility of creating multiple page types by assigning an appropriate class to the <body> element. In turn, the classes could trigger entirely different layouts, color schemes, and designs—all using similar markup structure and a single CSS file.

"You are here"

In addition to adding a class to the <body> element, you can achieve interesting results by adding an id as well.

For example, a crafty designer may use an id attached to the <body> element to trigger navigational elements that signify what page the user is on. Let's take a look at how this would work.

The navigation list

For this example, we're going to borrow the "tabs with shape" that were explained back in the "Extra credit" section of Chapter 1. The navigation uses a simple unordered list containing several links like this:

```
<ul id="minitabs">
  <li><a href="/apples/">Apples</a></li>
  <li><a href="/spaghetti/">Spaghetti</a></li>
  <li><a href="/greenbeans/">Green Beans</a></li>
  <li><a href="/milk/">Milk</a></li>
</ul>
```

15

249

Using CSS, you may remember we styled this list, making the items display horizontally and with a shaped tab that would appear when hovered over. Figure 15-3 shows how this would appear in a browser.

Apples **Spaghetti** Green Beans Milk

Figure 15-3. Horizontal navigation with shaped tabs

You may also remember that to achieve the "you are here" effect (with the tab sticking in the "on" position for a particular link), we added a class to the link that we'd like to stick:

```
<li><a href="/spaghetti/" class="active">spaghetti</a></li>
```

A CSS rule was added to apply the background-image to the link with the class="active" attached:

```
#minitabs a.active {
  color: #000;
  background: url(tab_pyra.gif) no-repeat bottom center;
  }
```

There is an alternative way to handle this, however, that leaves the navigation markup untouched, while still having the ability to mark which page the user is on: assigning an id to the <body> element.

Identify the parts

First, we'll need to add id attributes to each <li> element in our navigation. This is done once, and then the unordered list will remain unchanged on every page—even to achieve the "you are here" effect.

```
<ul id="minitabs">
  <li id="apples_tab"><a href="/apples/">Apples</a></li>
  <li id="spag_tab"><a href="/spaghetti/">Spaghetti</a></li>
  <li id="beans_tab"><a href="/greenbeans/">Green Beans</a></li>
  <li id="milk_tab"><a href="/milk/">Milk</a></li>
</ul>
```

In the preceding code snippet, we've added a short and sweet id to each <li>, suffixing each with a _tab so as not to repeat ourselves. This will make sense in a moment.

Now we're done with the list markup for good. We can forget about it—which can be rather convenient, depending on the templating or content management system you may be working with.

The variable in all of this is an id that will be attached to the <body> element only, signifying which page the user is on. For instance, if we wanted to tell the browser that we were on the Apples page, we may add an id to the <body> element like this:

```
<body id="apples">
```

Alternatively, we could add an id signifying we were on the Green Beans page:

```
<body id="beans">
```

and so on.

The magic CSS

To "light up" the tab, depending on which id is place in the <body>, we need only write a single CSS declaration that tells it to do so for each possible combination:

```
body#apples #apples_tab a,
body#spag #spag_tab a,
body#beans #beans_tab a,
body#milk #milk_tab a {
  color: #000;
  background: url(tab_pyra.gif) no-repeat bottom center;
  }
```

Essentially, we're saying, "When the <body> element has an id of apples, add the tab background and turn the link color black for the link within the #apples_tab list item." And then we're repeating that for each tab option.

All that's required now to "light up" the correct tab in the navigation is to change the id contained in the <body> element. The CSS declaration handles the rest, and could be modified to handle more combinations as future pages are added to a site.

For example, if we wanted to light up the Green Beans tab to signify to users that this is indeed the page they are on, we'd simply add the id to the <body> element like so:

```
<body id="beans_tab">
```

and the appropriate tab would be selected, as shown in Figure 15-4 (where we've applied the "mini-tab" styles that were explained back in Chapter 1).

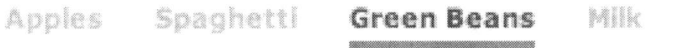

Figure 15-4. Tab selected by assigning an id to the <body> element

Alternatively, we could light up any tab we wish by choosing to add any one of the ids to the <body> that we've declared both in the list markup and the CSS.

Additionally, you could use this same concept to trigger other contextual events on the page—like subnavigation or alternating colors that rotate depending on the page's id. Because the <body> element is at the top level, the id contained within can be used to control *any* element below it on the page.

15

Summary

By migrating toward CSS-based layouts, you'll be amazed at the increased flexibility they bring. In this chapter, we've taken a look at one way to take advantage of that flexibility, by using a class or id on the <body> element to control a page's column structure, or to visually mark what page the user is currently on.

This is just a single example of how modular building sites with web standards can be—easily changing the layout, design, and style of an entire page or site with just one directive from the <body> element.

CHAPTER 16
NEXT STEPS

Now that you're armed with how web standards can improve your websites, remember that the learning never stops. Methods and techniques are constantly being tweaked, improved, and updated, even as I tap out the last few words of this chapter. What better way to stay on top of the game than on the Web itself? You'll find thousands of helpful sites out there exploring the wonders of standards-compliant design and development.

Where do you go from here?

To close this book, I've collected a few of my favorite resources, which I highly recommend visiting regularly to stay sharp on the latest developments of the web standards world.

Organizations and publications

W3C

www.w3.org

The World Wide Web Consortium is where it all happens. This is the organization that leads the Web and develops the standards that we all use every day. The site serves as a reference that is chock-full of technical details on anything and everything. Although it can be difficult to navigate and digest, this site is the definitive source for standards.

Especially helpful are the W3C's validation tools (validator.w3.org). Use them often to make sure your markup is in tip-top shape. You can validate by URL or by uploading a file you're working on locally.

Web Standards Project

www.webstandards.org

Formed in 1998, the Web Standards Project (WaSP) promotes web standards to the public and provides educational resources for web designers and developers to carry out standards-compliant methods. WaSP also works with and encourages browser and software makers to adhere to the standards that it promotes.

The Web Standards Project site is filled with resources on everything standards related.

A List Apart

www.alistapart.com

Founded by Jeffrey Zeldman and Brian Platz in 1998, *A List Apart* magazine explores the design, development, and meaning of web content, with a special focus on techniques and benefits of designing with web standards.

This indispensable online magazine has published many great tips and techniques on a wide variety of standards-compliant design, development, and business topics. A *must-read* "for people who make websites."

CSS Zen Garden

www.csszengarden.com

Planted and curated by standards guru and WaSP member Dave Shea, the CSS Zen Garden is "a demonstration of what can be accomplished visually through CSS-based design." Designers submit their own CSS designs that each reference the same markup structure. What results is a continually updated showcase of cutting-edge CSS design.

A fantastic inspiration—and also a great destination to point CSS naysayers to. (I'm referring to those who believe CSS is incapable of great design. Ha! And to think that would even cross someone's mind.)

Dive Into Accessibility

www.diveintoaccessibility.org

Mark Pilgrim published this online book to help people better understand how easy accessibility features can be to implement and also who benefits from these features.

Taking the perspective from five people, each with a different disability, the information is incredibly easy to understand. Read through Mark's explanations, and your sites will be better because of them.

css-discuss

www.css-discuss.org

css-discuss "is a mailing list devoted to talking about CSS and ways to use it in the real world." This is a great place to ask questions and get answers as you're exploring the benefits of CSS. Plenty of helpful folks are out there with the knowledge to get you through just about anything.

Digital Web Magazine

www.digital-web.com

Published by Nick Finck, *Digital Web Magazine* was an online magazine full of columns, news, and tutorials for web designers. The site "closed its doors" in March 2009, but its archive is well worth browsing.

Vitamin

www.thinkvitamin.com

Web design and development online publication with "in-depth features, audio interviews, training sessions and reviews," brought to you by the folks at Carsonified, a company that puts together popular conferences, workshops, and other web-related products.

16

Influential and inspirational weblogs

Many of the standards community's most talented designers and developers publish daily content on their own personal sites. By reading these weblogs regularly, you can learn from the masters as they pass on their knowledge.

Jeffrey Zeldman Presents: The Daily Report

www.zeldman.com

Jeffrey Zeldman, essentially the godfather of web standards, has been publishing web design news and information since 1995. Zeldman is cofounder of the aforementioned Web Standards Group, publisher of *A List Apart* magazine, and author of *Designing With Web Standards*, and this book wouldn't have been written if not for the work of this guy.

This site is a fountain of information regarding standards-compliant design, and a regular must-stop on your favorites list.

Stopdesign

www.stopdesign.com

Douglas Bowman, best known for his standards-based redesigns of Wired News (www.wired.com) and Adaptive Path (www.adaptivepath.com), publishes useful tutorials, commentary, and insights into the mind of a designer within the world of web standards. His work on Wired News was a huge influence on my redesigns of the sites for *Fast Company* and *Inc.*, and his attention to detail is second to none.

mezzoblue

www.mezzoblue.com

No one monitors the pulse of the standards community better than Dave Shea, curator of the aforementioned CSS Zen Garden. At mezzoblue, Dave tackles the cutting-edge issues of standards-compliant design head on, often getting the community involved to work out existing issues. A fantastic resource.

meyerweb.com

www.meyerweb.com

Recognized as the expert regarding anything CSS, Eric Meyer has written several great books on the subject and has long been an advocate of web standards through his consulting, speaking, and work with Netscape. His site contains great commentary on CSS as well as some great showcases and experiments.

Tantek Çelik

http://tantek.com/log

Weblog of Tantek Çelik, the author of the famed Box Model Hack described earlier in this book, as well as co-founder of microformats.org and W3C representative to the CSS and HTML working groups.

456 Berea Street

www.456bereastreet.com

The site of Swedish web developer Roger Johansson, focusing on accessible web design with web standards.

Jason Santa Maria

www.jasonsantamaria.com

Designer extraordinaire Jason Santa Maria's inspiring personal site.

Jina Bolton

www.sushiandrobots.com/journal

"...a visual interaction designer and artist working in Silicon Valley," Jina Bolton writes and speaks on web design.

Adactio

www.adactio.com/journal

Home to Jeremy Keith, a leading mind on all things markup, CSS, DOM scripting, and microformats.

Cameron Moll

www.cameronmoll.com

The site of Cameron Moll, author, speaker, and Super-Designer.

Mark Boulton

www.markboulton.co.uk

Home to Mark Boulton, designer and web typography whiz.

16

Molly.com

www.molly.com

Molly E. Holzschlag has done an enormous amount of work as a web standards advocate, instructor, and author over the years.

Shaun Inman

www.shauninman.com

Home to Shaun Inman, pioneer of CSS and JavaScript explorations, sIFR (Scalable Inman Flash Replacement) contributor, and designer.

Stuff and Nonsense

www.stuffandnonsense.co.uk

The site of author, speaker, and designer Andy Clarke.

Unstoppable Robot Ninja

www.unstoppablerobotninja.com/

Home to markup and style ninja Ethan Marcotte.

Subtraction

www.subtraction.com/

The site of the master of the grid-based web, Khoi Vinh.

Veerle's Blog

veerle.duoh.com/

The site of talented visual and web designer Veerle Pieters.

D. Keith Robinson

http://dkeithrobinson.com/

The site of web designer and developer D. Keith Robinson, who offers thoughts and questions on standards-related design and development topics.

Simon Willison's Weblog

http://simon.incutio.com

Developer and Web Standards Project member Simon Willison writes about "PHP, Python, CSS, XML, and general web development." He's always on top of web standards and how they relate to other aspects of web development.

Books

I need to mention a few books as well. All of these are fantastic books that will be nothing but indispensable resources for any practicing web designer.

- *Designing With Web Standards, Second Edition*, by Jeffrey Zeldman (New Riders, 2006)
- *Cascading Style Sheets: The Definitive Guide*, by Eric Meyer (O'Reilly, 2000)
- *Bulletproof Web Design, Second Edition*, by Dan Cederholm (New Riders, 2007)
- *CSS Mastery, Second Edition*, by Andy Budd, Simon Collison, Cameron Moll (friends of ED, 2009)
- *Professional CSS*, by Christopher Schmitt, Todd Dominey, Cindy Li, Ethan Marcotte, Dunstan Orchard, and Mark Trammell (Wrox, 2008)
- *Zen of CSS Design*, by Dave Shea and Molly E. Holzschlag (New Riders, 2005)
- *Transcending CSS*, by Andy Clarke and Molly E. Holzschlag (New Riders, 2006)
- *CSS Cookbook*, by Christopher Schmitt (O'Reilly, 2006)
- *Microformats: Empowering Your Markup for Web 2.0*, by John Allsopp (friends of ED, 2007)
- *Speed Up Your Site: Web Site Optimization*, by Andrew B. King (New Riders, 2003)
- *Don't Make Me Think: A Common Sense Approach to Web Usability, Second Edition*, by Steve Krug (New Riders, 2005)

Parting words

And we come to the end. My hope is that by working your way through this book, you've gained a new perspective on how building sites with web standards can be beneficial. By looking at multiple solutions that achieve the same results, you can start to make better choices on your own projects, and I believe you'll be better prepared to trade in bloated, old markup for lean, structured XHTML and CSS designs. Thanks for reading—it's been fun.

INDEX

456 Berea Street blog, 259

A

<a> element, 104–106, 235
abbr attribute, 36–37
<abbr> element, 89–99
accessibility, 30–32
accesskey attribute, 69–71, 80, 95
<acronym> element, 89–94
:active pseudo-class, 111, 114, 239
Adactio blog, 259
#advertising element, 172
aligning text, 214–215
alternate style sheets
    DOM, 163
    font sizing, 160–161
    overview, 159–160
"alternate stylesheet" value, 160
anchors
    options
        <a> element with name attribute, 104–106
        id and name attributes, 108
        id attribute, 107
        overview, 104
    overview, 104
    styling links
        :active pseudo-class, 114
        a:visited declaration, 113
        backgrounds, 112
        dotted borders, 112–113
        Fitts' Law, 115–116
        :hover pseudo-class, 113–114
        IE6, 116
        LoVe/HAte mnemonic, 114
        overview, 111
    title attribute, 110–111
#apples_tab element, 251
article page, 246–247
aural style sheet, 93
#author element, 55, 57
a:visited declaration, 113

B

<b> element, 19, 33
background property, 45–46, 54, 55, 125, 142, 224, 235
background:#ccc declaration, 46
background-color property, 115
background-image property, 55, 224–225, 239, 250
background-position property, 238
backgrounds
    forms, 78–79
    of headings, 23–25

images, headers with, 43–44
    links, 112
block-level elements, 6–8
<blockquote> element, 51–59, 139
blogs, 258–260
<body class="index"> element, 249
<body> element, 74, 173, 180, 203, 244–252
bold class, 88
bold font, 86–88
books, 261
border attribute, 39
border-bottom property, 112
border-collapse property, 40–42
border-left element, 39
border:none; rule, 144
borders
    backgrounds, 24
    forms, 78–79
border-top element, 39
Bowman, Douglas, 258
box model problem, 199–202

 (break) element, 4–7, 63–67, 124
braille media type, 168
bullets
    custom, 10–11
    numbered lists, 121
    turning off, 9–10
    validation, 6

C

Cameron Moll blog, 259
capitalization
    drop caps, 213–214
    small caps, 217
<caption> element, 32
captions, 31
cascade property, 156–157
Cascading Style Sheets. See CSS
CDATA comment syntax, 150
cite attribute, 52–53
<cite> element, 53, 89–91, 101
Clarke, Andy, 260
class attribute, 38, 138, 244
class labels, 137
class="quotation" declaration, 50
classified CSS, 135
clear property, 187, 193
clear: right; rule, 185
clickable area, 66
Code Creator, 97–99
<code> element, 89–95
collapse element, 40

columns
  box model problem, 199–202
  faux, 202–204
  three-column layout, 196–197, 244–248
  two-column layout, 180–195, 244–249
#content <div> element, 183–191
#content element, 136, 182, 192, 247–248
contrast, text, 219
CSS (Cascading Style Sheets)
  adding numbers to, 128–129
  alternate style sheets, 159–163
  applying to documents, 150–158
  assigning icons to IDs, 45–46
  classified, 135
  contextual, 136
  headers with background images, 43–44
  layouts
    box model problem, 199–202
    faux columns, 202–204
    overview, 180
    three-column layout, 196–197
    two-column layout, 180–195
  overview, 150
  reset style sheets, 163–165
CSS Zen Garden website, 257
css-discuss mailing list, 257
custom numbers, 128
custom.css style sheet, 156

D

D. Keith Robinson blog, 260
<dd> (description) element, 67, 125–126
decimal value, 122
default.css style sheet, 160
definition list (<dl>) element, 67, 125–126
definition lists, 67–68
descendant selectors
  applying to entire page, 136–137
  contextual CSS, 136
  easier maintenance, 137–138
  overview, 134–136
description (<dd>) element, 67, 125–126
<dfn> element, 89
Digital Web Magazine, 257
display: block property, 115
display property, 172, 225–229, 235
<div class="quotation"> element, 50–51
<div> element
  with classes attached, 50–51
  combined with <span> element, 98–99
  eliminating, 138–139
  floating sidebars, 181–182
  forms, 64–66
Dive Into Accessibility online book, 257

<dl> (definition list) element, 67, 125–126
Document Object Model (DOM) 163, 163
dotted borders, 112–113
drop caps, 213–214
drop class, 213
<dt> (term) element, 68, 125–126

E

em units, 209, 218
<em> element, 84–87, 101
embossed media type, 168
empty elements, 104
eXtensible HyperText Markup Language (XHTML), 28
external style sheets, 151–155

F

Fahrner Image Replacement (FIR)
  advantages of, 227–228
  assigning background, 226
  disadvantages of, 227–228
  extra element, 225
  markup, 225
  overview, 224–225
faux columns, 202–204
<fieldset> element, 69–76
Finck, Nick, 257
FIR. *See* Fahrner Image Replacement
Fitts' Law, 115–116
Flash, 230–232
float method, 186
float property, 181, 183, 187
floating content, 187–190
floating sidebar
  overview, 181–182
  styling headers and footers, 182–183
  true columns, 183–185
<font> element, 158, 208
font-family attribute, 74, 210
fonts
  bold and italic, 86–88
  changing, 210–211
  customizing with <label> element, 72–74
font-style property, 87, 95, 212
font-variant property, 217
#footer element, 182, 185–187, 247–248
for attribute, 65
<form> element, 72, 77, 139
forms
  accesskey attribute, 70–71
  options, 62–68
  overview, 62
  styling, 71–80
  tabindex attribute, 69–70

G

GIF layouts, 30
grids, creating, 39
<grocerylist> element, 31

H

<h1> through <h6> (heading) elements
    CSS, 156–157
    handling, 19–21
    images, 225–226
    negative letter-spacing, 212
handheld media type, 168
hCard example
    Code Creator, 97–98
    markup, 98–99
    overview, 97
    power of microformats, 99–100
<head> element, 150–157, 171
#header element, 181
headers
    with background images, 43–44
    customizing, 42
    table, 33–36
headers attribute, 35, 44
heading class, 18
heading elements. See <h1> through <h6> elements
headings
    methods, 18–21
    overview, 18
    styling, 22–27
height rule, 229
hi-fi styles, 155–156
hifi.css style sheet, 156
Holly Hack (* html hack), 116
horizontal navigation, 11–14
:hover pseudo-class, 111–114, 239
href attribute, 111, 138, 151
* html hack (Holly Hack), 116
<html> element, 150
hyperlinks. See links

I

icons
    adding to lists, 125–126
    assigning to ids, 44–47
id attribute
    anchors, 107–108
    assigning icons to, 44–47
    borders, 145
    headers, 35
    ordered lists, 127–129
IE6 (Internet Explorer 6), 116

image replacement
    Fahrner Image Replacement, 224–228
    image-tab rollovers, 236–241
    Langridge Image Replacement, 228–229
    logo swapping, 233–235
    overview, 224
    Phark Method, 229–230
    replacing text with images, 224
    Scalable Inman Flash Replacement, 230–231
<img> element, 26–27
@import rule, 152–155, 170
!important rule, 229
indenting, paragraphs, 218
index class, 248
index page, 247–248
inline quotations, 52–54
inline styles, 157–158
<input> element, 63, 71–72
input-bg.gif image, 79
Internet Explorer 6 (IE6), 116
italic font, 86–88

J

Jason Santa Maria blog, 259
Jeffrey Zeldman Presents: The Daily Report blog, 258
Jina Bolton blog, 259
Johansson, Roger, 259

K

<kbd> element, 89, 95
Keith, Jeremy, 259
kerning, 211–212
keywords, 21

L

<label> element
    accesskey attribute, 70
    customizing fonts, 72–74
    forms, 65–66
lang attribute, 53
Langridge Image Replacement (LIR), 228–229
large.css style sheet, 160
larger.css style sheet 160, 160
layouts. See CSS
leading, 209–210
<legend> element
    adding style to, 75
    overview, 74
    three-dimensional, 76–77
letter-spacing, 211–212
<li> element, 30, 138, 142, 238, 250

line-height, 209–210
:link pseudo-class, 106–111
<link> element, 151–152, 156, 159, 168, 171
links
    :active pseudo-class, 114
    a:visited declaration, 113
    backgrounds, 112
    dotted borders, 112–113
    Fitts' Law, 115–116
    :hover pseudo-class, 113–114
    IE6, 116
    LoVe/HAte mnemonic, 114
    overview, 111
    print styles, 173–174
LIR (Langridge Image Replacement), 228–229
List Apart, A magazine, 256
lists
    block-level elements, 6–8

 element, 4–5
    bullets, 9–11
    horizontal navigation, 11–14
    mini-tab shapes, 14–15
    numbered, 120–123
    overview, 4, 120
    term/definition pairs, 123–126
    <ul> element, 8
    wrapping, 5–6
list-style-type property, 122–123
lo-fi styles, 155–156
lofi.css style sheet, 156
logo swapping, 233–235
LoVe/HAte mnemonic, 114
lower-alpha value, 122
lower-roman value, 123

M

main.css style sheet, 157
Marcotte, Ethan, 260
margin-left values, 51
margin-right matching, 195
Mark Boulton blog, 259
master.css style sheet, 156–157
media attribute, 168–169, 171
@media rule, 170
<meta> element, 21
Meyer, Eric, 258
meyerweb.com blog, 258
mezzoblue blog, 258
microformats, 96–100
microformats.org, 96
Microsoft Internet Explorer 6 (IE6), 116
minimizing markup
    assigning classes, 135

    descendant selectors, 134–138
    eliminating <div> element, 138–139
    overview, 134
    site maps, 140–145
mini-tab shapes, 14–15
Molly.com blog, 260

N

name attribute, 104–108
#nav element, 172
navigational elements
    identify parts, 250–251
    navigation list, 249–250
    overview, 249
nesting inline quotations, 54
none value, 123
nonsemantic markup, 84
numbered lists
    ordered, 120–121
    unordered, 121–123

O

<ol> element, 121–123, 127
#opponent declaration, 46
ordered numbered lists, 120–121
organizations, 256–257

P

<p> (paragraph) element, 19, 73, 76, 209, 218
padding property, 115
padding value, 42
padding-left value, 51
paragraph (<p>) element, 19, 73, 76, 209, 218
paragraphs, indenting, 218
Perl script, 95
Phark Method, 229–230
phrase elements
    <abbr> element, 92–94
    <acronym> element, 92–94
    <cite> element, 90–91
    <code> element, 94–95
    <kbd> element, 95
    microformats, 96–100
    overview, 84
    presentational versus structural markups, 84–88
    <samp> element, 95
    <var> element, 95
Pilgrim, Mark, 257
point values, 172
presentational markup
    bold font, 86–88

<em> element, 84–86
  italic font, 86–88
  overview, 84
  <strong>, 84–85
Preview option, 174
Print dialog box, 174
print media type, 168, 172
print styles
  @import rule, 170
  @media rule, 170
  building sheet, 171–175
  media attribute, 169
  overview, 168
  recognized media types, 168–169
  separating screen styles from, 171
print value, 171
print.css file, 171
projection media type, 168
publications, 256–257

Q
<q> (quotation) element, 53–54
quotations
  <blockquote> element, 51–59
  cite attribute, 52–53
  <div class="quotation"> element, 50–51
  no markup, 50
  overview, 50
  <q> element, 53–54
#quote paragraph, 55–56

R
#record declaration, 46
red class, 137
rel attribute, 159
replacing images, 241
reset style sheets, 163–165
reset.css file, 163
resources
  blogs, 258–260
  books, 261
  organizations, 256–257
  publications, 256–257
#right element, 247
rollovers, image-tab, 236–241
Roman numerals, 123

S
<samp> element, 89, 95
Scalable Inman Flash Replacement (sIFR), 230–231
screen attribute, 171

screen media type, 168
screen readers, 85
screen styles, 171
screenstyles.css file, 169
#search element, 172
search engine robots, 21
semantic markup, 84, 96
Shaun Inman blog, 260
Shea, Dave, 258
shorthand method, 46
sidebar attribute, 87
sidebar class, 136
#sidebar declaration, 87, 136, 172, 183, 189
sidebar <div> element, 136, 138, 192–193
#sidecolumn element, 196–197
sideheading class, 135
sidelinks class, 135
sIFR (Scalable Inman Flash Replacement), 230–231
Simon Willison's Weblog, 260
SimpleBits, 97, 203, 240
site maps
  borders, 143–145
  bullets, 142–143
  raw markup, 140–141
  style, 141–142
size attribute, 71
small caps, 217
spacing, letter, 211–212
<span> element
  bold and italic fonts, 88
  drop caps, 213
  Fahrner Image Replacement, 225–228
  headings, 18–20
  logo swapping, 235
  Phark Method, 230
speech media type, 168
speech synthesizer user agents, 85
Stopdesign blog, 258
<strong> element, 58, 84–85, 101, 124
structural markup
  bold, 86–88
  <em> element, 84–86
  italic, 86–88
  overview, 84
  <strong> element, 84–85
Stuff and Nonsense blog, 260
style attribute, 157
<style> element, 150–151, 156–157, 170
styles.css file, 155, 165, 171
Subtraction blog, 260
summary attribute, 33
swappable icons, 25
swapping logos, 233–235
synthesis parameters, 85

T

tabindex attribute, 69–70, 80
table headers, 31
<table> element, 32, 39–40
tables
    abbr attribute, 36–37
    accessibility, 30–32
    assigning icons to ids, 44–47
    border-collapse property, 40–42
    forms, 62–63
    grids, creating, 39
    headers, 33–44
    overview, 30
    summary attribute, 33
    tabular data, 30
    <tbody> element, 37–38
    <tfoot> element, 37–38
    <thead> element, 37–38
tabular data, 30
Tantek Çelik blog, 259
<tbody> element, 37–38
<td> element, 35
term (<dt>) element, 68, 125–126
text
    alignment, 214–215
    captilization, 213–217
    contrast, 219
    fonts, 210–211
    kerning, 211–212
    leading, 209–210
    overview, 208
    paragraph indentation, 218
    replacing with images, 224
    transforming, 216
text-align property, 214
text/css value, 150
text-decoration property, 112
text-indent property, 218–219
text-transform property, 216
<tfoot> element, 37–38
th, td rule, 41
<th> element, 33, 43, 46
<thead> element, 37–38
#thisform label declaration, 74
three-column format
    assigning class to <body> element, 248
    layout, 196–197
    overview, 244–246
    style structure, 246–248
tiled backgrounds, 24–25
title attribute, 92–93, 104, 109–111, 117, 162
<title> element, 21, 110
tooltip titles, 110–111
top.gif image, 56

<tr> element, 38
transparency, heading, 26–27
tty media type, 169
tv media type 169, 169
two-column format
    assigning class to <body> element, 248
    floating content, 187–190
    floating sidebar, 181–187
    overview, 180–181, 244–246
    positioning, 191–195
    style structure, 246–248
type attribute, 123, 150

U

ul attribute, 145
<ul> element, 6, 8, 32, 135, 139
underline overline property, 111
unordered numbered lists, 121–123
Unstoppable Robot Ninja blog, 260
upper-alpha value, 122
upper-roman value, 123

V

validation tools, 256
<var> element, 89, 95
vCard markup, 100
Veerle's Blog, 260
Vinh, Khoi, 260
:visited pseudo-class, 111
visual browsers, 94
Vitamin online publication, 257
voice-family property, 201

W

W3C (World Wide Web Consortium), 28, 256
Web Standards Project (WaSP) 256, 256
weblogs, 258–260
width property, 199, 239
width rule, 201
World Wide Web Consortium (W3C), 28, 256
wrapping, 29–30, 122

X

XHTML (eXtensible HyperText Markup Language), 28

Y

#year declaration, 46

1-59059-543-2 $39.99 [US]

1-59059-518-1 $39.99 [US]

1-59059-542-4 $36.99 [US]

1-59059-517-3 $39.99 [US]

1-59059-651-X $44.99 [US]

EXPERIENCE THE
DESIGNER TO DESIGNER™
DIFFERENCE

1-59059-558-0 $49.99 [US]

1-59059-314-6 $59.99 [US]

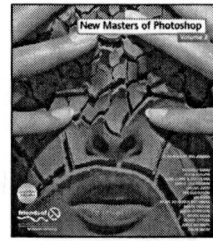

1-59059-315-4 $59.99 [US]

1-59059-619-6 $44.99 [US]

1-59059-304-9 $49.99 [US]

1-59059-355-3 $24.99 [US]

1-59059-409-6 $39.99 [US]

1-59059-748-6 $49.99 [US]

1-59059-593-9 $49.99 [US]

1-59059-555-6 $44.99 [US]

1-59059-533-5 $34.99 [US]

1-59059-638-2 $49.99 [US]

1-59059-765-6 $34.99 [US]

1-59059-581-5 $39.99 [US]

1-59059-614-5 $34.99 [US]

1-59059-594-7 $39.99 [US]

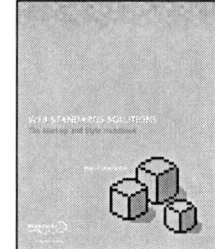

1-59059-381-2 $34.99 [US]

1-59059-554-8 $24.99 [US]